Christina

To someone special!

Blessings & Love ...

From:

~~Aunt Colene~~

Date:

December 25, 2014

The Bible in 366 Days

 For Girls

Carolyn Larsen

 christian art kids

The Bible in 366 Days for Girls

Copyright © 2013 by Christian Art Kids,
an imprint of Christian Art Publishers
PO Box 1599, Vereeniging, 1930, RSA

First edition 2013

Designed by Christian Art Publishers

Images used under license from Shutterstock.com

Scripture quotations are taken from the *Holy Bible*,
New Living Translation®. Copyright © 1996, 2004, 2007
by Tyndale House Foundation. Used by permission of
Tyndale House Publishers Inc., Carol Stream, Illinois 60188.
All rights reserved.

Set in 10 on 13pt Helvetica Neue LT Std
by Christian Art Kids

Printed in China

ISBN 978-1-77036-654-1

14 15 16 17 18 19 20 21 22 23 – 12 11 10 9 8 7 6 5 4 3

Your word is a lamp
to guide my feet and
a light for my path.

Psalm 119:105

January

The Beginning

*B*efore God started making things, there was nothing. The earth was just an empty, formless blob. Everything on earth – everything you see every day – everything you enjoy and appreciate is made by God. What an amazing, creative God!

¹ In the beginning God created the heavens and the earth. ² The earth was formless and empty, and darkness covered the deep waters.

³ Then God said, "Let there be light," and there was light. ⁴ And God saw that the light was good. Then he separated the light from the darkness. ⁵ God called the light "day" and the darkness "night."

And evening passed and morning came marking the first day.

⁶ Then God said, "Let there be a space between the waters, to separate the waters of the heavens from the waters of the earth."

⁹ Then God said, "Let the waters beneath the sky flow together into one place, so dry ground may appear." And that is what happened. ¹⁰ God called the dry ground "land" and the waters "seas." And God saw that it was good.

¹¹ Then God said, "Let the land sprout with vegetation – every sort of seed-bearing plant, and trees that grow seed-bearing fruit. These seeds will then produce the kinds of plants and trees from which they came." And that is what happened. ¹² The land produced vegetation – all sorts of seed-bearing plants, and trees with seed-bearing fruit. Their seeds produced plants and trees of the same kind. And God saw that it was good.

Genesis 1:1-6, 9-12

Everything You Need!

*G*od's most amazing creation was people! He created people to be like Him – able to think and make choices. Then God thought about what people would need to survive. He made sure they had everything they needed – He made everything YOU need!

²⁶ Then God said, "Let us make human beings in our image, to be like us. They will reign over the fish in the sea, the birds in the sky, the livestock, all the wild animals on the earth, and the small animals that scurry along the ground."

²⁷ So God created human beings in his own image. In the image of God he created them; male and female he created them.

²⁸ Then God blessed them and said, "Be fruitful and multiply. Fill the earth and govern it. Reign over the fish in the sea, the birds in the sky, and all the animals that scurry along the ground."

²⁹ Then God said, "Look! I have given you every seed-bearing plant throughout the earth and all the fruit trees for your food. ³⁰ And I have given every green plant as food for all the wild animals, the birds in the sky, and the small animals that scurry along the ground – everything that has life." And that is what happened.

³¹ Then God looked over all he had made, and he saw that it was very good!

2² On the seventh day God had finished his work of creation, so he rested from all his work. ³ And God blessed the seventh day and declared it holy, because it was the day when he rested from all his work of creation.

Genesis 1:26-31; 2:2-3

January 2

Adam's Perfect Mate

God gave Adam work to do but being busy wasn't enough for him. He was lonely. God made Adam to be in a relationship with another person. So, God made Eve, the first woman, to be a helper, a companion, a partner for Adam. God made you to be in relationships, too. You have friends and family members you can be a helper and encouragement to. You, my daughter, have work to do for God! He made you to do His work!

[18] Then the Lord God said, "It is not good for the man to be alone. I will make a helper who is just right for him." [19] So the Lord God formed from the ground all the wild animals and all the birds of the sky. He brought them to the man to see what he would call them, and the man chose a name for each one. [20] He gave names to all the livestock, all the birds of the sky, and all the wild animals. But still there was no helper just right for him.

[21] So the Lord God caused the man to fall into a deep sleep. While the man slept, the Lord God took out one of the man's ribs and closed up the opening. [22] Then the Lord God made a woman from the rib, and he brought her to the man.

[23] "At last!" the man exclaimed. "This one is bone from my bone, and flesh from my flesh! She will be called 'woman,' because she was taken from 'man.'"

[24] This explains why a man leaves his father and mother and is joined to his wife, and the two are united into one.

Genesis 2:18-24

January 3

A Bad Choice

*G*od gave Adam and Eve only one rule to obey but they chose to disobey it and that changed everything. There will be times when you disobey God, too, even if you try not to. Remember to tell Him you're sorry and ask Him to help you obey Him the next time.

¹ The serpent was the shrewdest of all the wild animals the Lord God had made. One day he asked the woman, "Did God really say you must not eat the fruit from any of the trees in the garden?"

³ "It's only the fruit from the tree in the middle of the garden that we are not allowed to eat. God said, 'You must not eat it or even touch it; if you do, you will die.'"

⁴ "You won't die!" the serpent replied to the woman.

⁵ "God knows that your eyes will be opened as soon as you eat it, and you will be like God." ⁶ The woman was convinced. She saw that the tree was beautiful and its fruit looked delicious, and she wanted the wisdom it would give her. So she took some of the fruit and ate it. Then she gave some to her husband.

⁸ When the cool evening breezes were blowing, the man and his wife heard the Lord God walking about in the garden. So they hid from the Lord God among the trees. ⁹ Then the Lord God called to the man, "Where are you?"

¹⁰ He replied, "I heard you walking in the garden, so I hid. I was afraid because I was naked."

¹¹ "Who told you that you were naked?" the Lord God asked. "Have you eaten from the tree whose fruit I commanded you not to eat?"

Genesis 3:1, 3-6, 8-11

Punishment Comes

*G*od punished Adam and Eve for disobeying Him. Every person since these first two has disobeyed God (except Jesus, of course) and God has to punish everyone's disobedience. But He also forgives if you ask Him to. He loves you that much!

^{12} The man replied, "It was the woman you gave me who gave me the fruit, and I ate it."

^{13} Then the Lord God asked the woman, "What have you done?"

"The serpent deceived me," she replied. "That's why I ate it."

^{14} Then the Lord God said to the serpent,

"Because you have done this, you are cursed more than all animals, domestic and wild. You will crawl on your belly, groveling in the dust as long as you live.

^{15} And I will cause hostility between you and the woman, and between your offspring and her offspring. He will strike your head, and you will strike his heel."

^{16} Then he said to the woman, "I will sharpen the pain of your pregnancy, and in pain you will give birth. And you will desire to control your husband, but he will rule over you."

^{17} And to the man he said, "Since you listened to your wife and ate from the tree whose fruit I commanded you not to eat, the ground is cursed because of you."

^{23} So the Lord God banished them from the Garden of Eden, and he sent Adam out to cultivate the ground from which he had been made. ^{24} After sending them out, the Lord God stationed mighty cherubim to the east of the Garden of Eden.

Genesis 3:12-17, 23-24

God Takes Care of Noah

*P*eople on earth completely stopped paying attention to God. He got tired of their disobedience. Only Noah obeyed God so God gave Noah instructions to keep him safe during the flood and He saved animals to repopulate the earth. Obeying God saved Noah's life!

⁹ Noah was a righteous man, the only blameless person living on earth at the time, and he walked in close fellowship with God. ¹⁰ Noah was the father of three sons: Shem, Ham, and Japheth.

¹¹ Now God saw that the earth had become corrupt and was filled with violence. ¹³ So God said to Noah, "I have decided to destroy all living creatures, for they have filled the earth with violence. Yes, I will wipe them all out along with the earth!

¹⁴ "Build a large boat from cypress wood and waterproof it with tar, inside and out. Then construct decks and stalls throughout its interior. ¹⁵ Make the boat 450 feet long, 75 feet wide, and 45 feet high. ¹⁶ Leave an 18-inch opening below the roof all the way around the boat. Put the door on the side, and build three decks inside the boat – lower, middle, and upper.

¹⁷ "Look! I am about to cover the earth with a flood that will destroy every living thing that breathes. Everything on earth will die. ¹⁸ But I will confirm my covenant with you. So enter the boat – you and your wife and your sons and their wives. ¹⁹ Bring a pair of every kind of animal – a male and a female – into the boat with you to keep them alive during the flood." ²² So Noah did everything exactly as God had commanded him.

Genesis 6:9-11, 13-19, 22

January 6

The Rainbow Promise

*A*fter the flood was over God told Noah and his sons to have babies and fill the earth with people again. Then, God made a promise to Noah. He promised to never send such a big flood again. God always keeps His promises ... always. Every time you see a beautiful rainbow, remember His precious promises. Remember His love!

¹³ On the first day of the new year, ten and a half months after the flood began, the floodwaters had almost dried up from the earth. Noah lifted back the covering of the boat and saw that the surface of the ground was drying.

¹⁵ Then God said to Noah, ¹⁶ "Leave the boat, all of you – you and your wife, and your sons and their wives. ¹⁷ Release all the animals – the birds, the livestock, and the small animals that scurry along the ground – so they can be fruitful and multiply throughout the earth."

²¹ And the Lord ... said to himself, "I will never again curse the ground because of the human race, even though everything they think or imagine is bent toward evil from childhood. I will never again destroy all living things."

9¹² Then God said, "I am giving you a sign of my covenant with you and with all living creatures, for all generations to come. ¹³ I have placed my rainbow in the clouds. It is the sign of my covenant with you and with all the earth. ¹⁵ I will remember my covenant with you and with all living creatures. Never again will the floodwaters destroy all life. ¹⁶ When I see the rainbow in the clouds, I will remember the eternal covenant between God and every living creature on earth."

Genesis 8:13, 15-17, 21; 9:12-13, 15-16

The Desire of Your Heart

*A*bram and Sarai wanted a child. Sarai wanted to be a mother! God promised to give them a child ... a son. They served God, loved God and obeyed God. He rewarded their love by giving them something they wanted very much.

¹ When Abram was ninety-nine years old, the Lord appeared to him and said, "I am El-Shaddai – 'God Almighty.' Serve me faithfully and live a blameless life. ² I will make a covenant with you, by which I will guarantee to give you countless descendants."

⁴ "This is my covenant with you: I will make you the father of a multitude of nations! ⁵ What's more, I am changing your name. It will no longer be Abram. Instead, you will be called Abraham, for you will be the father of many nations." ¹⁵ Then God said to Abraham, "Regarding Sarai, your wife – her name will no longer be Sarai. From now on her name will be Sarah. ¹⁶ And I will bless her and give you a son from her! Yes, I will bless her richly, and she will become the mother of many nations. Kings of nations will be among her descendants."

¹⁷ Then Abraham bowed down to the ground, but he laughed to himself in disbelief. "How could I become a father at the age of 100?" he thought. "And how can Sarah have a baby when she is ninety years old?" ¹⁸ So Abraham said to God, "May Ishmael live under your special blessing!"

¹⁹ But God replied, "No – Sarah, your wife, will give birth to a son for you. You will name him Isaac, and I will confirm my covenant with him and his descendants as an everlasting covenant. ²¹ My covenant will be confirmed with Isaac."

Genesis 17:1-2, 4-5, 15-19, 21

January 8

No Laughter!

Sarah heard God's promise that she would have a baby. She knew that would take a miracle because she was so old. Sarah didn't believe God's promise – she laughed at Him. Do you believe the promises in God's Word?

¹ One day Abraham was sitting at the entrance to his tent during the hottest part of the day. ² He looked up and noticed three men standing nearby. When he saw them, he ran to meet them and welcomed them, bowing low to the ground.

³ "My lord," he said, "if it pleases you, stop here for a while. ⁵ And since you've honored your servant with this visit, let me prepare some food to refresh you before you continue on your journey."

"All right," they said. "Do as you have said."

⁸ As they ate, Abraham waited on them in the shade of the trees.

¹⁰ Then one of them said, "I will return to you about this time next year, and your wife, Sarah, will have a son!"

Sarah was listening to this conversation from the tent.

¹¹ Abraham and Sarah were both very old by this time, and Sarah was long past the age of having children. ¹² So she laughed silently to herself and said, "How could a worn-out woman like me enjoy such pleasure, especially when my master – my husband – is also so old?"

¹³ Then the Lord said to Abraham, "Why did Sarah laugh? Why did she say, 'Can an old woman like me have a baby?' ¹⁴ Is anything too hard for the Lord? I will return about this time next year, and Sarah will have a son."

Genesis 18:1-3, 5, 8, 10-14

God Can Change You

Jacob was not an honest man. He cheated his brother and he wasn't nice to other people either. But God had big plans for Jacob's life. He just needed to get Jacob's attention. He did. Then Jacob changed his ways and began serving God.

[22] During the night Jacob got up and took his two wives, his two servant wives, and his eleven sons and crossed the Jabbok River with them. [23] After taking them to the other side, he sent over all his possessions.

[24] This left Jacob all alone in the camp, and a man came and wrestled with him until the dawn began to break. [25] When the man saw that he would not win the match, he touched Jacob's hip and wrenched it out of its socket. [26] Then the man said, "Let me go, for the dawn is breaking!"

But Jacob said, "I will not let you go unless you bless me."

[27] "What is your name?" the man asked.

He replied, "Jacob."

[28] "Your name will no longer be Jacob," the man told him. "From now on you will be called Israel, because you have fought with God and with men and have won."

[29] "Please tell me your name," Jacob said.

"Why do you want to know my name?" the man replied. Then he blessed Jacob there.

[30] Jacob named the place Peniel (which means "face of God"), for he said, "I have seen God face to face, yet my life has been spared."

Genesis 32:22-30

Playing Favorites

*J*acob had twelve sons. But, he loved his son, Joseph, more than any of his other boys. Maybe he knew that God had big plans for this son. Joseph did make some bad choices but in his heart he truly wanted to serve God. And, God did have plans to use Joseph for His work!

3 Jacob loved Joseph more than any of his other children because Joseph had been born to him in his old age. So one day Jacob had a special gift made for Joseph – a beautiful robe.

4 But his brothers hated Joseph because their father loved him more than the rest of them. They couldn't say a kind word to him.

5 One night Joseph had a dream, and when he told his brothers about it, they hated him more than ever. 7 "We were out in the field, tying up bundles of grain. Suddenly my bundle stood up, and your bundles all gathered around and bowed low before mine!"

8 His brothers responded, "So you think you will be our king, do you? Do you actually think you will reign over us?" And they hated him all the more because of his dreams and the way he talked about them.

9 Soon Joseph had another dream, and again he told his brothers about it. "Listen, I have had another dream," he said. "The sun, moon, and eleven stars bowed low before me!"

10 This time he told the dream to his father as well as to his brothers. 11 But while his brothers were jealous of Joseph, his father wondered what the dreams meant.

Genesis 37:3-5, 7-11

Bad-Good-Bad-Good

Joseph ended up in prison but he hadn't done anything wrong. That's bad for Joseph. But, God used him there to do good things. That's good for Joseph. And, God wasn't finished! He had more good-bad things for Joseph.

¹ Pharaoh's chief cup-bearer and chief baker offended their royal master ³ and he put them in the prison where Joseph was. ⁵ While they were in prison, Pharaoh's cup-bearer and baker each had a dream one night, and each dream had its own meaning. ⁶ When Joseph saw them the next morning, he noticed that they both looked upset. ⁷ "Why do you look so worried today?" he asked them.

⁹ So the chief cup-bearer told Joseph his dream first. ¹² "This is what the dream means," Joseph said. ¹³ "Within three days Pharaoh will lift you up and restore you to your position as his chief cup-bearer. ¹⁴ And please remember me and do me a favor when things go well for you. Mention me to Pharaoh, so he might let me out of this place." ¹⁶ When the chief baker saw that Joseph had given the first dream such a positive interpretation, he said to Joseph, "I had a dream, too." ¹⁸ "This is what the dream means," Joseph told him. ¹⁹ "Three days from now Pharaoh will lift you up and impale your body."

²⁰ Pharaoh's birthday came three days later, and he prepared a banquet for all his officials and staff. He summoned his chief cup-bearer and chief baker to join the other officials. ²¹ He then restored the chief cup-bearer to his former position, so he could again hand Pharaoh his cup.

²³ Pharaoh's chief cup-bearer, however, forgot all about Joseph.

Genesis 40:1, 3, 5-7, 9, 12-14, 16, 18-21, 23

Trusting God

*B*ad things happened to Joseph but he kept trusting God anyway. Then the king of Egypt noticed Joseph. That changed everything for Joseph. Keep trusting God even when you can't see where He is leading you.

¹Two full years later, Pharaoh dreamed that he was standing on the bank of the Nile River. ² In his dream he saw seven fat, healthy cows come up out of the river and begin grazing in the marsh grass. ³ Then he saw seven more cows come up behind them from the Nile, but these were scrawny and thin. These cows stood beside the fat cows on the riverbank. ⁴ Then the scrawny, thin cows ate the seven healthy, fat cows!

⁸ The next morning Pharaoh ... called for all the magicians and wise men of Egypt. When Pharaoh told them his dreams, not one of them could tell him what they meant.

¹⁵ Then Pharaoh said to Joseph, "I had a dream last night, and no one here can tell me what it means. But I have heard that when you hear about a dream you can interpret it."

²⁵ Joseph responded, "God is telling Pharaoh in advance what he is about to do."

³³ "Therefore, Pharaoh should find an intelligent and wise man and put him in charge of the entire land of Egypt. ³⁴ Then Pharaoh should appoint supervisors over the land and let them collect one-fifth of all the crops during the seven good years. ³⁶ That way there will be enough to eat when the seven years of famine come to the land of Egypt."

Genesis 41:1-4, 8, 15, 25, 33-34, 36

From Prison to Ruler

Joseph was a prisoner who became a ruler. He may have been scared but Joseph had trusted God his whole life and now he could look back and see how something good came out of bad experiences. God always knows what He is doing!

[39] Then Pharaoh said to Joseph, "Since God has revealed the meaning of the dreams to you, clearly no one else is as intelligent or wise as you are. [40] You will be in charge of my court, and all my people will take orders from you."

[47] As predicted, for seven years the land produced bumper crops. [48] During those years, Joseph gathered all the crops grown in Egypt and stored the grain from the surrounding fields in the cities. [49] He piled up huge amounts of grain like sand on the seashore. Finally, he stopped keeping records because there was too much to measure.

[53] At last the seven years of bumper crops throughout the land of Egypt came to an end. [54] Then the seven years of famine began, just as Joseph had predicted. The famine also struck all the surrounding countries, but throughout Egypt there was plenty of food. [55] Eventually, however, the famine spread throughout the land of Egypt as well. And when the people cried out to Pharaoh for food, he told them, "Go to Joseph, and do whatever he tells you." [56] So with severe famine everywhere, Joseph opened up the storehouses and distributed grain to the Egyptians, for the famine was severe throughout the land of Egypt. [57] And people from all around came to Egypt to buy grain from Joseph.

Genesis 41:39-40, 47-49, 53-57

Forgive and Forget

Joseph's life is a good example of forgiving and forgetting. He didn't hold a grudge against his brothers for what they did to him. He was able to see God's purposes in all his life.

¹When Jacob heard that grain was available in Egypt, he said to his sons, "Why are you standing around looking at one another? ²I have heard there is grain in Egypt. Go down there, and buy enough grain to keep us alive. Otherwise we'll die."

⁸Although Joseph recognized his brothers, they didn't recognize him.

45³ "I am Joseph!" he said to his brothers. "Is my father still alive?" But his brothers were speechless! They were stunned to realize that Joseph was standing there in front of them. ⁵But don't be upset, and don't be angry with yourselves for selling me to this place. It was God who sent me here ahead of you to preserve your lives. ⁷God has sent me ahead of you to keep you and your families alive and to preserve many survivors. ⁸So it was God who sent me here, not you! And he is the one who made me an adviser to Pharaoh – the manager of his entire palace and the governor of all Egypt.

⁹"Now hurry back to my father and tell him, 'This is what your son Joseph says: God has made me master over all the land of Egypt. So come down to me immediately! ¹⁰You can live in the region of Goshen, where you can be near me with all your children and grandchildren, your flocks and herds, and everything you own. ¹¹I will take care of you there, for there are still five years of famine ahead of us.'"

Genesis 42:1-2, 8; 45:3, 5, 7-11

Taking a Chance!

*M*oses was God's man to lead His people out of slavery. But, the Pharaoh ordered that all Hebrew boy babies be killed! Moses' mother took a chance and saved his life ... so he could lead God's people to freedom.

¹A man and woman from the tribe of Levi got married. ² The woman became pregnant and gave birth to a son. She saw that he was a special baby and kept him hidden for three months. ³ But when she could no longer hide him, she got a basket made of papyrus reeds and waterproofed it with tar and pitch. She put the baby in the basket and laid it among the reeds along the bank of the Nile River. ⁵ Soon Pharaoh's daughter came down to bathe in the river, and her attendants walked along the riverbank. When the princess saw the basket among the reeds, she sent her maid to get it for her.

⁶ When the princess opened it, she saw the baby. "This must be one of the Hebrew children," she said.

⁷ Then the baby's sister approached the princess. "Should I go and find one of the Hebrew women to nurse the baby for you?" she asked.

⁸ "Yes, do!" the princess replied. So the girl went and called the baby's mother.

⁹ "Take this baby and nurse him for me," the princess told the baby's mother. "I will pay you for your help." So the woman took her baby home and nursed him.

¹⁰ Later, when the boy was older, his mother brought him back to Pharaoh's daughter, who adopted him as her own son. The princess named him Moses.

January 16

Exodus 2:1-3, 5-10

Your Mission Is …

God spoke to Moses from a burning bush. He told Moses He had a job for him to do. Moses wasn't sure he was the one for this job, but God promised to be with him every step of the way.

¹ One day Moses was tending the flock of his father-in-law, Jethro, the priest of Midian. He led the flock far into the wilderness and came to Sinai, the mountain of God. ² There the angel of the Lord appeared to him in a blazing fire from the middle of a bush. Moses stared in amazement. Though the bush was engulfed in flames, it didn't burn up. ⁴ When the Lord saw Moses coming to take a closer look, God called to him from the middle of the bush, "Moses! Moses!"

"Here I am!" Moses replied.

⁵ "Do not come any closer," the Lord warned. "Take off your sandals, for you are standing on holy ground. ⁶ I am the God of your father – the God of Abraham, the God of Isaac, and the God of Jacob." When Moses heard this, he covered his face because he was afraid to look at God.

⁷ Then the Lord told him, "I have certainly seen the oppression of my people in Egypt. I have heard their cries of distress because of their harsh slave drivers. Yes, I am aware of their suffering. ⁸ So I have come down to rescue them from the power of the Egyptians and lead them out of Egypt into their own fertile land. ¹⁰ Now go, for I am sending you to Pharaoh. You must lead my people Israel out of Egypt."

¹¹ But Moses protested to God, "Who am I to lead the people of Israel out of Egypt?"

¹² God answered, "I will be with you."

Exodus 3:1-2, 4-8, 10-12

Convince Me!

God had an important job for Moses to do but Moses didn't believe in himself. He didn't believe that God would give him the skill and authority to do the job. God had to convince him.

¹ Moses protested, "What if they won't believe me?"

² Then the Lord asked him, "What is that in your hand?"

"A shepherd's staff," Moses replied.

³ "Throw it down on the ground," the Lord told him. So Moses threw down the staff, and it turned into a snake!

⁴ Then the Lord told him, "Reach out and grab its tail." So Moses reached out and grabbed it, and it turned back into a shepherd's staff in his hand.

⁵ "Perform this sign," the Lord told him. "Then they will believe that the Lord really has appeared to you."

⁶ Then the Lord said to Moses, "Now put your hand inside your cloak." So Moses put his hand inside his cloak, and when he took it out again, his hand was white as snow with a severe skin disease. ⁷ "Now put your hand back into your cloak," the Lord said. So Moses put his hand back in, and when he took it out again, it was as healthy as the rest of his body. ⁸ The Lord said to Moses, "If they are not convinced by the first sign, they will be convinced by the second."

¹⁰ But Moses pleaded, "O Lord, I'm not very good with words. I never have been, and I'm not now, even though you have spoken to me."

¹¹ Then the Lord asked, "Who decides whether people speak or do not speak, hear or do not hear, see or do not see? Is it not I, the Lord? ¹² Now go! I will be with you as you speak."

Exodus 4:1-8, 10-12

"I Need Help"

God promised several times to be with Moses, but still Moses didn't believe he could do the job. So, God sent Aaron to do the part that Moses didn't think he could do. God never sends you into a job without giving you what you need to accomplish it.

[13] But Moses again pleaded, "Lord, please! Send anyone else."

[14] Then the Lord became angry with Moses. "All right," he said. "What about your brother, Aaron? I know he speaks well. [15] I will be with both of you as you speak, and I will instruct you both in what to do. [16] Aaron will be your spokesman to the people. He will be your mouthpiece, and you will stand in the place of God for him, telling him what to say. [17] Take your shepherd's staff with you, and use it to perform the miraculous signs I have shown you."

[27] Now the Lord had said to Aaron, "Go out into the wilderness to meet Moses." So Aaron went and met Moses at the mountain of God, and he embraced him. [28] Moses then told Aaron everything the Lord had commanded him to say. And he told him about the miraculous signs the Lord had commanded him to perform.

[29] Then Moses and Aaron returned to Egypt and called all the elders of Israel together. [30] Aaron told them everything the Lord had told Moses, and Moses performed the miraculous signs as they watched. [31] Then the people of Israel were convinced that the Lord had sent Moses and Aaron. When they heard that the Lord was concerned about them and had seen their misery, they bowed down and worshiped.

Exodus 4:13-17, 27-31

God's Power Wins!

*G*od sent Moses and Aaron to demand that the Egyptian pharaoh let the Hebrews leave Egypt. The pharaoh continually lied – saying "Yes, they can go" but then changing his mind. God sent terrible plagues each time the pharaoh lied. Finally, the last one was so awful that the Hebrews were released. God's power won!

[1] The Lord said to Moses, "Pay close attention to this. I will make you seem like God to Pharaoh, and your brother, Aaron, will be your prophet. [2] Tell Aaron everything I command you, and Aaron must command Pharaoh to let the people of Israel leave his country. [5] When I raise my powerful hand and bring out the Israelites, the Egyptians will know that I am the Lord."

[6] So Moses and Aaron did just as the Lord had commanded them. [8] Then the Lord said to Moses and Aaron,

[9] "Pharaoh will demand, 'Show me a miracle.' When he does this, say to Aaron, 'Take your staff and throw it down in front of Pharaoh, and it will become a serpent.'" [10] So Moses and Aaron went to Pharaoh and did what the Lord had commanded them. [14] Then the Lord said to Moses, "Pharaoh's heart is stubborn, and he still refuses to let the people go." [17] So this is what the Lord says: "I will show you that I am the Lord."

11[1] Then the Lord said to Moses, "I will strike Pharaoh and the land of Egypt with one more blow. After that, Pharaoh will let you leave this country. In fact, he will be so eager to get rid of you that he will force you all to leave."

Exodus 7:1-2, 5-6, 8-10, 14, 17; 11:1

God Meets Your Needs

*T*he people were hungry. They had been walking a long time since leaving Egypt and they had no food. Instead of asking God for help, they complained about Moses. But, God was the One who led them out of Egypt so He met their needs. He sent food for them. God cares about all your needs.

² The whole community of Israel complained about Moses and Aaron.

³ "If only the Lord had killed us back in Egypt," they moaned. "There we sat around pots filled with meat and ate all the bread we wanted. But now you have brought us into this wilderness to starve us all to death." ⁴ The Lord said to Moses, "I'm going to rain down food from heaven for you. Each day the people can go out and pick up as much food as they need for that day."

⁶ So Moses and Aaron said to the people of Israel, ⁸ "The Lord will give you meat to eat in the evening and bread to satisfy you in the morning, for he has heard all your complaints against him."

¹³ That evening vast numbers of quail flew in and covered the camp. And the next morning the area around the camp was wet with dew. ¹⁴ When the dew evaporated, a flaky substance as fine as frost blanketed the ground. ¹⁵ The Israelites were puzzled when they saw it. "What is it?" they asked each other. They had no idea what it was. Moses told them, "It is the food the Lord has given you to eat." ³¹ The Israelites called the food manna. It was white like coriander seed, and it tasted like honey wafers.

Exodus 16:2-4, 6, 8, 13-15, 31

Whatever It Takes

*T*he people didn't learn, did they? God took care of them in amazing ways but they still complained when they didn't have exactly what they wanted exactly when they needed it. Now they were thirsty but there was no water around. No problem, God can provide whatever is needed!

¹ At the Lord's command, the whole community of Israel left the wilderness of Sin and moved from place to place. Eventually they camped at Rephidim, but there was no water there for the people to drink. ² So once more the people complained against Moses. "Give us water to drink!" they demanded.

"Quiet!" Moses replied. "Why are you complaining against me? And why are you testing the Lord?"

³ But tormented by thirst, they continued to argue with Moses. "Why did you bring us out of Egypt? Are you trying to kill us, our children, and our livestock with thirst?"

⁴ Then Moses cried out to the Lord, "What should I do with these people? They are ready to stone me!"

⁵ The Lord said to Moses, "Walk out in front of the people. Take your staff, the one you used when you struck the water of the Nile, and call some of the elders of Israel to join you. ⁶ I will stand before you on the rock at Mount Sinai. Strike the rock, and water will come gushing out. Then the people will be able to drink." So Moses struck the rock as he was told, and water gushed out as the elders looked on.

⁷ Moses named the place Massah (which means "test") and Meribah (which means "arguing") because the people of Israel argued with Moses and tested the Lord.

Exodus 17:1-7

Helping One Another

*I*t was not unusual for enemies to attack God's people. Many, many times He protected them. The cool thing about this story is that as long as Moses held his arms up the Israelites were winning. But, he got tired and his arms sagged. So, Aaron and Hur stood on each side of him and held his arms up. God gives family and friends to help us through difficulties!

[8] While the people of Israel were still at Rephidim, the warriors of Amalek attacked them. [9] Moses commanded Joshua, "Choose some men to go out and fight the army of Amalek for us. Tomorrow, I will stand at the top of the hill, holding the staff of God in my hand."

[10] So Joshua did what Moses had commanded and fought the army of Amalek. Meanwhile, Moses, Aaron, and Hur climbed to the top of a nearby hill. [11] As long as Moses held up the staff in his hand, the Israelites had the advantage. But whenever he dropped his hand, the Amalekites gained the advantage.

[12] Moses' arms soon became so tired he could no longer hold them up. So Aaron and Hur found a stone for him to sit on. Then they stood on each side of Moses, holding up his hands. So his hands held steady until sunset.

[13] As a result, Joshua overwhelmed the army of Amalek in battle.

[14] After the victory, the Lord instructed Moses, "Write this down on a scroll as a permanent reminder, and read it aloud to Joshua: I will erase the memory of Amalek from under heaven." [15] Moses built an altar there and named it Yahweh-Nissi (which means "the Lord is my banner").

Exodus 17:8-15

Ten Rules to Follow

*T*he Ten Commandments were not given to make the people miserable. Guidelines for how to live actually make life easier. If everyone followed the Ten Commandments our world would be a much more peaceful place where people love and help one another and honor God in their lives.

[3] "You must not have any other god but me.

[4] "You must not make for yourself an idol of any kind or an image of anything in the heavens or on the earth or in the sea.

[7] "You must not misuse the name of the Lord your God. The Lord will not let you go unpunished if you misuse his name.

[8] "Remember to observe the Sabbath day by keeping it holy. [9] You have six days each week for your ordinary work, [10] but the seventh day is a Sabbath day of rest dedicated to the Lord your God. On that day no one in your household may do any work. [11] For in six days the Lord made the heavens, the earth, the sea, and everything in them; but on the seventh day he rested.

[12] "Honor your father and mother. Then you will live a long, full life in the land the Lord your God is giving you.

[13] "You must not murder.

[14] "You must not commit adultery.

[15] "You must not steal.

[16] "You must not testify falsely against your neighbor.

[17] "You must not covet your neighbor's house. You must not covet your neighbor's wife, male or female servant, ox or donkey, or anything else that belongs to your neighbor."

Exodus 20:3-4, 7-17

Cloud Watching

*G*od instructed the people in building the Tabernacle where His presence would dwell. He led the people by His Spirit in a cloud above the Tabernacle. The people followed Him by watching the cloud and moving when it told them to move. They obeyed God and followed Him.

¹⁵ On the day the Tabernacle was set up, the cloud covered it. But from evening until morning the cloud over the Tabernacle looked like a pillar of fire. ¹⁶ This was the regular pattern – at night the cloud that covered the Tabernacle had the appearance of fire.

¹⁷ Whenever the cloud lifted from over the sacred tent, the people of Israel would break camp and follow it. And wherever the cloud settled, the people of Israel would set up camp.

¹⁸ In this way, they traveled and camped at the Lord's command wherever he told them to go. Then they remained in their camp as long as the cloud stayed over the Tabernacle. ¹⁹ If the cloud remained over the Tabernacle for a long time, the Israelites stayed and performed their duty to the Lord. ²⁰ Sometimes the cloud would stay over the Tabernacle for only a few days, so the people would stay for only a few days, as the Lord commanded. Then at the Lord's command they would break camp and move on. ²¹ Sometimes the cloud stayed only overnight and lifted the next morning. But day or night, when the cloud lifted, the people broke camp and moved on.

²³ So they camped or traveled at the Lord's command, and they did whatever the Lord told them through Moses.

Numbers 9:15-21, 23

Perfect Obedience

*M*oses obeyed God almost all the time. But the thing about obeying God is that you must obey EXACTLY what He says. One time Moses "sort of" obeyed … but that wasn't good enough and he was punished for that.

¹ In the first month of the year, the whole community of Israel camped at Kadesh. ² There was no water for the people to drink at that place, so they rebelled against Moses and Aaron. ³ The people blamed Moses and said, "⁴ Why have you brought the congregation of the Lord's people into this wilderness to die, along with all our livestock? ⁵ Why did you make us leave Egypt and bring us here to this terrible place? This land has no grain, no figs, no grapes, no pomegranates, and no water to drink!"

⁶ Moses and Aaron turned away from the people and went to the entrance of the Tabernacle, where they fell face down on the ground. Then the glorious presence of the Lord appeared to them, ⁷ and the Lord said to Moses, ⁸ "You and Aaron must take the staff and assemble the entire community. As the people watch, speak to the rock over there, and it will pour out its water. You will provide enough water from the rock to satisfy the whole community and their livestock."

¹¹ Then Moses raised his hand and struck the rock twice with the staff, and water gushed out. So the entire community and their livestock drank their fill.

¹² But the Lord said to Moses and Aaron, "Because you did not trust me enough to demonstrate my holiness to the people of Israel, you will not lead them into the land I am giving them!"

Numbers 20:1-8,11-12

A Talking Donkey?

*B*alaam was going to do something that God told him NOT to do. God stopped him though. Listen to God. He will do whatever He can to keep you from disobeying!

²³ Balaam's donkey saw the angel of the Lord standing in the road with a drawn sword in his hand. The donkey bolted off the road into a field, but Balaam beat it and turned it back onto the road. ²⁴ Then the angel of the Lord stood at a place where the road narrowed between two vineyard walls. ²⁵ When the donkey saw the angel of the Lord, it tried to squeeze by and crushed Balaam's foot against the wall. So Balaam beat the donkey again. ²⁶ Then the angel of the Lord moved farther down the road and stood in a place too narrow for the donkey to get by at all. ²⁷ This time when the donkey saw the angel, it lay down under Balaam. In a fit of rage Balaam beat the animal again with his staff.

²⁸ Then the Lord gave the donkey the ability to speak. "What have I done to you that deserves your beating me three times?" it asked Balaam.

²⁹ "You have made me look like a fool!" Balaam shouted. "If I had a sword with me, I would kill you!"

³⁰ "But I am the same donkey you have ridden all your life," the donkey answered. "Have I ever done anything like this before?"

"No," Balaam admitted.

³¹ Then the Lord opened Balaam's eyes, and he saw the angel of the Lord standing in the roadway with a drawn sword in his hand. Balaam bowed his head and fell face down on the ground before him.

Numbers 22:23-31

Good Parenting

*G*od instructed parents to teach their children about Him. So, when your parents talk about God and obeying Him ... listen to them. They are doing exactly what God told them to do. Learn from your parents to love, obey and trust God.

[1]"These are the commands, decrees, and regulations that the Lord your God commanded me to teach you. You must obey them in the land you are about to enter and occupy, [2] and you and your children and grandchildren must fear the Lord your God as long as you live. If you obey all his decrees and commands, you will enjoy a long life. [3] Listen closely, Israel, and be careful to obey. Then all will go well with you, and you will have many children in the land flowing with milk and honey, just as the Lord, the God of your ancestors, promised you. [4]"Listen, O Israel! The Lord is our God, the Lord alone. [5] And you must love the Lord your God with all your heart, all your soul, and all your strength.

[6] And you must commit yourselves wholeheartedly to these commands that I am giving you today.

[7] Repeat them again and again to your children. Talk about them when you are at home and when you are on the road, when you are going to bed and when you are getting up. [8] Tie them to your hands and wear them on your forehead as reminders.

[9] Write them on the doorposts of your house and on your gates.

Deuteronomy 6:1-9

Know Your History

*S*ince the beginning of time God has taken care of His children. He has protected them, guided them and loved them. By studying the Bible and learning the stories of what He has already done, you will learn to trust Him, too!

[20] "In the future your children will ask you, 'What is the meaning of these laws, decrees, and regulations that the Lord our God has commanded us to obey?'

[21] "Then you must tell them, 'We were Pharaoh's slaves in Egypt, but the Lord brought us out of Egypt with his strong hand.

[22] The Lord did miraculous signs and wonders before our eyes, dealing terrifying blows against Egypt and Pharaoh and all his people. [23] He brought us out of Egypt so he could give us this land he had sworn to give our ancestors. [24] And the Lord our God commanded us to obey all these decrees and to fear him so he can continue to bless us and preserve our lives, as he has done to this day. [25] For we will be counted as righteous when we obey all the commands the Lord our God has given us.'

[7] "The Lord did not set his heart on you and choose you because you were more numerous than other nations, for you were the smallest of all nations! [8] Rather, it was simply that the Lord loves you, and he was keeping the oath he had sworn to your ancestors. That is why the Lord rescued you with such a strong hand from your slavery and from the oppressive hand of Pharaoh, king of Egypt. [9] Understand, therefore, that the Lord your God is indeed God. He is the faithful God who keeps his covenant for a thousand generations and lavishes his unfailing love on those who love him and obey his commands."

Deuteronomy 6:20-25; 7:7-9

God Will Take Care of You

*G*od took care of His people when they were traveling to the land He promised to give them. They walked for forty years but their clothes never wore out! He will take care of you, too. Be careful to obey Him!

[1] "Be careful to obey all the commands I am giving you today. Then you will live and multiply, and you will enter and occupy the land the Lord swore to give your ancestors. [2] Remember how the Lord your God led you through the wilderness for these forty years, humbling you and testing you to prove your character, and to find out whether or not you would obey his commands. [3] Yes, he humbled you by letting you go hungry and then feeding you with manna, a food previously unknown to you and your ancestors. He did it to teach you that people do not live by bread alone; rather, we live by every word that comes from the mouth of the Lord. [4] For all these forty years your clothes didn't wear out, and your feet didn't blister or swell. [5] Think about it: Just as a parent disciplines a child, the Lord your God disciplines you for your own good.

[6] "So obey the commands of the Lord your God by walking in his ways and fearing him. [7] For the Lord your God is bringing you into a good land of flowing streams and pools of water, with fountains and springs that gush out in the valleys and hills. [8] It is a land of wheat and barley; of grapevines, fig trees, and pomegranates; of olive oil and honey. [9] It is a land where food is plentiful and nothing is lacking. It is a land where iron is as common as stone, and copper is abundant in the hills.

Deuteronomy 8:1-9

Choose to Obey

*M*oses spoke these words to the Israelites. He begged them to choose to obey God. Obeying would bring them wonderful blessings. Have you chosen to obey God? It's a decision you may have to make every day.

[11] "This command I am giving you today is not too difficult for you to understand, and it is not beyond your reach. [12] It is not kept in heaven, so distant that you must ask, 'Who will go up to heaven and bring it down so we can hear it and obey?' [13] It is not kept beyond the sea, so far away that you must ask, 'Who will cross the sea to bring it to us so we can hear it and obey?' [14] No, the message is very close at hand; it is on your lips and in your heart so that you can obey it.

[15] "Now listen! Today I am giving you a choice between life and death, between prosperity and disaster. [16] For I command you this day to love the Lord your God and to keep his commands, decrees, and regulations by walking in his ways. If you do this, you will live and multiply, and the Lord your God will bless you and the land you are about to enter and occupy.

[19] "Today I have given you the choice between life and death, between blessings and curses. Now I call on heaven and earth to witness the choice you make. Oh, that you would choose life, so that you and your descendants might live! [20] You can make this choice by loving the Lord your God, obeying him, and committing yourself firmly to him. This is the key to your life. And if you love and obey the Lord, you will live long in the land the Lord swore to give your ancestors Abraham, Isaac, and Jacob."

Deuteronomy 30:11-16, 19-20

February

A Job for Joshua

Joshua was Moses' assistant for a while. Now God gave him the job of leading the people – but he had learned the job by watching Moses. God never gives you a job to do without helping you know how to do it!

[1] After the death of Moses the Lord's servant, the Lord spoke to Joshua son of Nun, Moses' assistant. He said, [2] "Moses my servant is dead. Therefore, the time has come for you to lead these people, the Israelites, across the Jordan River into the land I am giving them. [3] I promise you what I promised Moses: 'Wherever you set foot, you will be on land I have given you – [4] from the Negev wilderness in the south to the Lebanon mountains in the north, from the Euphrates River in the east to the Mediterranean Sea in the west, including all the land of the Hittites.' [5] No one will be able to stand against you as long as you live. For I will be with you as I was with Moses. I will not fail you or abandon you.

[6] "Be strong and courageous, for you are the one who will lead these people to possess all the land I swore to their ancestors I would give them. [7] Be strong and very courageous. Be careful to obey all the instructions Moses gave you. Do not deviate from them, turning either to the right or to the left. Then you will be successful in everything you do. [8] Study this Book of Instruction continually. Meditate on it day and night so you will be sure to obey everything written in it. Only then will you prosper and succeed in all you do. [9] This is my command – be strong and courageous! Do not be afraid or discouraged. For the Lord your God is with you wherever you go."

Joshua 1:1-9

Seeing God's Power

*G*od told Joshua exactly what the people should do. If they obeyed God then they would capture Jericho. They did and … they did! Do you obey all the way? Or do you sometimes make excuses when you obey half way but hope that God will bless you anyway?

¹ Now the gates of Jericho were tightly shut because the people were afraid of the Israelites. No one was allowed to go out or in. ² But the Lord said to Joshua, "I have given you Jericho, its king, and all its strong warriors. ³ You and your fighting men should march around the town once a day for six days. ⁴ Seven priests will walk ahead of the Ark, each carrying a ram's horn. On the seventh day you are to march around the town seven times, with the priests blowing the horns.

⁵ When you hear the priests give one long blast on the rams' horns, have all the people shout as loud as they can. Then the walls of the town will collapse, and the people can charge straight into the town."

¹⁵ On the seventh day the Israelites got up at dawn and marched around the town as they had done before. But this time they went around the town seven times. ¹⁶ The seventh time around, as the priests sounded the long blast on their horns, Joshua commanded the people, "Shout! For the Lord has given you the town!"

²⁰ When the people heard the sound of the rams' horns, they shouted as loud as they could. Suddenly, the walls of Jericho collapsed, and the Israelites charged straight into the town and captured it.

Joshua 6:1-5, 15-16, 20

February 2

An Important Woman

*I*n Bible times women did not get much respect, but Deborah had an important job as a judge for the people. God still uses women to do His work. Are you willing to do whatever job God has for you?

⁴ Deborah was a prophet who was judging Israel at that time.

⁶ One day she sent for Barak. She said to him, "This is what the Lord, the God of Israel, commands you: Call out 10,000 warriors from the tribes of Naphtali and Zebulun at Mount Tabor. ⁷ And I will call out Sisera, commander of Jabin's army, along with his chariots and warriors, to the Kishon River. There I will give you victory over him."

⁸ Barak told her, "I will go, but only if you go with me."

⁹ "Very well," she replied, "I will go with you. But you will receive no honor in this venture, for the Lord's victory over Sisera will be at the hands of a woman." So Deborah went with Barak to Kedesh. ¹⁴ So Barak led his 10,000 warriors down the slopes of Mount Tabor into battle. ¹⁵ When Barak attacked, the Lord threw Sisera and all his chariots and warriors into a panic. Sisera leaped down from his chariot and escaped on foot.

¹⁷ Meanwhile, Sisera ran to the tent of Jael. ¹⁸ Jael went out to meet Sisera and said to him, "Come into my tent, sir. Come in. Don't be afraid." So he went into her tent, and she covered him with a blanket.

²² When Barak came looking for Sisera, Jael went out to meet him. She said, "Come, and I will show you the man you are looking for." So he followed her into the tent and found Sisera lying there dead.

Judges 4:4, 6-9, 14-15, 17-18, 22

Partnership with God

God asked Gideon to lead a battle to free the Israelites from slavery. Gideon didn't think he could do it because he wasn't strong enough or important enough. God promised Gideon something that you can trust, too! When God gives you a job to do, He goes with you to do it. You have HIS strength, HIS power and HIS wisdom. So ... trust Him!

[11] Then the angel of the Lord came and sat beneath the great tree at Ophrah, which belonged to Joash of the clan of Abiezer. Gideon son of Joash was threshing wheat at the bottom of a winepress to hide the grain from the Midianites. [12] The angel of the Lord appeared to him and said, "Mighty hero, the Lord is with you!"

[13] "Sir," Gideon replied, "if the Lord is with us, why has all this happened to us? And where are all the miracles our ancestors told us about? Didn't they say, 'The Lord brought us up out of Egypt'? But now the Lord has abandoned us and handed us over to the Midianites."

[14] Then the Lord turned to him and said, "Go with the strength you have, and rescue Israel from the Midianites. I am sending you!"

[15] "But Lord," Gideon replied, "how can I rescue Israel? My clan is the weakest in the whole tribe of Manasseh, and I am the least in my entire family!"

[16] The Lord said to him, "I will be with you. And you will destroy the Midianites as if you were fighting against one man."

Judges 6:11-16

God Alone!

*G*od wanted everyone to know that the Israelites' victory over their enemy was from His strength alone – not because they had a huge army. God made the odds look impossible, then He helped them win the battle! Trust God – even when things look impossible, He will accomplish His will for you.

² The Lord said to Gideon, "You have too many warriors with you. If I let all of you fight the Midianites, the Israelites will boast to me that they saved themselves by their own strength. ³ Therefore, tell the people, 'Whoever is timid or afraid may leave this mountain and go home.'" So 22,000 of them went home, leaving only 10,000 who were willing to fight.

⁴ But the Lord told Gideon, "There are still too many! Bring them down to the spring, and I will test them to determine who will go with you and who will not." ⁵ When Gideon took his warriors down to the water, the Lord told him, "Divide the men into two groups. In one group put all those who cup water in their hands and lap it up with their tongues like dogs. In the other group put all those who kneel down and drink with their mouths in the stream." ⁶ Only 300 of the men drank from their hands. All the others got down on their knees and drank with their mouths in the stream.

⁷ The Lord told Gideon, "With these 300 men I will rescue you and give you victory. Send all the others home."

²² When the 300 Israelites blew their rams' horns, the Lord caused the warriors in the camp to fight against each other with their swords.

Judges 7:2-7, 22

Losing Your Focus

*A*s long as Samson kept his focus on God, he had God's strength. But, he took his focus off God and put it on Delilah, then God's strength left him. Where is your focus today? On God or something else?

⁴ Samson fell in love with Delilah. ⁵ The rulers of the Philistines went to her and said, "Entice Samson to tell you how he can be tied up securely. Then each of us will give you 1,100 pieces of silver."

⁶ So Delilah said to Samson, "Please tell me what makes you so strong."

⁷ Samson replied, "If I were tied up with seven new bowstrings, I would become as weak as anyone else."

⁸ So she tied Samson up. ⁹ But Samson snapped the bowstrings.

¹⁵ Then Delilah pouted, "How can you tell me, 'I love you,' when you don't share your secrets with me? ¹⁶ She tormented him with her nagging day after day until he was sick to death of it.

¹⁷ Finally, Samson shared his secret with her. "If my head were shaved, my strength would leave me, and I would become as weak as anyone else."

¹⁸ Delilah realized he had finally told her the truth, so she sent for the Philistine rulers. ¹⁹ Delilah lulled Samson to sleep with his head in her lap, and then she called in a man to shave off the seven locks of his hair. His strength left him.

²⁰ Then she cried out, "Samson! The Philistines have come to capture you!" When he woke up, he didn't realize the Lord had left him.

²¹ So the Philistines captured him.

Judges 16:4-9, 15-21

February 6

Second Chances

God's strength had left Samson when he disobeyed God. But, Samson was sorry for his actions and asked for a second chance. He was obedient again so God's strength returned. God never gives up on His children!

²² Before long, Samson's hair began to grow back.

²³ The Philistine rulers held a great festival, offering sacrifices and praising their god, Dagon. They said, "Our god has given us victory over our enemy Samson!"

²⁵ Half drunk by now, the people demanded, "Bring out Samson so he can amuse us!" So he was brought from the prison to amuse them, and they had him stand between the pillars supporting the roof.

²⁶ Samson said to the young servant who was leading him by the hand, "Place my hands against the pillars that hold up the temple. I want to rest against them." ²⁷ Now the temple was completely filled with people. All the Philistine rulers were there, and there were about 3,000 men and women on the roof who were watching as Samson amused them.

²⁸ Then Samson prayed to the Lord, "Sovereign Lord, remember me again. O God, please strengthen me just one more time. With one blow let me pay back the Philistines for the loss of my two eyes." ²⁹ Then Samson put his hands on the two center pillars that held up the temple. Pushing against them with both hands, ³⁰ he prayed, "Let me die with the Philistines." And the temple crashed down on the Philistine rulers and all the people. So he killed more people when he died than he had during his entire lifetime.

Judges 16:22-23, 25-29

Broken Hearts

*N*aomi is sometimes called the female Job because she lost everything – her homeland, husband, children, friends. She felt like God had abandoned her. She even tried to change her name. But, God had not turned away from her. She just had to be patient to see what He was doing.

¹ A man from Bethlehem left his home and went to live in the country of Moab. ² The man's name was Elimelech, and his wife was Naomi.

³ Then Elimelech died, and Naomi was left with her two sons.

⁴ The two sons married Moabite women. One married Orpah, and the other a woman named Ruth. But about ten years later, ⁵ both Mahlon and Kilion died. ⁷ With her two daughters-in-law Naomi took the road that would lead them back to Judah. ⁸ But on the way, Naomi said, "Go back to your mothers' homes. ¹⁰ "No," they said. "We want to go with you to your people." ¹¹ But Naomi replied, "Can I still give birth to other sons who could grow up to be your husbands? ¹³ Would you wait for them to grow up and refuse to marry someone else? No, of course not! Things are far more bitter for me than for you."

¹⁴ Orpah kissed her mother-in-law good-bye.

¹⁶ But Ruth replied, "Wherever you go, I will go; wherever you live, I will live. Your people will be my people, and your God will be my God."

¹⁹ When they came to Bethlehem, the entire town was excited by their arrival. "Is it really Naomi?" the women asked.

²⁰ "Don't call me Naomi," she responded. "Instead, call me Mara, for the Almighty has made life very bitter for me. ²¹ I went away full, but the Lord has brought me home empty."

Ruth 1:1-5, 7-8, 10-11, 13-14, 16, 19-21

God's Planned Care

*G*od used Boaz to help Ruth and Naomi. His care comes from surprising places sometimes. When you have a need in your life, pay attention to how God takes care of you – who He uses to help you.

[1] There was a wealthy and influential man in Bethlehem named Boaz. [2] One day Ruth said to Naomi, "Let me go out into the harvest fields to pick up the stalks of grain left behind by anyone who is kind enough to let me do it." [3] So Ruth went out to gather grain behind the harvesters. She found herself working in a field that belonged to Boaz.

[5] Boaz asked his foreman, "Who is that young woman?"

[6] And the foreman replied, "She is the young woman from Moab who came back with Naomi.

[8] Boaz went over and said to Ruth, "Stay right here with us when you gather grain; don't go to any other fields. [9] See which part of the field they are harvesting, and then follow them. I have warned the young men not to treat you roughly. And when you are thirsty, help yourself to the water they have drawn."

[10] Ruth fell at his feet and thanked him warmly. "What have I done to deserve such kindness?" she asked. "I am only a foreigner."

[11] "Yes, I know," Boaz replied. "But I know about everything you have done for your mother-in-law. I have heard how you left your father and mother and your own land to live here among complete strangers. [12] May the Lord, the God of Israel, under whose wings you have come to take refuge, reward you fully for what you have done."

Ruth 2:1-3, 5-6, 8-12

A Happy Ending

*A*t one time Naomi thought God had turned against her. But then Ruth and Boaz got married. Ruth had not been able to have children before but now she had a son. Nothing is ever final until God says it is. He can change circumstances and even people. Trust Him and wait patiently for Him to act.

⁹ Then Boaz said to the elders and to the crowd standing around, "You are witnesses that today I have bought from Naomi all the property of Elimelech, Kilion, and Mahlon.

¹⁰ And with the land I have acquired Ruth, the Moabite widow of Mahlon, to be my wife. This way she can have a son to carry on the family name of her dead husband and to inherit the family property here in his hometown. You are all witnesses today."

¹³ So Boaz took Ruth into his home, and she became his wife. The Lord enabled her to become pregnant, and she gave birth to a son. ¹⁴ Then the women of the town said to Naomi, "Praise the Lord, who has now provided a redeemer for your family! May this child be famous in Israel. ¹⁵ May he restore your youth and care for you in your old age. For he is the son of your daughter-in-law who loves you and has been better to you than seven sons!"

¹⁶ Naomi took the baby and cuddled him to her breast. And she cared for him as if he were her own. ¹⁷ The neighbor women said, "Now at last Naomi has a son again!" And they named him Obed. He became the father of Jesse and the grandfather of David.

Ruth 4:9-10, 13-17

Where to Turn

*T*he prayer of Hannah's heart was to have a child. She wanted to be a mom more than anything. Where did she go with the cry of her heart? To God. She prayed and prayed for God's help. Where do you go with the cries of your heart?

² Elkanah had two wives, Hannah and Peninnah. Peninnah had children, but Hannah did not.

⁷ Year after year it was the same – Peninnah would taunt Hannah as they went to the Tabernacle. Each time, Hannah would be reduced to tears and would not even eat.

⁹ Once after a sacrificial meal at Shiloh, Hannah got up and went to pray. Eli the priest was sitting at his customary place beside the entrance of the Tabernacle. ¹⁰ Hannah was in deep anguish, crying bitterly as she prayed to the Lord. ¹¹ And she made this vow: "O Lord of Heaven's Armies, if you will look upon my sorrow and answer my prayer and give me a son, then I will give him back to you. He will be yours for his entire lifetime."

¹² As she was praying to the Lord, Eli watched her. ¹³ Seeing her lips moving but hearing no sound, he thought she had been drinking. ¹⁴ "Must you come here drunk?" he demanded.

¹⁵ "Oh no, sir!" she replied. "I haven't been drinking wine or anything stronger. But I am very discouraged, and I was pouring out my heart to the Lord. ¹⁶ Don't think I am a wicked woman! For I have been praying out of great anguish and sorrow."

¹⁷ "In that case," Eli said, "go in peace! May the God of Israel grant the request you have asked of him."

1 Samuel 1:2, 7, 9-17

Answered Prayer and Kept Promise

*H*annah promised that if God gave her a child, she would give Him to God's service. God answered her prayer and gave her Samuel. Hannah kept her promise and gave Samuel to God's service. Trying to make a deal with God is never a good idea. But it's an even worse idea to make a deal but not keep your end of the bargain.

¹⁹ The entire family got up early the next morning and went to worship the Lord once more. Then they returned home to Ramah. The Lord remembered Hannah's plea, ²⁰ and in due time she gave birth to a son. She named him Samuel, for she said, "I asked the Lord for him."

²¹ The next year Elkanah and his family went on their annual trip to offer a sacrifice to the Lord. ²² But Hannah did not go. She told her husband, "Wait until the boy is weaned. Then I will take him to the Tabernacle and leave him there with the Lord permanently."

²³ "Whatever you think is best," Elkanah agreed. So she stayed home and nursed the boy until he was weaned.

²⁴ When the child was weaned, Hannah took him to the Tabernacle in Shiloh. They brought along a three-year-old bull for the sacrifice and a basket of flour and some wine. ²⁵ After sacrificing the bull, they brought the boy to Eli. ²⁶ "Sir, do you remember me?" Hannah asked. "I am the woman who stood here several years ago praying to the Lord. ²⁷ I asked the Lord to give me this boy, and he has granted my request. ²⁸ Now I am giving him to the Lord, and he will belong to the Lord his whole life."

1 Samuel 1:19-28

Praising God

Not only did Hannah keep her promise, she recognized God's power, strength and control in her life ... and in everyone's lives. She praised Him and thanked Him for answering her prayer and for being a just and loving God.

¹ Then Hannah prayed:

"My heart rejoices in the Lord! The Lord has made me strong. I rejoice because you rescued me.

² No one is holy like the Lord! There is no one besides you; there is no Rock like our God.

³ "Stop acting so proud and haughty! Don't speak with such arrogance! For the Lord is a God who knows what you have done; he will judge your actions.

⁴ The bow of the mighty is now broken, and those who stumbled are now strong.

⁶ The Lord gives both death and life; he brings some down to the grave but raises others up.

⁷ The Lord makes some poor and others rich; he brings some down and lifts others up.

⁸ He lifts the poor from the dust and the needy from the garbage dump. He sets them among princes, placing them in seats of honor. For all the earth is the Lord's.

⁹ "He will protect his faithful ones, but the wicked will disappear in darkness. No one will succeed by strength alone.

¹⁰ Those who fight against the Lord will be shattered. He thunders against them from heaven; the Lord judges throughout the earth. He gives power to his king; he increases the strength of his anointed one."

1 Samuel 2:1-4, 6-10

God Speaks

Samuel was just a little boy but God wanted to speak to him personally. This is a good example of why you should never discount how God may want to use you in His work. Sometimes a child is the exact right person to hear God speak and to do His work.

¹ Meanwhile, the boy Samuel served the Lord by assisting Eli. Now in those days messages from the Lord were very rare, and visions were quite uncommon. ² One night Eli, who was almost blind by now, had gone to bed. ³ The lamp of God had not yet gone out, and Samuel was sleeping in the Tabernacle near the Ark of God. ⁴ Suddenly the Lord called out, "Samuel!"

"Yes?" Samuel replied. "What is it?" ⁵ He got up and ran to Eli. "Here I am. Did you call me?"

"I didn't call you," Eli replied. "Go back to bed." So he did.
⁶ Then the Lord called out again, "Samuel!"

Again Samuel got up and went to Eli. "Here I am. Did you call me?"

"I didn't call you," Eli said. "Go back to bed."

⁷ Samuel did not yet know the Lord because he had never had a message from the Lord before. ⁸ So the Lord called a third time, and once more Samuel got up and went to Eli. "Here I am. Did you call me?"

Then Eli realized it was the Lord who was calling the boy. ⁹ So he said to Samuel, "Go and lie down again, and if someone calls again, say, 'Speak, Lord, your servant is listening.'" So Samuel went back to bed.

¹⁰ And the Lord came and called as before, "Samuel! Samuel!" And Samuel replied, "Speak, your servant is listening."

1 Samuel 3:1-10

Obedience Is the Best

God gave specific instructions to King Saul about how to defeat God's enemies and how to behave around them. He gave the instructions through His prophet, Samuel. But, Saul did things his own way and then tried to justify his actions. That doesn't work with God. Disobey Him and be punished. Plain and simple.

19 "Why haven't you obeyed the Lord? Why did you rush for the plunder and do what was evil in the Lord's sight?"

20 "But I did obey the Lord," Saul insisted. "I carried out the mission he gave me. I brought back King Agag, but I destroyed everyone else. 21 Then my troops brought in the best of the sheep, goats, cattle, and plunder to sacrifice to the Lord your God in Gilgal."

22 But Samuel replied,

"What is more pleasing to the Lord: your burnt offerings and sacrifices or your obedience to his voice? Listen! Obedience is better than sacrifice, and submission is better than offering the fat of rams.

23 Rebellion is as sinful as witchcraft, and stubbornness as bad as worshiping idols. So because you have rejected the command of the Lord, he has rejected you as king."

27 As Samuel turned to go, Saul tried to hold him back and tore the hem of his robe. 28 And Samuel said to him, "The Lord has torn the kingdom of Israel from you today and has given it to someone else – one who is better than you. 29 And he who is the Glory of Israel will not lie, nor will he change his mind, for he is not human that he should change his mind!"

1 Samuel 15:19-23, 27-29

A Healthy Heart

*G*od chose a new king for Israel. But He didn't choose the strongest, tallest, most powerful man. None of that mattered to God. He looked at the hearts of men and chose the man who was most submitted to Him. How's your heart? Are you willing to be God's servant?

¹ The Lord said to Samuel, "Go to Bethlehem. Find a man named Jesse who lives there, for I have selected one of his sons to be my king." ⁶ When they arrived, Samuel took one look at Eliab and thought, "Surely this is the Lord's anointed!"

⁷ But the Lord said to Samuel, "Don't judge by his appearance or height, for I have rejected him. The Lord doesn't see things the way you see them. People judge by outward appearance, but the Lord looks at the heart."

⁸ Then Jesse told his son Abinadab to step forward. But Samuel said, "This is not the one the Lord has chosen." ¹⁰ In the same way all seven of Jesse's sons were presented to Samuel. But Samuel said to Jesse, "The Lord has not chosen any of these." ¹¹Then Samuel asked, "Are these all the sons you have?"

"There is still the youngest," Jesse replied. "But he's out in the fields watching the sheep and goats."

"Send for him at once," Samuel said.

¹² So Jesse sent for him. He was dark and handsome, with beautiful eyes. And the Lord said, "This is the one; anoint him." ¹³ So as David stood there among his brothers, Samuel took the flask of olive oil he had brought and anointed David with the oil. And the Spirit of the Lord came powerfully upon David from that day on.

1 Samuel 16:1, 6-8, 10-13

Big vs. Little

*G*oliath was a giant. David was a young boy. Goliath was a soldier. David was a shepherd. Goliath had weapons. David had God. Enough said! (Psst ... do you have God?)

[8] Goliath stood and shouted a taunt across to the Israelites. "Why are you all coming out to fight?" he called. "Choose one man to come down here and fight me!" [11] When Saul and the Israelites heard this, they were terrified and deeply shaken. [16] For forty days, every morning and evening, the Philistine champion strutted in front of the Israelite army.

[32] "Don't worry about this Philistine," David told Saul. "I'll go fight him!"

[40] He picked up five smooth stones from a stream and put them into his shepherd's bag. Then, armed only with his shepherd's staff and sling, he started across the valley to fight the Philistine.

[41] Goliath walked out toward David with his shield bearer ahead of him. [44] "Come over here, and I'll give your flesh to the birds and wild animals!" Goliath yelled. [45] David replied to the Philistine, "You come to me with sword, spear, and javelin, but I come to you in the name of the Lord of Heaven's Armies – the God of the armies of Israel, whom you have defied. [47] And everyone assembled here will know that the Lord rescues his people, but not with sword and spear. This is the Lord's battle, and he will give you to us!" [49] Reaching into his shepherd's bag and taking out a stone, he hurled it with his sling and hit the Philistine in the forehead. The stone sank in, and Goliath stumbled and fell face down on the ground.

1 Samuel 17:8, 11, 16, 32, 40-41, 44-45, 47, 49

True Friendship

*J*onathan's dad was king, so Jonathan should be the next king. However, God chose David to be the next king. Jonathan wasn't jealous, though. He promised loyalty to David. They promised each other to be friends forever.

5 David replied, "Tomorrow we celebrate the new moon festival. I've always eaten with the king on this occasion, but tomorrow I'll hide in the field and stay there. 6 If your father asks where I am, tell him I asked permission to go home to Bethlehem for an annual family sacrifice. 7 If he says, 'Fine!' you will know all is well. But if he is angry and loses his temper, you will know he is determined to kill me.

17 Jonathan made David reaffirm his vow of friendship again, for Jonathan loved David as he loved himself.

35 The next morning, as agreed, Jonathan went out into the field and took a young boy with him to gather his arrows.

36 "Start running," he told the boy, "so you can find the arrows as I shoot them." So the boy ran, and Jonathan shot an arrow beyond him. 37 When the boy had almost reached the arrow, Jonathan shouted, "The arrow is still ahead of you. 38 Hurry, hurry, don't wait." 39 He, of course, suspected nothing; only Jonathan and David understood the signal. 41 As soon as the boy was gone, David came out from where he had been hiding near the stone pile. Both of them were in tears as they embraced each other and said good-bye, especially David. 42 At last Jonathan said to David, "Go in peace, for we have sworn loyalty to each other in the Lord's name. The Lord is the witness of a bond between us and our children forever."

1 Samuel 20:5-7, 17, 36-39, 41-42

Doing the Right Thing

*K*ing Saul was chasing David. He wanted to hurt him. David had a chance to get even with Saul. But, he didn't. Getting even is not the God way of doing things.

³ Saul went into a cave. But as it happened, David and his men were hiding farther back in that very cave!

⁴ "Now's your opportunity!" David's men whispered to him. So David crept forward and cut off a piece of the hem of Saul's robe.

⁶ "The Lord knows I shouldn't have done that to my lord the king," he said to his men. "The Lord forbid that I should do this to my lord the king and attack the Lord's anointed one, for the Lord himself has chosen him." ⁷ After Saul had left the cave and gone on his way, ⁸ David came out and shouted after him, "My lord the king!" And when Saul looked around, David bowed low before him.

⁹ Then he shouted to Saul, "Why do you listen to the people who say I am trying to harm you? ¹⁰ This very day you can see with your own eyes it isn't true. For the Lord placed you at my mercy back there in the cave. Some of my men told me to kill you, but I spared you. For I said, 'I will never harm the king – he is the Lord's anointed one.' ¹¹ Look at what I have in my hand. It is a piece of the hem of your robe! I cut it off, but I didn't kill you. This proves that I am not trying to harm you and that I have not sinned against you, even though you have been hunting for me to kill me."

1 Samuel 24:3-4, 6-11

Making Peace

*A*bigail protected her husband. She also protected David from doing something he would regret. She kept the peace between them. Being a peacemaker is a good thing.

² There was a wealthy man from Maon. ³ This man's name was Nabal, and his wife, Abigail, was a sensible and beautiful woman. But Nabal was crude and mean.

⁵ David sent this message for Nabal: ⁸ "Please share any provisions you might have on hand with us and with your friend David." ¹⁰ "Who is this fellow David?" Nabal sneered.

¹¹ "Should I take my bread and my water and my meat and give it to a band of outlaws?" ¹³ "Get your swords!" was David's reply as he strapped on his own. Then 400 men started off with David. ¹⁴ Meanwhile, one of Nabal's servants went to Abigail and told her, "David sent messengers from the wilderness to greet our master, but he screamed insults at them. ¹⁸ Abigail wasted no time. She quickly gathered 200 loaves of bread, two wineskins full of wine, five sheep that had been slaughtered, nearly a bushel of roasted grain, 100 clusters of raisins, and 200 fig cakes. She packed them on donkeys.

²³ When Abigail saw David, she ²⁴ fell at his feet and said, ²⁷ "Here is a present that I have brought to you and your young men. ³¹ Don't let this be a blemish on your record. Then your conscience won't have to bear the staggering burden of needless bloodshed and vengeance."

³² David replied to Abigail, ³³ "Thank God for your good sense! Bless you for keeping me from murder and from carrying out vengeance with my own hands."

1 Samuel 25:2-3, 5, 8, 10-11, 13-14, 18, 23-24, 27, 31-33

February 20

Keeping a Promise

*D*avid promised his friend, Jonathan, that he would take care of Jonathan's family. Years later David still remembered his promise. And, he kept it. Are you as good as your word? Do you keep your promises?

¹ One day David asked, "Is anyone in Saul's family still alive – anyone to whom I can show kindness for Jonathan's sake?"
³ Ziba replied, "Yes, one of Jonathan's sons is still alive. He is crippled in both feet."

⁵ So David sent for him. ⁶ His name was Mephibosheth; he was Jonathan's son and Saul's grandson. David said, "Greetings, Mephibosheth."

⁷ "Don't be afraid!" David said. "I intend to show kindness to you because of my promise to your father, Jonathan. I will give you all the property that once belonged to your grandfather Saul, and you will eat here with me at the king's table!"

⁹ Then the king summoned Saul's servant Ziba and said, "I have given your master's grandson everything that belonged to Saul and his family. ¹⁰ You and your sons and servants are to farm the land for him. But Mephibosheth, your master's grandson, will eat here at my table."

¹¹ And from that time on, Mephibosheth ate regularly at David's table, like one of the king's own sons.

¹² Mephibosheth had a young son named Mica. From then on, all the members of Ziba's household were Mephibosheth's servants. ¹³ And Mephibosheth, who was crippled in both feet, lived in Jerusalem and ate regularly at the king's table.

2 Samuel 9:1, 3, 5-7, 9-13

Thankfulness

*D*avid had enemies who tried to hurt him. But, God protected him and blessed him. David remembered to thank God for His care. Your prayers should not always be only requests. Remember to thank God for all He gives you, too.

¹ David sang this song to the Lord. ² "The Lord is my rock, my fortress, and my savior; ³ my God is my rock, in whom I find protection. He is my shield, the power that saves me, and my place of safety. He is my refuge.

²⁰ He led me to a place of safety; he rescued me because he delights in me. ²⁵ The Lord rewarded me for doing right.

²⁶ "To the faithful you show yourself faithful; to those with integrity you show integrity.

²⁷ To the pure you show yourself pure, but to the wicked you show yourself hostile.

²⁸ You rescue the humble, but your eyes watch the proud and humiliate them.

²⁹ O Lord, you are my lamp. The Lord lights up my darkness.

³⁰ In your strength I can crush an army; with my God I can scale any wall.

³¹ God's way is perfect. All the Lord's promises prove true. He is a shield for all who look to him for protection.

³² For who is God except the Lord? Who but our God is a solid rock?

³³ God is my strong fortress, and he makes my way perfect.

³⁴ He makes me as surefooted as a deer, enabling me to stand on mountain heights."

2 Samuel 22:1-3, 20, 25-34

Request Wisdom

*G*od would give Solomon whatever he asked for. Solomon wisely requested wisdom to rule the people well. What would you ask for if God offered to give you anything?

³ Solomon loved the Lord and followed all the decrees of his father, David. ⁵ The Lord appeared to Solomon in a dream, and God said, "What do you want? Ask, and I will give it to you!"

⁶ Solomon replied, "You showed faithful love to your servant my father, David, because he was honest and true and faithful to you. And you have continued your faithful love to him today by giving him a son to sit on his throne.

⁷ "Now, O Lord my God, you have made me king instead of my father, David, but I am like a little child who doesn't know his way around. ⁸ And here I am in the midst of your own chosen people, a nation so great and numerous they cannot be counted! ⁹ Give me an understanding heart so that I can govern your people well and know the difference between right and wrong. For who by himself is able to govern this great people of yours?"

¹⁰ The Lord was pleased that Solomon had asked for wisdom. ¹¹ So God replied, "Because you have asked for wisdom in governing my people with justice and have not asked for a long life or wealth or the death of your enemies – ¹² I will give you what you asked for! I will give you a wise and understanding heart such as no one else has had or ever will have! ¹³ And I will also give you what you did not ask for – riches and fame! No other king in all the world will be compared to you for the rest of your life!

1 Kings 3:3, 5-13

Putting It to Use

God gave Solomon wisdom like no one had ever had before or has had since. Solomon put it to good use right away in dealing with two women. How do you use the gifts and skills God has given you?

¹⁶ Some time later two prostitutes came to have an argument settled. ¹⁷ One of them began, "I gave birth to a baby while she was with me in the house. ¹⁸ Three days later this woman also had a baby. ¹⁹ But her baby died during the night when she rolled over on it. ²⁰ Then she took my son from beside me while I was asleep. She laid her dead child in my arms and took mine to sleep beside her. ²¹ And in the morning when I tried to nurse my son, he was dead! But when I looked more closely in the morning light, I saw that it wasn't my son at all."

²³ Then the king said, "Let's get the facts straight. Both of you claim the living child is yours, and each says that the dead one belongs to the other. ²⁴ All right, bring me a sword." So a sword was brought to the king.

²⁵ Then he said, "Cut the living child in two, and give half to one woman and half to the other!"

²⁶ Then the woman who was the real mother of the living child, and who loved him very much, cried out, "Oh no, my lord! Give her the child – please do not kill him!"

But the other woman said, "All right, he will be neither yours nor mine; divide him between us!"

²⁷ Then the king said, "Do not kill the child, but give him to the woman who wants him to live, for she is his mother!"

1 Kings 3:16-21, 23-27

God's Care

*T*rusting God enough to do something scary often brings His love and care. The woman in this story found that to be true.

¹ Elijah told King Ahab, "As surely as the God of Israel, lives there will be no dew or rain during the next few years until I give the word!"

² Then the Lord said to Elijah, ³ "Hide by Kerith Brook. ⁴ Drink from the brook and eat what the ravens bring you."

⁷ But after a while the brook dried up.

⁸ Then the Lord said to Elijah, ⁹ "Go and live in the village of Zarephath. I have instructed a widow there to feed you."

¹⁰ So he went to Zarephath. As he arrived, he saw a widow gathering sticks, and he asked her, "Would you please bring me a little water in a cup?" ¹¹ As she was going to get it, he called to her, "Bring me a bite of bread, too."

¹² But she said, "I swear by the Lord your God that I don't have a single piece of bread in the house. And I have only a handful of flour left in the jar and a little cooking oil in the bottom of the jug. I was just gathering a few sticks to cook this last meal, and then my son and I will die."

¹³ But Elijah said to her, "Make a little bread for me. Then use what's left to prepare a meal for yourself and your son. ¹⁴ For this is what the Lord says: There will always be flour and oil left in your containers until the time when the Lord sends rain and the crops grow again!"

¹⁵ So she did as Elijah said, and her family continued to eat for many days. ¹⁶ There was always enough flour and oil left, just as the Lord had promised through Elijah.

1 Kings 17:1-4, 7-16

The Real God

*T*he prophet Elijah challenged the prophets of a fake god to a contest. He wanted all the people to know that God is the true God and He is the most powerful!

²³ "Now bring two bulls. The prophets of Baal may choose one and lay it on their altar, but without setting fire to it. I will prepare the other bull and lay it on the altar, but not set fire to it. ²⁴ Then call on the name of your god, and I will call on the name of the Lord. The god who answers by setting fire to the wood is the true God!" And all the people agreed.

²⁵ Then Elijah said to the prophets of Baal, "You go first."

²⁶ So they prepared one of the bulls and placed it on the altar. Then they called from morning until noontime, shouting, "O Baal, answer us!" But there was no reply of any kind. ³⁰ Then Elijah repaired the altar of the Lord. ³² Then he dug a trench around the altar large enough to hold about three gallons. ³³ He cut the bull into pieces and laid the pieces on the wood. Then he said, "Fill four large jars with water, and pour the water over the offering and the wood."

³⁴ After they had done this, he said, "Do the same thing again!" And, "Now do it a third time!" ³⁵ The water ran around the altar and even filled the trench.

³⁶ Elijah prayed, "O God, prove today that you are God in Israel and that I am your servant."

³⁸ Immediately the fire of the Lord flashed down and burned up the bull, the wood, the stones, and the dust. It even licked up all the water in the trench! ³⁹ And the people cried out, "The Lord – he is God!"

1 Kings 18:23-26, 30, 32-36, 38-39

God's Presence

*E*lijah was depressed. He felt alone in the world. But God showed him that He was with him. However, Elijah learned that the best way to hear God is to be still – He comes in a quiet whisper. Take time to be quiet and listen for God's voice.

[7] Then the angel of the Lord came again and touched Elijah and said, "Get up and eat some more, or the journey ahead will be too much for you."

[8] So he got up and ate and drank, and the food gave him enough strength to travel forty days and forty nights to Mount Sinai. [9] There he came to a cave, where he spent the night. But the Lord said to him, "What are you doing here, Elijah?"

[10] Elijah replied, "The people of Israel have broken their covenant with you, torn down your altars, and killed every one of your prophets. I am the only one left, and now they are trying to kill me, too."

[11] "Go out and stand before me on the mountain," the Lord told him. And as Elijah stood there, the Lord passed by, and a mighty windstorm hit the mountain. It was such a terrible blast that the rocks were torn loose, but the Lord was not in the wind. After the wind there was an earthquake, but the Lord was not in the earthquake. [12] And after the earthquake there was a fire, but the Lord was not in the fire. And after the fire there was the sound of a gentle whisper. [13] When Elijah heard it, he wrapped his face in his cloak and went out and stood at the entrance of the cave.

1 Kings 19:7-13

Helping Others

*E*lisha was God's prophet. He could have been concerned only with helping important people or people who were influential in some way, but he wasn't. Elisha helped a poor widow who just wanted to save her children from harm. God helped him do a miracle to save these children. Elisha showed God's love to this woman by helping her.

¹ One day the widow of a member of the group of prophets came to Elisha and cried out, "My husband who served you is dead, and you know how he feared the Lord. But now a creditor has come, threatening to take my two sons as slaves."

² "What can I do to help you?" Elisha asked. "Tell me, what do you have in the house?"

"Nothing at all, except a flask of olive oil," she replied.

³ And Elisha said, "Borrow as many empty jars as you can from your friends and neighbors. ⁴ Then go into your house with your sons and shut the door behind you. Pour olive oil from your flask into the jars, setting each one aside when it is filled."

⁵ So she did as she was told. Her sons kept bringing jars to her, and she filled one after another. ⁶ Soon every container was full to the brim!

"Bring me another jar," she said to one of her sons.

"There aren't any more!" he told her. And then the olive oil stopped flowing.

⁷ When she told the man of God what had happened, he said to her, "Now sell the olive oil and pay your debts, and you and your sons can live on what is left over."

2 Kings 4:1-7

Taking Care of God's Servants

*E*lisha traveled from town to town doing God's work, teaching about God and encouraging people to follow God. One woman took it upon herself to make life a little bit easier for Elisha. She made sure he always had a place to stay when he came to her town and she didn't ask for anything in return. She unselfishly helped Elisha. She thought about his needs and saw how she could help meet them. That's a good thing to do.

⁸ One day Elisha went to the town of Shunem. A wealthy woman lived there, and she urged him to come to her home for a meal. After that, whenever he passed that way, he would stop there for something to eat.

⁹ She said to her husband, "I am sure this man who stops in from time to time is a holy man of God. ¹⁰ Let's build a small room for him on the roof and furnish it with a bed, a table, a chair, and a lamp. Then he will have a place to stay whenever he comes by."

¹¹ One day Elisha returned to Shunem, and he went up to this upper room to rest. ¹² He said to his servant Gehazi, "Tell the woman from Shunem I want to speak to her." When she appeared, ¹³ Elisha said to Gehazi, "Tell her, 'We appreciate the kind concern you have shown us. What can we do for you? Can we put in a good word for you to the king or to the commander of the army?'"

"No," she replied, "my family takes good care of me."

2 Kings 4:8-13

March

A Child Helps

*C*an a child make a difference? Yes! This story shows that a child who encouraged her master to visit God's prophet played a big role in his healing from leprosy. A child who follows God and shares her faith with others is serving God and others!

¹ The king of Aram had great admiration for Naaman, the commander of his army, because through him the Lord had given Aram great victories. But though Naaman was a mighty warrior, he suffered from leprosy.

² At this time Aramean raiders had invaded the land of Israel, and among their captives was a young girl who had been given to Naaman's wife as a maid. ³ One day the girl said to her mistress, "I wish my master would go to see the prophet in Samaria. He would heal him of his leprosy."

⁴ So Naaman told the king what the young girl from Israel had said. ⁵ "Go and visit the prophet," the king of Aram told him. "I will send a letter of introduction for you to take to the king of Israel." So Naaman started out, carrying as gifts 750 pounds of silver, 150 pounds of gold, and ten sets of clothing.

⁹ So Naaman went with his horses and chariots and waited at the door of Elisha's house. ¹⁰ But Elisha sent a messenger out to him with this message: "Go and wash yourself seven times in the Jordan River. Then your skin will be restored, and you will be healed of your leprosy." ¹⁴ So Naaman went down to the Jordan River and dipped himself seven times, as the man of God had instructed him. And his skin became as healthy as the skin of a young child's, and he was healed!

2 Kings 5:1-5, 9-10, 14

A Bad Decision

*N*aaman was healed of leprosy and offered gifts to Elisha. God's prophet refused the gifts but his servant, Gehazi, wanted them and lied to get them. Because of his greed he was punished. God doesn't want his servants to be greedy or selfish.

²⁰ Gehazi, the servant of Elisha, said to himself, "My master should not have let this Aramean get away without accepting his gifts." ²¹ So Gehazi set off after Naaman.

When Naaman saw Gehazi running after him, he climbed down from his chariot and went to meet him.

²² Gehazi said, "My master has sent me to tell you that two young prophets from the hill country of Ephraim have just arrived. He would like 75 pounds of silver and two sets of clothing to give to them."

²³ "By all means, take twice as much silver," Naaman insisted. He gave him two sets of clothing, tied up the money in two bags, and sent two of his servants to carry the gifts for Gehazi. ²⁴ Then he went and hid the gifts inside the house.

²⁵ When he went in to his master, Elisha asked him, "Where have you been, Gehazi?"

"I haven't been anywhere," he replied.

²⁶ But Elisha asked him, "Don't you realize that I was there in spirit? Is this the time to receive money and clothing, olive groves and vineyards, sheep and cattle, and male and female servants? ²⁷ Because you have done this, you and your descendants will suffer from Naaman's leprosy forever." When Gehazi left the room, he was covered with leprosy; his skin was white as snow.

2 Kings 5:20-27

March 2

God's Protection

A king was mad at Elisha. How does one man defeat a king and his armies? Well, Elisha didn't have to worry about it because God was on his side. God's army is the biggest ever! God is on your side, too. When you need help, call on Him!

¹³ "Go and find out where he is," the king commanded, "so I can send troops to seize him." And the report came back: "Elisha is at Dothan."

¹⁵ When the servant of the man of God got up early the next morning and went outside, there were troops, horses, and chariots everywhere. "Oh, sir, what will we do now?" the young man cried to Elisha. ¹⁶ "Don't be afraid!" Elisha told him. ¹⁷ Then Elisha prayed, "O Lord, open his eyes and let him see!" When he looked up, he saw that the hillside was filled with horses and chariots of fire.

¹⁸ As the Aramean army advanced toward him, Elisha prayed, "O Lord, please make them blind." So the Lord struck them with blindness as Elisha had asked.

¹⁹ Then Elisha went out and told them, "You have come the wrong way! This isn't the right city! Follow me, and I will take you to the man you are looking for." And he led them to the city of Samaria. ²⁰ Elisha prayed, "O Lord, now open their eyes and let them see." So the Lord opened their eyes, and they discovered that they were in the middle of Samaria.

²¹ When the king of Israel saw them, he shouted to Elisha, "My father, should I kill them? Should I kill them?"

²² Elisha replied, "Do we kill prisoners of war? Give them food and drink and send them home again to their master."

2 Kings 6:13, 15-22

God Answers Prayer

*G*od doesn't always do what we ask in prayer. But this time He did. Hezekiah was dying and he asked God to help and God did heal him. Praying always gets results – maybe not the one we always want, but God always knows what's best!

¹ About that time Hezekiah became deathly ill, and the prophet Isaiah son of Amoz went to visit him. He gave the king this message: "This is what the Lord says: Set your affairs in order, for you are going to die. You will not recover from this illness."

² When Hezekiah heard this, he turned his face to the wall and prayed to the Lord, ³ "Remember, O Lord, how I have always been faithful to you and have served you single-mindedly, always doing what pleases you." Then he broke down and wept bitterly.

⁴ But before Isaiah had left the middle courtyard, this message came to him from the Lord: ⁵ "Go back to Hezekiah, the leader of my people. Tell him, 'This is what the Lord, the God of your ancestor David, says: I have heard your prayer and seen your tears. I will heal you, and three days from now you will get out of bed and go to the Temple of the Lord. ⁶ I will add fifteen years to your life, and I will rescue you and this city from the king of Assyria. I will defend this city for my own honor and for the sake of my servant David.'"

⁷ Then Isaiah said, "Make an ointment from figs." So Hezekiah's servants spread the ointment over the boil, and Hezekiah recovered!

2 Kings 20:1-7

March 4

Following God's Plan

*E*ven while Saul was king of Israel, God chose David to be the next king. He was just a boy at that time. But, the people paid attention to God. They followed His plan. David accepted the position God gave him, too. It must have been kind of scary to become king of a nation, but he knew God was on his side. When you know what God wants, are you willing to follow His plan?

¹ Then all Israel gathered before David at Hebron and told him, "We are your own flesh and blood.

² In the past, even when Saul was king, you were the one who really led the forces of Israel. And the Lord your God told you, 'You will be the shepherd of my people Israel. You will be the leader of my people Israel.'"

³ So there at Hebron, David made a covenant before the Lord with all the elders of Israel. And they anointed him king of Israel, just as the Lord had promised through Samuel.

1 Chronicles 11:1-3

Praising God

*T*he Ark of the Covenant was a very holy thing to the Israelites because it was God's dwelling place. King David made a special place for it to be kept. When it was brought there, everyone praised God. David led the people in their praises!

¹ They brought the Ark of God and placed it inside the special tent David had prepared for it. And they presented burnt offerings and peace offerings to God. ⁷ On that day David gave this song of thanksgiving to the Lord:

⁸ Give thanks to the Lord and proclaim his greatness. Let the whole world know what he has done.

⁹ Sing to him; yes, sing his praises. Tell everyone about his wonderful deeds.

¹⁰ Exult in his holy name; rejoice, you who worship the Lord.

²³ Let the whole earth sing to the Lord! Each day proclaim the good news that he saves.

²⁴ Publish his glorious deeds among the nations. Tell everyone about the amazing things he does.

²⁵ Great is the Lord! He is most worthy of praise! He is to be feared above all gods.

²⁶ The gods of other nations are mere idols, but the Lord made the heavens!

²⁷ Honor and majesty surround him; strength and joy fill his dwelling.

²⁹ Give to the Lord the glory he deserves! Bring your offering and come into his presence. Worship the Lord in all his holy splendor.

³⁶ Praise the Lord, the God of Israel, who lives from everlasting to everlasting!

1 Chronicles 16:1, 7-10, 23-27, 29, 36

God's Amazing Provisions

When the plans were made to build God's temple, many people gave gifts to the project. David didn't take their generosity lightly. He stopped and praised God and thanked Him for everything.

[10] Then David praised the Lord:

"O Lord, the God of our ancestor Israel, may you be praised forever and ever! [11] Yours, O Lord, is the greatness, the power, the glory, the victory, and the majesty. Everything in the heavens and on earth is yours, O Lord, and this is your kingdom. We adore you as the one who is over all things. [12] Wealth and honor come from you alone, for you rule over everything. Power and might are in your hand, and at your discretion people are made great and given strength.

[13] "O our God, we thank you and praise your glorious name! [14] Everything we have has come from you, and we give you only what you first gave us! [15] We are here for only a moment. Our days on earth are like a passing shadow, gone so soon without a trace.

[16] "O Lord our God, even this material we have gathered to build a Temple to honor your holy name comes from you! It all belongs to you! [17] I know, my God, that you examine our hearts and rejoice when you find integrity there. You know I have done all this with good motives, and I have watched your people offer their gifts willingly and joyously.

[18] "O Lord, the God of our ancestors Abraham, Isaac, and Israel, make your people always want to obey you. See to it that their love for you never changes."

1 Chronicles 29:10-18

Praying for Blessing

$\mathcal{N}$ehemiah heard that terrible things had happened to Jerusalem. Immediately he prayed, asking God's forgiveness and blessing of the people. Confessing and asking forgiveness is a good thing to do. It opens the doorway to God's blessings!

[1] In late autumn, in the month of Kislev, in the twentieth year of King Artaxerxes' reign, I was at the fortress of Susa. [2] Hanani, one of my brothers, came to visit me with some other men who had just arrived from Judah. I asked them about the Jews who had returned there from captivity and about how things were going in Jerusalem.

[3] They said to me, "Things are not going well. They are in great trouble and disgrace. The wall of Jerusalem has been torn down, and the gates have been destroyed by fire."

[4] When I heard this, I sat down and wept. In fact, for days I mourned, fasted, and prayed to the God of heaven. [5] Then I said,

"O Lord, God of heaven, the great and awesome God who keeps his covenant of unfailing love with those who love him and obey his commands, [6] listen to my prayer! Look down and see me praying night and day for your people Israel. I confess that we have sinned against you. Yes, even my own family and I have sinned!

[8] "Please remember what you told your servant Moses: 'If you are unfaithful to me, I will scatter you among the nations. [9] But if you return to me and obey my commands and live by them, then even if you are exiled to the ends of the earth, I will bring you back to the place I have chosen for my name to be honored.'"

Nehemiah 1:1-6, 8-9

Asking for Help

*N*ehemiah was sad that Jerusalem, God's city, had been destroyed. The king he served didn't really care about the city or about God. But, Nehemiah asked for his help anyway and the king helped! He let Nehemiah go to rebuild the city. When you need help – ask for it. You never know where help may come from!

⁴ The king asked, "Well, how can I help you?"

With a prayer to the God of heaven, ⁵ I replied, "If it please the king, and if you are pleased with me, your servant, send me to Judah to rebuild the city where my ancestors are buried."

⁶ The king, with the queen sitting beside him, asked, "How long will you be gone? When will you return?" After I told him how long I would be gone, the king agreed to my request.

¹⁶ The city officials did not know I had been out there or what I was doing, for I had not yet said anything to anyone about my plans. I had not yet spoken to the Jewish leaders – the priests, the nobles, the officials, or anyone else in the administration.

¹⁷ But now I said to them, "You know very well what trouble we are in. Jerusalem lies in ruins, and its gates have been destroyed by fire. Let us rebuild the wall of Jerusalem and end this disgrace!"

¹⁸ Then I told them about how the gracious hand of God had been on me, and about my conversation with the king.

They replied at once, "Yes, let's rebuild the wall!" So they began the good work.

Nehemiah 2:4-6, 16-18

Work Then Celebrate

*N*ehemiah led the work of rebuilding the wall around Jerusalem. Then he led the people in celebrating and praising God. This is a good reminder to work first, then celebrate – don't let the party get in the way of the work!

[15] So on October 2 the wall was finished – just fifty-two days after we had begun. [16] When our enemies and the surrounding nations heard about it, they were frightened and humiliated. They realized this work had been done with the help of our God.

7[4] At that time the city was large and spacious, but the population was small, and none of the houses had been rebuilt. [5] So my God gave me the idea to call together all the nobles and leaders of the city, along with the ordinary citizens, for registration. I had found the genealogical record of those who had first returned to Judah.

8[1] All the people assembled with a unified purpose at the square just inside the Water Gate. They asked Ezra the scribe to bring out the Book of the Law of Moses, which the Lord had given for Israel to obey.

[2] So on October 8 Ezra the priest brought the Book of the Law before the assembly, which included the men and women and all the children old enough to understand.

[6] Then Ezra praised the Lord, the great God, and all the people chanted, "Amen! Amen!" as they lifted their hands. Then they bowed down and worshiped the Lord with their faces to the ground.

Nehemiah 6:15-16; 7:4-5; 8:1-2, 6

Confessing Sin

*T*he people of Israel gathered to confess their sin. This was not a 2-minute prayer – they stood for more than three hours to confess and worship God! They recognized God's goodness so they thanked Him and praised Him. Confess ... be thankful ... and offer praise.

¹ On October 31 the people assembled again, and this time they fasted and dressed in burlap and sprinkled dust on their heads. ² Those of Israelite descent separated themselves from all foreigners as they confessed their own sins and the sins of their ancestors. ³ They remained standing in place for three hours while the Book of the Law of the Lord their God was read aloud to them. Then for three more hours they confessed their sins and worshiped the Lord their God.

⁵ Then they prayed: "May your glorious name be praised! May it be exalted above all blessing and praise! ⁶ "You alone are the Lord. You made the skies and the heavens and all the stars. You made the earth and the seas and everything in them.

¹⁶ "But our ancestors were proud and stubborn, and they paid no attention to your commands. ¹⁷ They refused to obey and did not remember the miracles you had done for them. But you are a God of forgiveness, gracious and merciful, slow to become angry, and rich in unfailing love. You did not abandon them.

²⁰ You sent your good Spirit to instruct them, and you did not stop giving them manna from heaven or water for their thirst.

²¹ For forty years you sustained them in the wilderness, and they lacked nothing. Their clothes did not wear out, and their feet did not swell!

Nehemiah 9:1-3, 5-6, 16-17, 20-21

God Paves the Way

Sometimes things that happen seem unfair. Queen Vashti refused to be paraded before a bunch of men to show off her beauty. Wasn't she just respecting herself? Her actions got her kicked off the throne. Why did God allow that? He was paving the way to solve a problem that was coming – He was already preparing the answer for that next thing. Trust Him. He knows what's coming!

[10] On the seventh day of the feast, when King Xerxes was in high spirits because of the wine, he told the seven eunuchs who attended him [11] to bring Queen Vashti to him with the royal crown on her head. He wanted the nobles and all the other men to gaze on her beauty, for she was a very beautiful woman. [12] But when they conveyed the king's order to Queen Vashti, she refused to come. This made the king furious, and he burned with anger.

[15] "What must be done to Queen Vashti?" the king demanded. "What penalty does the law provide for a queen who refuses to obey the king's orders, properly sent through his eunuchs?" [19] "So if it please the king, we suggest that you issue a written decree, a law of the Persians and Medes that cannot be revoked. It should order that Queen Vashti be forever banished from the presence of King Xerxes, and that the king should choose another queen more worthy than she. [20] When this decree is published throughout the king's vast empire, husbands everywhere, whatever their rank, will receive proper respect from their wives!" [21] The king and his nobles thought this made good sense, so he followed Memucan's counsel.

Esther 1:10-12, 15, 19, 20-21

The Plan Moves Forward

*A*fter Queen Vashti was removed from the palace, the king searched for a new queen. The woman he chose was Esther. This was all part of God's plan to save the Jewish people. Many times God makes something good from a situation that seems bad.

⁵ At that time there was a Jewish man in the fortress of Susa whose name was Mordecai son of Jair. He was from the tribe of Benjamin. ⁷ This man had a very beautiful and lovely young cousin, Hadassah, who was also called Esther. When her father and mother died, Mordecai adopted her into his family and raised her as his own daughter. ⁸ As a result of the king's decree, Esther, along with many other young women, was brought to the king's harem at the fortress of Susa and placed in Hegai's care.

¹⁶ Esther was taken to King Xerxes ¹⁷ and the king loved Esther more than any of the other young women. He was so delighted with her that he set the royal crown on her head and declared her queen instead of Vashti.

3⁵ When Haman saw that Mordecai would not bow down or show him respect, he was filled with rage. ⁶ He had learned of Mordecai's nationality, so he decided it was not enough to lay hands on Mordecai alone. Instead, he looked for a way to destroy all the Jews throughout the entire empire of Xerxes.

4⁸ Mordecai gave Hathach a copy of the decree issued in Susa that called for the death of all Jews. He asked Hathach to show it to Esther and explain the situation to her. He also asked Hathach to direct her to go to the king to beg for mercy and plead for her people.

Esther 2:5, 7-8, 16-17; 3:5-6; 4:8

The Challenge

*T*he pieces of God's plan are beginning to come together. The Jewish people are in trouble. No one knows that Queen Esther is Jewish. But now she can save her people ... but she has to risk her own life to do it. Is she up for the challenge? Would you be?

[11] "All the king's officials and the people know that anyone who appears before the king without being invited is doomed to die unless the king holds out his gold scepter. And the king has not called for me to come to him for thirty days." [13] Mordecai sent this reply to Esther: "Don't think for a moment that because you're in the palace you will escape when all other Jews are killed. [14] Who knows if perhaps you were made queen for just such a time as this?"

5[1] Esther put on her royal robes and entered the inner court. [2] The king welcomed her and held out the gold scepter. So Esther approached. [8] "If I have found favor with the king, please come with Haman tomorrow to the banquet I will prepare."

7[1] So the king and Haman went to Queen Esther's banquet. [2] While they were drinking wine, the king said, "Tell me what you want, Queen Esther. What is your request?" [3] Queen Esther replied, "If I have found favor with the king, I ask that my life and the lives of my people will be spared.

8[7] Then King Xerxes said, "I have given Esther the property of Haman, and he has been impaled on a pole because he tried to destroy the Jews. [8] Now go ahead and send a message to the Jews in the king's name." [16] The Jews were filled with joy and gladness and were honored everywhere.

Esther 4:11, 13; 5:1-2, 8; 7:1-3; 8:7-8,16

When Everything Goes Wrong

*G*od allowed Job to lose everything he had – possessions and children. But, Job trusted God very much and he kept praising and worshiping God. Are you able to praise God when things go wrong?

⁸ The Lord asked Satan, "Have you noticed my servant Job? He is blameless – a man of complete integrity. "

¹⁰ "You have always put a wall of protection around him. You have made him prosper in everything he does. ¹¹ But reach out and take away everything he has, and he will surely curse you to your face!"

¹² "All right," the Lord said. "Do whatever you want with everything he possesses, but don't harm him physically."

¹⁴ A messenger arrived at Job's home with this news: ¹⁵ "the Sabeans raided us. They stole all the animals and killed all the farmhands." ¹⁶ While he was still speaking, another messenger arrived with this news: "The fire of God has fallen from heaven and burned up your sheep and all the shepherds."

¹⁷ While he was still speaking, a third messenger arrived with this news: "Three bands of Chaldean raiders have stolen your camels and killed your servants."

¹⁸ While he was still speaking, another messenger arrived: "Your sons and daughters were feasting in their oldest brother's home. ¹⁹ Suddenly, a powerful wind swept in and hit the house. The house collapsed, and all your children are dead."

²⁰ Job stood up and tore his robe in grief. He shaved his head and fell to the ground to worship. ²¹ He said, "The Lord gave me what I had, and the Lord has taken it away. Praise the name of the Lord!" ²² In all of this, Job did not sin by blaming God.

Job 1:8, 10-12, 14-22

More Troubles

*J*ob had lost his wealth and his children but he kept praising God. Satan wondered if Job would still praise God if he lost his health. So God let him make Job sick. Did Job get angry at God now? No way! Job knew he must accept trouble from God as well as blessings.

¹ One day the members of the heavenly court came again to present themselves before the Lord, and the Accuser, Satan, came with them. ² "Where have you come from?" the Lord asked Satan.

Satan answered the Lord, "I have been patrolling the earth, watching everything that's going on."

³ Then the Lord asked Satan, "Have you noticed my servant Job? He fears God and stays away from evil. And he has maintained his integrity, even though you urged me to harm him without cause."

⁴ Satan replied to, "Skin for skin! A man will give up everything he has to save his life. ⁵ But take away his health, and he will surely curse you to your face!"

⁶ "All right, do with him as you please," the Lord said to Satan. "But spare his life." ⁷ So Satan left the Lord's presence, and he struck Job with terrible boils from head to foot.

⁸ Job scraped his skin with a piece of broken pottery as he sat among the ashes. ⁹ His wife said to him, "Are you still trying to maintain your integrity? Curse God and die."

¹⁰ But Job replied, "You talk like a foolish woman. Should we accept only good things from the hand of God and never anything bad?" So in all this, Job said nothing wrong.

Job 2:1-10

Friends Who Care

*J*ob's friends heard about his problems and they came to comfort him. Sometimes when you know a friend is having a hard time you want to stay away from her. But that's when your friend needs you the most – even if you don't know what to say. Just by being with her you let her know you care.

[11] When three of Job's friends heard of the tragedy he had suffered, they got together and traveled from their homes to comfort and console him. Their names were Eliphaz the Temanite, Bildad the Shuhite, and Zophar the Naamathite. [12] When they saw Job from a distance, they scarcely recognized him. Wailing loudly, they tore their robes and threw dust into the air over their heads to show their grief. [13] Then they sat on the ground with him for seven days and nights. No one said a word to Job, for they saw that his suffering was too great for words.

3[1] At last Job spoke, and he cursed the day of his birth.

[23] "Why is life given to those with no future, those God has surrounded with difficulties?

[24] I cannot eat for sighing; my groans pour out like water.

[25] What I always feared has happened to me. What I dreaded has come true.

[26] I have no peace, no quietness.
I have no rest; only trouble comes."

Job 2:11-13; 3:1, 23-26

Honest Words

*J*ob was going through a really tough time. He spoke his mind to God as he struggled to understand what was happening. He was honest – and God could take it. But, don't stop reading here. Job came to a new understanding of God's love!

¹ "Is not all human life a struggle? Our lives are like that of a hired hand, ² like a worker who longs for the shade, like a servant waiting to be paid.

⁶ My days fly faster than a weaver's shuttle. They end without hope. ⁷ O God, remember that my life is but a breath, and I will never again feel happiness.

⁸ You see me now, but not for long. You will look for me, but I will be gone.

¹¹ "I cannot keep from speaking. I must express my anguish. My bitter soul must complain. ¹² Am I a sea monster or a dragon that you must place me under guard?

¹³ I think, 'My bed will comfort me, and sleep will ease my misery,' ¹⁴ but then you shatter me with dreams and terrify me with visions. ¹⁵ I would rather be strangled – rather die than suffer like this.

¹⁷ "What are people, that you should make so much of us, that you should think of us so often?

¹⁸ For you examine us every morning and test us every moment. ¹⁹ Why won't you leave me alone, at least long enough for me to swallow! ²⁰ If I have sinned, what have I done to you, O watcher of all humanity? Why make me your target? Am I a burden to you? ²¹ Why not just forgive my sin and take away my guilt? For soon I will lie down in the dust and die. When you look for me, I will be gone."

Job 7:1-2, 6-8, 11-15, 17-21

God's Power and Creativity

*G*od reminded Job of His amazing power and His creativity. When you stop and think about everything that God planned and created, how can you question His power?

¹ Then the Lord answered Job from the whirlwind:

² "Who is this that questions my wisdom with such ignorant words? ³ Brace yourself like a man, because I have some questions for you. ⁴ "Where were you when I laid the foundations of the earth? Tell me, if you know so much.

⁵ Who determined its dimensions and stretched out the surveying line? ⁶ What supports its foundations, and who laid its cornerstone?

⁸ "Who kept the sea inside its boundaries as it burst from the womb, ⁹ and as I clothed it with clouds and wrapped it in thick darkness? ¹⁰ For I locked it behind barred gates, limiting its shores. ¹¹ I said, 'This far and no farther will you come. Here your proud waves must stop!' ²² "Have you visited the storehouses of the snow or seen the storehouses of hail?

²⁴ Where is the path to the source of light? Where is the home of the east wind? ²⁵ "Who created a channel for the torrents of rain? Who laid out the path for the lightning? ²⁶ Who makes the rain fall on barren land, in a desert where no one lives? ²⁷ Who sends rain to satisfy the parched ground and make the tender grass spring up?

³⁶ Who gives intuition to the heart and instinct to the mind? ³⁷ Who is wise enough to count all the clouds? Who can tilt the water jars of heaven ³⁸ when the parched ground is dry and the soil has hardened into clods?

Job 38:1-6, 8-11, 22, 24-27, 36-38

Good Choices

*W*hat makes you happy? Do you find joy in choosing to be with those who love and serve God? Or, do you hang out with friends who do not care about Him at all? Remember that spending lots of time with sinners could easily drag you into their attitudes and actions. Make good choices – including which friends have the most influence over you.

[1] Oh, the joys of those who do not follow the advice of the wicked, or stand around with sinners, or join in with mockers.

[2] But they delight in the law of the Lord, meditating on it day and night.

[3] They are like trees planted along the riverbank, bearing fruit each season. Their leaves never wither, and they prosper in all they do.

[4] But not the wicked! They are like worthless chaff, scattered by the wind.

[5] They will be condemned at the time of judgment. Sinners will have no place among the godly.

[6] For the Lord watches over the path of the godly, but the path of the wicked leads to destruction.

Psalm 1

Protection

*T*he writer of this psalm was scared. But he knew where to turn for protection. Are you ever afraid? When you are scared do you turn to God and ask for His protection from your enemies? Try it … He is always ready to help you.

¹ O Lord, I have so many enemies; so many are against me.

² So many are saying, "God will never rescue him!"

³ But you, O Lord, are a shield around me; you are my glory, the one who holds my head high.

⁴ I cried out to the Lord, and he answered me from his holy mountain.

⁵ I lay down and slept, yet I woke up in safety, for the Lord was watching over me.

⁶ I am not afraid of ten thousand enemies who surround me on every side.

⁷ Arise, O Lord! Rescue me, my God! Slap all my enemies in the face! Shatter the teeth of the wicked!

⁸ Victory comes from you, O Lord May you bless your people.

Psalm 3

Peaceful Sleep

*W*hen you know God there is no reason to ever be afraid. The psalmist knew he could sleep peacefully because God was on duty watching over him. He also knew that it is important to live for God so that your life reflects Him to others. Living for God equals God's protection equals peace.

³ You can be sure of this: The Lord set apart the godly for himself. The Lord will answer when I call to him.

⁴ Don't sin by letting anger control you. Think about it overnight and remain silent.

⁵ Offer sacrifices in the right spirit, and trust the Lord.

⁶ Many people say, "Who will show us better times?" Let your face smile on us, Lord.

⁷ You have given me greater joy than those who have abundant harvests of grain and new wine.

⁸ In peace I will lie down and sleep, for you alone, O Lord, will keep me safe.

Psalm 4:3-8

Crying Out to God

*W*here do you turn when life gets tough? The psalmist started his morning by crying out to God. He knew that God heard his prayers. He knew that God would direct his thoughts and actions to help him be the best person he could be. Do you start your day with God?

1 O Lord, hear me as I pray; pay attention to my groaning.

2 Listen to my cry for help, my King and my God, for I pray to no one but you.

3 Listen to my voice in the morning, Lord. Each morning I bring my requests to you and wait expectantly.

4 O God, you take no pleasure in wickedness; you cannot tolerate the sins of the wicked.

5 Therefore, the proud may not stand in your presence, for you hate all who do evil.

6 You will destroy those who tell lies. The Lord detests murderers and deceivers.

7 Because of your unfailing love, I can enter your house; I will worship at your Temple with deepest awe.

8 Lead me in the right path, O Lord, or my enemies will conquer me. Make your way plain for me to follow.

11 But let all who take refuge in you rejoice; let them sing joyful praises forever. Spread your protection over them, that all who love your name may be filled with joy.

12 For you bless the godly, O Lord; you surround them with your shield of love.

Psalm 5:1-8, 11-12

You Are Important to God

$\mathcal{D}$oes life ever get you down to the point where you wonder if you matter to anyone ... even God? Well, wonder no more! This psalm reports how important you are to God. He gave people ... humans (that's you) a lot of authority over the earth and created you only a little lower than Himself. He wouldn't do that if you didn't matter!

¹ O Lord, our Lord, your majestic name fills the earth! Your glory is higher than the heavens.

² You have taught children and infants to tell of your strength, silencing your enemies and all who oppose you.

³ When I look at the night sky and see the work of your fingers – the moon and the stars you set in place –

⁴ what are mere mortals that you should think about them, human beings that you should care for them?

⁵ Yet you made them only a little lower than God and crowned them with glory and honor.

⁶ You gave them charge of everything you made, putting all things under their authority –

⁷ the flocks and the herds and all the wild animals,

⁸ the birds in the sky, the fish in the sea, and everything that swims the ocean currents.

⁹ O Lord, our Lord, your majestic name fills the earth!

Psalm 8

God's Girl

OK, so you know you want to follow God. You want to live for Him but sometimes you wonder what that actually looks like. What does it mean to live for God? This psalm gives you a pretty good checklist. How many things can you find on this list that describe living for God?

¹ Who may worship in your sanctuary, Lord? Who may enter your presence on your holy hill?

² Those who lead blameless lives and do what is right, speaking the truth from sincere hearts.

³ Those who refuse to gossip or harm their neighbors or speak evil of their friends.

⁴ Those who despise flagrant sinners, and honor the faithful followers of the Lord, and keep their promises even when it hurts.

⁵ Those who lend money without charging interest, and who cannot be bribed to lie about the innocent. Such people will stand firm forever.

Psalm 15

God Is My Rock!

*W*hat issue are you facing today? Problems in your family? A bully at school? A broken friendship? Health issues? How are you handling your issues? The best place to turn ... the One who can always help ... is God. He is your strength, Rock, Savior.

¹ I love you, Lord; you are my strength. ² The Lord is my rock, my fortress, and my savior; my God is my rock, in whom I find protection. He is my shield, the power that saves me, and my place of safety. ³ I called on the Lord, who is worthy of praise, and he saved me from my enemies.

³⁰ God's way is perfect. All the Lord's promises prove true. He is a shield for all who look to him for protection. ³¹ For who is God except the Lord? Who but our God is a solid rock? ³² God arms me with strength, and he makes my way perfect. ³³ He makes me as surefooted as a deer, enabling me to stand on mountain heights. ³⁴ He trains my hands for battle; he strengthens my arm to draw a bronze bow.

³⁵ You have given me your shield of victory. Your right hand supports me; your help has made me great. ³⁶ You have made a wide path for my feet to keep them from slipping.

⁴⁶ The Lord lives! Praise to my Rock! May the God of my salvation be exalted! ⁴⁷ He is the God who pays back those who harm me; he subdues the nations under me ⁴⁸ and rescues me from my enemies. You hold me safe beyond the reach of my enemies; you save me from violent opponents.

⁴⁹ For this, O Lord, I will praise you among the nations; I will sing praises to your name.

Psalm 18:1-3, 30-36, 46-49

The Greatness of God

The psalmist recognizes God's greatness then asks God to keep him from sinning and to keep his heart focused on God. That's a good prayer – think about praying it yourself.

¹ The heavens proclaim the glory of God. The skies display his craftsmanship.

² Day after day they continue to speak; night after night they make him known.

⁶ The sun rises at one end of the heavens and follows its course to the other end. Nothing can hide from its heat.

⁷ The instructions of the Lord are perfect, reviving the soul. The decrees of the Lord are trustworthy, making wise the simple.

⁸ The commandments of the Lord are right, bringing joy to the heart. The commands of the Lord are clear, giving insight for living.

⁹ Reverence for the Lord is pure, lasting forever. The laws of the Lord are true; each one is fair.

¹⁰ They are more desirable than gold, even the finest gold. They are sweeter than honey, even honey dripping from the comb.

¹¹ They are a warning to your servant, a great reward for those who obey them.

¹² How can I know all the sins lurking in my heart? Cleanse me from these hidden faults.

¹³ Keep your servant from deliberate sins! Don't let them control me. Then I will be free of guilt and innocent of great sin.

¹⁴ May the words of my mouth and the meditation of my heart be pleasing to you, O Lord, my rock and my redeemer.

Psalm 19:1-2, 6-14

Where Is God When You Need Him?

*H*ere's the scene: A bully picks on you day after day. You beg God to help but nothing changes. Is God ignoring you? Doesn't He care about what you're going through? Yes, He does. Continue to trust Him. Continue to praise Him. He will come through for you!

¹ My God, my God, why have you abandoned me? Why are you so far away when I groan for help? ² Every day I call to you, my God, but you do not answer. Every night you hear my voice, but I find no relief. ³ Yet you are holy, enthroned on the praises of Israel.

²³ Praise the Lord, all you who fear him! Honor him, all you descendants of Jacob! Show him reverence, all you descendants of Israel! ²⁴ For he has not ignored or belittled the suffering of the needy. He has not turned his back on them, but has listened to their cries for help. ²⁵ I will praise you in the great assembly. ²⁶ The poor will eat and be satisfied. All who seek the Lord will praise him. Their hearts will rejoice with everlasting joy.

²⁷ The whole earth will acknowledge the Lord and return to him. All the families of the nations will bow down before him. ²⁸ For royal power belongs to the Lord. He rules all the nations. ²⁹ Bow before him, all who are mortal, all whose lives will end as dust. ³⁰ Our children will also serve him. Future generations will hear about the wonders of the Lord. ³¹ His righteous acts will be told to those not yet born. They will hear about everything he has done.

Psalm 22:1-3, 23-31

March 28

The Lord Is My Shepherd

A shepherd guides and protects his sheep. That's his job and he takes it very seriously. Did you know that you have a shepherd? The Lord is your shepherd. He guides, guards and protects you. He makes sure you have what you need. He is always with you and loves you more than you can even imagine.

[1] The Lord is my shepherd; I have all that I need.

[2] He lets me rest in green meadows; he leads me beside peaceful streams.

[3] He renews my strength. He guides me along right paths, bringing honor to his name.

[4] Even when I walk through the darkest valley, I will not be afraid, for you are close beside me. Your rod and your staff protect and comfort me.

[5] You prepare a feast for me in the presence of my enemies. You honor me by anointing my head with oil. My cup overflows with blessings.

[6] Surely your goodness and unfailing love will pursue me all the days of my life, and I will live in the house of the Lord forever.

Psalm 23

Who Is in Charge?

*I*mportant and powerful people may think they don't need God. They may think they have more power than Him and can run their own lives. They are wrong. God is in charge. He is the most powerful. Only people who give their hearts to Him and live for Him will enter His kingdom. He is the king of glory!

¹ The earth is the Lord's, and everything in it. The world and all its people belong to him.

² For he laid the earth's foundation on the seas and built it on the ocean depths.

³ Who may climb the mountain of the Lord? Who may stand in his holy place?

⁴ Only those whose hands and hearts are pure, who do not worship idols and never tell lies.

⁵ They will receive the Lord's blessing and have a right relationship with God their savior.

⁶ Such people may seek you and worship in your presence, O God of Jacob.

⁷ Open up, ancient gates! Open up, ancient doors, and let the King of glory enter.

⁸ Who is the King of glory? The Lord, strong and mighty; the Lord, invincible in battle.

⁹ Open up, ancient gates! Open up, ancient doors, and let the King of glory enter.

¹⁰ Who is the King of glory? The Lord of Heaven's Armies – he is the King of glory.

Psalm 24

Choose God

*T*here are many things you could choose to devote your time and energy to. There are many things that may seem important – being popular, being successful – but the truth is that nothing and no one deserves your devotion more than God. Is He in charge of your life?

¹ O Lord, I give my life to you.

² I trust in you, my God! Do not let me be disgraced, or let my enemies rejoice in my defeat. ³ No one who trusts in you will ever be disgraced, but disgrace comes to those who try to deceive others. ⁴ Show me the right path, O Lord; point out the road for me to follow. ⁵ Lead me by your truth and teach me, for you are the God who saves me. All day long I put my hope in you.

⁶ Remember, O Lord, your compassion and unfailing love, which you have shown from long ages past.

⁷ Do not remember the rebellious sins of my youth. Remember me in the light of your unfailing love, for you are merciful, O Lord. ⁸ The Lord is good and does what is right; he shows the proper path to those who go astray.

⁹ He leads the humble in doing right, teaching them his way.

¹⁰ The Lord leads with unfailing love and faithfulness all who keep his covenant and obey his demands.

¹¹ For the honor of your name, O Lord, forgive my many, many sins. ¹² Who are those who fear the Lord? He will show them the path they should choose.

¹³ They will live in prosperity, and their children will inherit the land. ¹⁴ The Lord is a friend to those who fear him.

¹⁵ My eyes are always on the Lord, for he rescues me.

Psalm 25:1-15

April

What Lights Your World?

*W*hat is the most important thing to you? Now, you can say that it's God because you think that is the right answer, but if your life doesn't prove that you feel that way by your actions and words, then maybe you need to think about what is truly important to you ... and make some changes!

[1] The Lord is my light and my salvation – so why should I be afraid? The Lord is my fortress, protecting me from danger, so why should I tremble?

[7] Hear me as I pray, O Lord. Be merciful and answer me!

[8] My heart has heard you say, "Come and talk with me." And my heart responds, "Lord, I am coming."

[9] Do not turn your back on me. Do not reject your servant in anger. You have always been my helper. Don't leave me now; don't abandon me, O God of my salvation!

[11] Teach me how to live, O Lord. Lead me along the right path, for my enemies are waiting for me.

[12] Do not let me fall into their hands. For they accuse me of things I've never done; with every breath they threaten me with violence.

[13] Yet I am confident I will see the Lord's goodness while I am here in the land of the living.

[14] Wait patiently for the Lord. Be brave and courageous. Yes, wait patiently for the Lord.

Psalm 27:1, 7-9, 11-14

The Joy of Forgiveness

*H*ow easily do you forgive someone who hurts you? Do you find that difficult? Well, how good does it feel when a friend you've hurt gives you forgiveness? Even more awesome than that is the fact that God – the Creator of everything – lovingly forgives your sins. He loves you that much!

¹ Oh, what joy for those whose disobedience is forgiven, whose sin is put out of sight! ² Yes, what joy for those whose record the Lord has cleared of guilt, whose lives are lived in complete honesty!

³ When I refused to confess my sin, my body wasted away, and I groaned all day long.

⁴ Day and night your hand of discipline was heavy on me. My strength evaporated like water in the summer heat.

⁵ Finally, I confessed all my sins to you and stopped trying to hide my guilt. I said to myself, "I will confess my rebellion to the Lord." And you forgave me! All my guilt is gone.

⁶ Therefore, let all the godly pray to you while there is still time, that they may not drown in the floodwaters of judgment.

⁷ For you are my hiding place; you protect me from trouble. You surround me with songs of victory.

⁸ The Lord says, "I will guide you along the best pathway for your life. I will advise you and watch over you. ⁹ Do not be like a senseless horse or mule that needs a bit and bridle to keep it under control."

¹⁰ Many sorrows come to the wicked, but unfailing love surrounds those who trust the Lord.

Psalm 32:1-10

April 2

Hope for Everyone

*H*ope is an important thing. Like when you have a big math test that you forgot to study for, but you hope that you remember enough from class to pass the test. Where does real hope that things in life will work out come from? God and God alone. He loves you very much so you know He will take care of you, no matter what.

⁴ For the word of the Lord holds true, and we can trust everything he does. ⁵ He loves whatever is just and good; the unfailing love of the Lord fills the earth.

⁶ The Lord merely spoke, and the heavens were created. He breathed the word, and all the stars were born.

⁷ He assigned the sea its boundaries and locked the oceans in vast reservoirs.

⁸ Let the whole world fear the Lord, and let everyone stand in awe of him. ⁹ For when he spoke, the world began! It appeared at his command.

¹¹ But the Lord's plans stand firm forever; his intentions can never be shaken. ¹² What joy for the nation whose God is the Lord, whose people he has chosen as his inheritance. ¹³ The Lord looks down from heaven and sees the whole human race.

¹⁴ From his throne he observes all who live on the earth. ¹⁵ He made their hearts, so he understands everything they do.

¹⁸ But the Lord watches over those who fear him, those who rely on his unfailing love. ²⁰ We put our hope in the Lord. He is our help and our shield. ²¹ In him our hearts rejoice, for we trust in his holy name. ²² Let your unfailing love surround us, Lord, for our hope is in you alone.

Psalm 33:4-9, 11-15, 18, 20-22

April 3

The Honest Truth

*Y*ou can fool people. You can make others think you are loving, kind and honest, but you can't fool God. He sees your heart and knows what your true motivations are. Be righteous before God. Obey Him and love Him. And He will always help you.

¹ I will praise the Lord at all times. I will constantly speak his praises.

² I will boast only in the Lord; let all who are helpless take heart.

³ Come, let us tell of the Lord's greatness; let us exalt his name together.

⁸ Taste and see that the Lord is good. Oh, the joys of those who take refuge in him!

¹¹ Come, my children, and listen to me, and I will teach you to fear the Lord.

¹² Does anyone want to live a life that is long and prosperous?

¹³ Then keep your tongue from speaking evil and your lips from telling lies!

¹⁴ Turn away from evil and do good. Search for peace, and work to maintain it.

¹⁵ The eyes of the Lord watch over those who do right; his ears are open to their cries for help.

¹⁶ But the Lord turns his face against those who do evil; he will erase their memory from the earth.

¹⁷ The Lord hears his people when they call to him for help. He rescues them from all their troubles.

¹⁸ The Lord is close to the brokenhearted; he rescues those whose spirits are crushed.

Psalm 34:1-3, 8, 11-18

April 4

Real Love

*E*veryone wants to be loved, right? Unfortunately sometimes the love that your friends have for you may fade away. But the love of God will never stop. You can count on God's love surrounding you and encouraging you forever! There is nothing that will make Him stop loving you and His love is bigger than anything you can ever imagine!

5 Your unfailing love, O Lord, is as vast as the heavens; your faithfulness reaches beyond the clouds.

6 Your righteousness is like the mighty mountains, your justice like the ocean depths. You care for people and animals alike, O Lord.

7 How precious is your unfailing love, O God! All humanity finds shelter in the shadow of your wings.

8 You feed them from the abundance of your own house, letting them drink from your river of delights.

9 For you are the fountain of life, the light by which we see.

10 Pour out your unfailing love on those who love you; give justice to those with honest hearts.

11 Don't let the proud trample me or the wicked push me around.

12 Look! Those who do evil have fallen! They are thrown down, never to rise again.

Psalm 36:5-12

Let Go of Anger

*W*hat makes you angry? What do you do when you are angry? Unfortunately, anger usually means you strike out against the one who made you angry. It means bad things happen. God says to just stop being angry, let God take care of the situation and let Him control your words. Let Him calm you down.

⁵ Commit everything you do to the Lord. Trust him, and he will help you.

⁶ He will make your innocence radiate like the dawn, and the justice of your cause will shine like the noonday sun.

⁷ Be still in the presence of the Lord, and wait patiently for him to act. Don't worry about evil people who prosper or fret about their wicked schemes.

⁸ Stop being angry! Turn from your rage! Do not lose your temper – it only leads to harm.

⁹ For the wicked will be destroyed, but those who trust in the Lord will possess the land.

²³ The Lord directs the steps of the godly. He delights in every detail of their lives.

²⁴ Though they stumble, they will never fall, for the Lord holds them by the hand.

³⁹ The Lord rescues the godly; he is their fortress in times of trouble.

⁴⁰ The Lord helps them, rescuing them from the wicked. He saves them, and they find shelter in him.

Psalm 37:5-9, 23-24, 39-40

What Is Your Song?

*W*hat's your favorite song? Music usually makes you feel good or says something that you agree with. Did you know that God has given you a new song of praise to Him? Make a list of all the things He does for you … there's your song!

³ He has given me a new song to sing, a hymn of praise to our God. Many will see what he has done and be amazed. They will put their trust in the Lord.

⁴ Oh, the joys of those who trust the Lord, who have no confidence in the proud or in those who worship idols.

⁵ O Lord my God, you have performed many wonders for us. Your plans for us are too numerous to list. You have no equal. If I tried to recite all your wonderful deeds, I would never come to the end of them.

⁶ You take no delight in sacrifices or offerings. Now that you have made me listen, I finally understand – you don't require burnt offerings or sin offerings.

⁷ Then I said, "Look, I have come. As is written about me in the Scriptures:

⁸ I take joy in doing your will, my God, for your instructions are written on my heart."

¹⁶ But may all who search for you be filled with joy and gladness in you. May those who love your salvation repeatedly shout, "The Lord is great!"

¹⁷ As for me, since I am poor and needy, let the Lord keep me in his thoughts. You are my helper and my savior. O my God, do not delay.

Psalm 40:3-8, 16-17

Your Heart's Longing

*W*hat do you long for? Would you like to be super popular? Do you want to be a good athlete or musician? Are you longing to be loved? Or, like the psalmist, does your heart long to know God better? That's a really good thing to long for!

¹ As the deer longs for streams of water, so I long for you, O God. ² I thirst for God, the living God. When can I go and stand before him?

³ Day and night I have only tears for food, while my enemies continually taunt me, saying, "Where is this God of yours?"

⁵ Why am I discouraged? Why is my heart so sad? I will put my hope in God! I will praise him again – my Savior and ⁶ my God! Now I am deeply discouraged, but I will remember you – even from distant Mount Hermon, the source of the Jordan, from the land of Mount Mizar.

⁷ I hear the tumult of the raging seas as your waves and surging tides sweep over me.

⁸ But each day the Lord pours his unfailing love upon me, and through each night I sing his songs, praying to God who gives me life.

⁹ "O God my rock," I cry, "Why have you forgotten me? Why must I wander around in grief, oppressed by my enemies?"

¹⁰ Their taunts break my bones. They scoff, "Where is this God of yours?"

¹¹ Why am I discouraged? Why is my heart so sad? I will put my hope in God! I will praise him again – my Savior and my God!

Psalm 42:1-3, 5-11

Be Still and Know

*Y*ou may know all the right Bible verses about God's power and strength and even about His love for you. But do you know God? It's pretty hard to know Him if you don't spend time reading His Word, then being quiet and listening for His voice.

¹ God is our refuge and strength, always ready to help in times of trouble.

² So we will not fear when earthquakes come and the mountains crumble into the sea.

³ Let the oceans roar and foam. Let the mountains tremble as the waters surge!

⁴ A river brings joy to the city of our God, the sacred home of the Most High.

⁵ God dwells in that city; it cannot be destroyed. From the very break of day, God will protect it.

⁶ The nations are in chaos, and their kingdoms crumble! God's voice thunders, and the earth melts!

⁷ The Lord of Heaven's Armies is here among us; the God of Israel is our fortress.

⁸ Come, see the glorious works of the Lord: See how he brings destruction upon the world.

⁹ He causes wars to end throughout the earth. He breaks the bow and snaps the spear; he burns the shields with fire.

¹⁰ "Be still, and know that I am God! I will be honored by every nation. I will be honored throughout the world."

¹¹ The Lord of Heaven's Armies is here among us; the God of Israel is our fortress.

Psalm 46

The Great Clean-Up

*T*he truth is that everyone sins. No matter how hard you try to do things right, sin happens. The wonderful thing is that when you ask God's forgiveness, He gives it. He forgives and cleans up your heart so you can start fresh, every time.

¹ Have mercy on me, O God, because of your unfailing love. Because of your great compassion, blot out the stain of my sins.

² Wash me clean from my guilt. Purify me from my sin.

³ For I recognize my rebellion; it haunts me day and night.

⁴ Against you, and you alone, have I sinned; I have done what is evil in your sight. You will be proved right in what you say, and your judgment against me is just.

⁵ For I was born a sinner – yes, from the moment my mother conceived me.

⁶ But you desire honesty from the womb, teaching me wisdom even there.

⁷ Purify me from my sins, and I will be clean; wash me, and I will be whiter than snow.

⁸ Oh, give me back my joy again; you have broken me – now let me rejoice.

⁹ Don't keep looking at my sins. Remove the stain of my guilt.

¹⁰ Create in me a clean heart, O God. Renew a loyal spirit within me.

¹¹ Do not banish me from your presence, and don't take your Holy Spirit from me.

¹² Restore to me the joy of your salvation, and make me willing to obey you.

Psalm 51:1-12

Mercy

*D*o you know what mercy is? Mercy is being forgiven when you don't deserve forgiveness. Mercy is what God gives when you ask – mercy to give you forgiveness, protection and love. How awesome is that?

¹ Have mercy on me, O God, have mercy! I look to you for protection. I will hide beneath the shadow of your wings until the danger passes by.

² I cry out to God Most High, to God who will fulfill his purpose for me.

³ He will send help from heaven to rescue me, disgracing those who hound me. My God will send forth his unfailing love and faithfulness.

⁵ Be exalted, O God, above the highest heavens! May your glory shine over all the earth.

⁷ My heart is confident in you, O God; my heart is confident. No wonder I can sing your praises!

⁸ Wake up, my heart! Wake up, O lyre and harp! I will wake the dawn with my song.

⁹ I will thank you, Lord, among all the people. I will sing your praises among the nations.

¹⁰ For your unfailing love is as high as the heavens. Your faithfulness reaches to the clouds.

¹¹ Be exalted, O God, above the highest heavens. May your glory shine over all the earth.

Psalm 57:1-3, 5, 7-11

All Tired Out

*L*ife can be full of pressure. You have the pressures of school, of friendships, of thinking about your future. How do you get out from under the pressure? Turn to God. No, don't just turn to Him … cling to Him. Let Him hold you up, protect you and guide you.

¹ O God, you are my God; I earnestly search for you. My soul thirsts for you; my whole body longs for you in this parched and weary land where there is no water.

² I have seen you in your sanctuary and gazed upon your power and glory.

³ Your unfailing love is better than life itself; how I praise you!

⁴ I will praise you as long as I live, lifting up my hands to you in prayer.

⁵ You satisfy me more than the richest feast. I will praise you with songs of joy.

⁶ I lie awake thinking of you, meditating on you through the night.

⁷ Because you are my helper, I sing for joy in the shadow of your wings.

⁸ I cling to you; your strong right hand holds me securely.

⁹ But those plotting to destroy me will come to ruin. They will go down into the depths of the earth.

¹⁰ They will die by the sword and become the food of jackals.

¹¹ But the king will rejoice in God. All who trust in him will praise him, while liars will be silenced.

Psalm 63

What You Need

*G*od takes care of His creation by providing what it needs. He takes care of you by providing what you need. Notice that He provides what you NEED – not what you WANT. Praise Him for providing your needs. Thank Him for when He gives you what you want.

5 You faithfully answer our prayers with awesome deeds, O God our savior. You are the hope of everyone on earth, even those who sail on distant seas.

6 You formed the mountains by your power and armed yourself with mighty strength.

7 You quieted the raging oceans with their pounding waves and silenced the shouting of the nations.

8 Those who live at the ends of the earth stand in awe of your wonders. From where the sun rises to where it sets, you inspire shouts of joy.

9 You take care of the earth and water it, making it rich and fertile. The river of God has plenty of water; it provides a bountiful harvest of grain, for you have ordered it so.

10 You drench the plowed ground with rain, melting the clods and leveling the ridges. You soften the earth with showers and bless its abundant crops.

11 You crown the year with a bountiful harvest; even the hard pathways overflow with abundance.

12 The grasslands of the wilderness become a lush pasture, and the hillsides blossom with joy.

13 The meadows are clothed with flocks of sheep, and the valleys are carpeted with grain. They all shout and sing for joy!

Psalm 65:5-13

Miracles

*H*ave you ever thought about what miracles God does to take care of you? You probably don't know how often He does something amazing to provide for you or protect you. Your life is completely in His hands. Praise Him for all He does – both what you see and what you don't see.

¹ Shout joyful praises to God, all the earth! ² Sing about the glory of his name! Tell the world how glorious he is.

³ Say to God, "How awesome are your deeds! Your enemies cringe before your mighty power. ⁴ Everything on earth will worship you; they will sing your praises, shouting your name in glorious songs."

⁵ Come and see what our God has done, what awesome miracles he performs for people!

⁶ He made a dry path through the Red Sea, and his people went across on foot. There we rejoiced in him.

⁷ For by his great power he rules forever. He watches every movement of the nations; let no rebel rise in defiance.

⁸ Let the whole world bless our God and loudly sing his praises.

¹⁸ If I had not confessed the sin in my heart, the Lord would not have listened. ¹⁹ But God did listen! He paid attention to my prayer. ²⁰ Praise God, who did not ignore my prayer or withdraw his unfailing love from me.

Psalm 66:1-8, 18-20

May the Whole World Know

*G*od's desire has always been for the whole world – every person – to know Him and to love Him. As you live for Him, worship Him, praise Him and love Him, others around you will become aware of His power, strength and love. You are part of God's plan for the whole world to know!

[1] May God be merciful and bless us. May his face smile with favor on us.

[2] May your ways be known throughout the earth, your saving power among people everywhere.

[3] May the nations praise you, O God. Yes, may all the nations praise you.

[4] Let the whole world sing for joy, because you govern the nations with justice and guide the people of the whole world.

[5] May the nations praise you, O God. Yes, may all the nations praise you.

[6] Then the earth will yield its harvests, and God, our God, will richly bless us.

[7] Yes, God will bless us, and people all over the world will fear him.

Psalm 67

Your Future!

*D*o you find yourself getting caught up in daily life so that you focus on stuff like grades, popularity, maybe even a future career? You may find yourself becoming so "now" focused that you forget there is a greater future – heaven.

¹ How lovely is your dwelling place, O Lord of Heaven's Armies.

² I long, yes, I faint with longing to enter the courts of the Lord. With my whole being, body and soul, I will shout joyfully to the living God.

³ Even the sparrow finds a home, and the swallow builds her nest and raises her young at a place near your altar, O Lord of Heaven's Armies, my King and my God!

⁴ What joy for those who can live in your house, always singing your praises.

⁵ What joy for those whose strength comes from the Lord, who have set their minds on a pilgrimage to Jerusalem.

¹⁰ A single day in your courts is better than a thousand anywhere else! I would rather be a gatekeeper in the house of my God than live the good life in the homes of the wicked.

¹¹ For the Lord God is our sun and our shield. He gives us grace and glory. The Lord will withhold no good thing from those who do what is right.

¹² O Lord of Heaven's Armies, what joy for those who trust in you.

Psalm 84:1-5, 10-12

Speaking Peace

*W*hat beautiful words the psalmist put together here – that God speaks peace to His faithful people. Are you faithful to Him? Do you seek to know Him better and better? Do you read His Word and spend time talking to Him? Do you trust Him with your life? It's hard to have His peace if you don't trust Him completely.

⁷ Show us your unfailing love, O Lord, and grant us your salvation.

⁸ I listen carefully to what God the Lord is saying, for he speaks peace to his faithful people. But let them not return to their foolish ways.

⁹ Surely his salvation is near to those who fear him, so our land will be filled with his glory.

¹⁰ Unfailing love and truth have met together. Righteousness and peace have kissed!

¹¹ Truth springs up from the earth, and righteousness smiles down from heaven.

¹² Yes, the Lord pours down his blessings. Our land will yield its bountiful harvest.

¹³ Righteousness goes as a herald before him, preparing the way for his steps.

Psalm 85:7-13

The Power of Prayer

To whom do you go when you are scared, lonely, nervous, stressed? Who do you talk to when you have a problem or a need? It's good to talk with your parents. It's good to have close friends to talk with, too. But, don't forget to talk to God. Ultimately, He is the One who can and will help you. He wants to. He loves you very much.

[1] Bend down, O Lord, and hear my prayer; answer me, for I need your help.

[2] Protect me, for I am devoted to you. Save me, for I serve you and trust you. You are my God.

[3] Be merciful to me, O Lord, for I am calling on you constantly. [4] Give me happiness, O Lord, for I give myself to you.

[5] O Lord, you are so good, so ready to forgive, so full of unfailing love for all who ask for your help.

[6] Listen closely to my prayer, O Lord; hear my urgent cry. [7] I will call to you whenever I'm in trouble, and you will answer me.

[10] For you are great and perform wonderful deeds. You alone are God.

[11] Teach me your ways, O Lord, that I may live according to your truth! Grant me purity of heart, so that I may honor you.

[12] With all my heart I will praise you, O Lord my God. I will give glory to your name forever, [13] for your love for me is very great. You have rescued me from the depths of death.

Psalm 86:1-7, 10-13

The Words You Speak

*W*hat kinds of words come out of your mouth on a typical day? Mean words about someone else? Unkind words about a friend? Half truths about a class-mate? Complaints, whines or defeated words? How many of your words are about God? How often do you speak about His unfailing love? How often do you speak of His forgiveness, protection, provisions? Use your voice to sing His praises today! Others will hear that praise.

¹ I will sing of the Lord's unfailing love forever! Young and old will hear of your faithfulness.

² Your unfailing love will last forever. Your faithfulness is as enduring as the heavens.

⁹ You rule the oceans. You subdue their storm-tossed waves.

¹⁰ You crushed the great sea monster. You scattered your enemies with your mighty arm.

¹¹ The heavens are yours, and the earth is yours; everything in the world is yours – you created it all.

¹⁵ Happy are those who hear the joyful call to worship, for they will walk in the light of your presence, Lord.

¹⁶ They rejoice all day long in your wonderful reputation. They exult in your righteousness.

¹⁷ You are their glorious strength.

Psalm 89:1-2, 9-11, 15-17

A Thankful Heart

*D*o you appreciate being thanked when you help someone else? Sure you do. It shows that they noticed your effort. Guess what? God appreciates being thanked, too. Remember to thank Him for all He does for you. It shows you are paying attention.

[1] It is good to give thanks to the Lord, to sing praises to the Most High.

[2] It is good to proclaim your unfailing love in the morning, your faithfulness in the evening, [3] accompanied by the ten-stringed harp and the melody of the lyre.

[4] You thrill me, Lord, with all you have done for me! I sing for joy because of what you have done.

[5] O Lord, what great works you do! And how deep are your thoughts.

[8] But you, O Lord, will be exalted forever.

[9] Your enemies, Lord, will surely perish; all evildoers will be scattered.

[10] But you have made me as strong as a wild ox. You have anointed me with the finest oil.

[11] My eyes have seen the downfall of my enemies; my ears have heard the defeat of my wicked opponents.

Psalm 92:1-5, 8-11

Who Is in Charge?

Some people think they are in charge of pretty much everything. But the truth is that God is in control of everything. He is the king. The cool thing is that you can trust Him with your life because He loves you very much.

¹ The Lord is king! He is robed in majesty. Indeed, the Lord is robed in majesty and armed with strength. The world stands firm and cannot be shaken.

² Your throne, O Lord, has stood from time immemorial. You yourself are from the everlasting past.

³ The floods have risen up, O Lord. The floods have roared like thunder; the floods have lifted their pounding waves.

⁴ But mightier than the violent raging of the seas, mightier than the breakers on the shore – the Lord above is mightier than these!

⁵ Your royal laws cannot be changed. Your reign, O Lord, is holy forever and ever.

Psalm 93

Worship and Bow Down

*W*hat is a natural response to recognizing how great God is? Worship! Yeah, when you stop and think about how great God is and all He has done, your heart just automatically wants to worship Him. Worship in joy!

¹ Come, let us sing to the Lord! Let us shout joyfully to the Rock of our salvation.

² Let us come to him with thanksgiving. Let us sing psalms of praise to him.

³ For the Lord is a great God, a great King above all gods.

⁴ He holds in his hands the depths of the earth and the mightiest mountains.

⁵ The sea belongs to him, for he made it. His hands formed the dry land, too.

⁶ Come, let us worship and bow down. Let us kneel before the Lord our maker, ⁷ for he is our God.

We are the people he watches over, the flock under his care.

If only you would listen to his voice today!

⁸ The Lord says, "Don't harden your hearts as Israel did at Meribah, as they did at Massah in the wilderness.

⁹ For there your ancestors tested and tried my patience, even though they saw everything I did.

¹⁰ For forty years I was angry with them, and I said, 'They are a people whose hearts turn away from me. They refuse to do what I tell them.'

¹¹ So in my anger I took an oath: 'They will never enter my place of rest.'"

Psalm 95

Joy! Joy! Joy!

*P*salm 100 is a very popular psalm. Why? Because it encourages praise and worship to God. The psalmist says to acknowledge that God is God. He is the most awesome, powerful God. Praise Him for making you. Praise Him for loving you. Praise Him for His faithfulness to His people.

¹ Shout with joy to the Lord, all the earth!

² Worship the Lord with gladness. Come before him, singing with joy.

³ Acknowledge that the Lord is God! He made us, and we are his. We are his people, the sheep of his pasture.

⁴ Enter his gates with thanksgiving; go into his courts with praise. Give thanks to him and praise his name.

⁵ For the Lord is good. His unfailing love continues forever, and his faithfulness continues to each generation.

Psalm 100

Justice!

*W*ould you like to be sure that the people who hurt you or cheat you will pay for their behavior? Well, you can be sure. God gives justice. You don't have to try to get even. Just trust God to hold others accountable.

¹ Let all that I am praise the Lord; with my whole heart, I will praise his holy name.

² Let all that I am praise the Lord; may I never forget the good things he does for me.

³ He forgives all my sins and heals all my diseases.

⁴ He redeems me from death and crowns me with love and tender mercies.

⁵ He fills my life with good things. My youth is renewed like the eagle's!

⁶ The Lord gives righteousness and justice to all who are treated unfairly.

⁷ He revealed his character to Moses and his deeds to the people of Israel.

⁸ The Lord is compassionate and merciful, slow to get angry and filled with unfailing love.

⁹ He will not constantly accuse us, nor remain angry forever.

¹⁰ He does not punish us for all our sins; he does not deal harshly with us, as we deserve.

¹¹ For his unfailing love toward those who fear him is as great as the height of the heavens above the earth.

¹² He has removed our sins as far from us as the east is from the west.

Psalm 103:1-12

Remember Me!

*T*he psalms are filled with reminders to praise God, no matter what may be going on in your life. Remember to praise Him because He is good. Praise Him for His faithful love. Praise Him for taking care of you.

¹ Praise the Lord! Give thanks to the Lord, for he is good! His faithful love endures forever. ² Who can list the glorious miracles of the Lord? Who can ever praise him enough?

³ There is joy for those who deal justly with others and always do what is right.

⁴ Remember me, Lord, when you show favor to your people; come near and rescue me.

⁵ Let me share in the prosperity of your chosen ones. Let me rejoice in the joy of your people; let me praise you with those who are your heritage.

⁷ Our ancestors in Egypt were not impressed by the Lord's miraculous deeds. They soon forgot his many acts of kindness to them. Instead, they rebelled against him at the Red Sea.

⁸ Even so, he saved them – to defend the honor of his name and to demonstrate his mighty power.

⁹ He commanded the Red Sea to dry up. He led Israel across the sea as if it were a desert.

¹⁰ So he rescued them from their enemies and redeemed them from their foes.

¹¹ Then the water returned and covered their enemies; not one of them survived.

¹² Then his people believed his promises. Then they sang his praise.

Psalm 106:1-5, 7-12

Cry Out!

*C*ry out to God when you have trouble. He is waiting to hear your voice. God encourages you throughout Scripture to pray to Him. So, talk to Him. Tell Him what you need. Thank Him for what you have.

¹ I love the Lord because he hears my voice and my prayer for mercy.

² Because he bends down to listen, I will pray as long as I have breath!

⁵ How kind the Lord is! How good he is! So merciful, this God of ours!

⁶ The Lord protects those of childlike faith; I was facing death, and he saved me.

⁷ Let my soul be at rest again, for the Lord has been good to me.

⁸ He has saved me from death, my eyes from tears, my feet from stumbling.

⁹ And so I walk in the Lord's presence as I live here on earth!

¹⁰ I believed in you, so I said, "I am deeply troubled, Lord." ¹¹ In my anxiety I cried out to you, "These people are all liars!"

¹² What can I offer the Lord for all he has done for me?

¹³ I will lift up the cup of salvation and praise the Lord's name for saving me.

¹⁴ I will keep my promises to the Lord in the presence of all his people.

¹⁵ The Lord cares deeply when his loved ones die.

¹⁶ O Lord, I am your servant; yes, I am your servant, born into your household; you have freed me from my chains.

Psalm 116:1-2, 5-16

The Safest Place

*G*od is the safest place to hide. The psalmist talks about taking refuge in the Lord – that means He is your hiding place. He will protect you from anything and everything.

¹ Give thanks to the Lord, for he is good! His faithful love endures forever.

⁵ In my distress I prayed to the Lord, and the Lord answered me and set me free.

⁶ The Lord is for me, so I will have no fear. What can mere people do to me?

⁷ Yes, the Lord is for me; he will help me. I will look in triumph at those who hate me.

⁸ It is better to take refuge in the Lord than to trust in people.

⁹ It is better to take refuge in the Lord than to trust in princes.

²² The stone that the builders rejected has now become the cornerstone.

²³ This is the Lord's doing, and it is wonderful to see.

²⁴ This is the day the Lord has made. We will rejoice and be glad in it.

²⁵ Please, Lord, please save us. Please, Lord, please give us success.

²⁶ Bless the one who comes in the name of the Lord. We bless you from the house of the Lord.

²⁷ The Lord is God, shining upon us. Take the sacrifice and bind it with cords on the altar.

²⁸ You are my God, and I will praise you! You are my God, and I will exalt you!

Psalm 118:1, 5-9, 22-28

Not Perfect

You don't have to be perfect to come to God. Good thing, right? No one is perfect. But if you try to keep God's commandments and your heart desires to obey God, then He will forgive you and just keep on loving you!

¹ Joyful are people of integrity, who follow the instructions of the Lord.

² Joyful are those who obey his laws and search for him with all their hearts.

³ They do not compromise with evil, and they walk only in his paths.

⁴ You have charged us to keep your commandments carefully.

⁵ Oh, that my actions would consistently reflect your decrees! ⁶ Then I will not be ashamed when I compare my life with your commands.

⁷ As I learn your righteous regulations, I will thank you by living as I should!

⁸ I will obey your decrees. Please don't give up on me!

⁹ How can a young person stay pure? By obeying your word.

¹⁰ I have tried hard to find you – don't let me wander from your commands.

¹¹ I have hidden your word in my heart, that I might not sin against you.

¹² I praise you, O Lord; teach me your decrees.

Psalm 119:1-12

Eager to Learn

*A*re you eager to learn from God's instructions? Do you read His Word and try to understand it so that you can grow in obeying Him? Keep searching and learning so that you become stronger in living for God.

³³ Teach me your decrees, O Lord; I will keep them to the end.

³⁴ Give me understanding and I will obey your instructions; I will put them into practice with all my heart.

³⁵ Make me walk along the path of your commands, for that is where my happiness is found.

³⁶ Give me an eagerness for your laws rather than a love for money!

³⁷ Turn my eyes from worthless things, and give me life through your word.

⁴¹ Lord, give me your unfailing love, the salvation that you promised me.

⁴² Then I can answer those who taunt me, for I trust in your word.

⁴³ Do not snatch your word of truth from me, for your regulations are my only hope.

⁴⁴ I will keep on obeying your instructions forever and ever.

⁴⁵ I will walk in freedom, for I have devoted myself to your commandments.

⁴⁶ I will speak to kings about your laws, and I will not be ashamed.

⁴⁷ How I delight in your commands! How I love them!

⁴⁸ I honor and love your commands. I meditate on your decrees.

Psalm 119:33-37, 41-48

Not On Your Own

*T*he cool thing about living for God is that you don't have to do it alone. God's power is always available to help you along the journey. He loves you that much!

⁷⁵ I know, O Lord, that your regulations are fair; you disciplined me because I needed it.

⁷⁶ Now let your unfailing love comfort me, just as you promised me, your servant.

⁷⁷ Surround me with your tender mercies so I may live, for your instructions are my delight.

⁷⁸ Bring disgrace upon the arrogant people who lied about me; meanwhile, I will concentrate on your commandments.

⁷⁹ Let me be united with all who fear you, with those who know your laws.

⁸⁰ May I be blameless in keeping your decrees; then I will never be ashamed.

⁹⁷ Oh, how I love your instructions! I think about them all day long.

⁹⁸ Your commands make me wiser than my enemies, for they are my constant guide.

¹⁰¹ I have refused to walk on any evil path, so that I may remain obedient to your word.

¹⁰² I haven't turned away from your regulations, for you have taught me well.

¹⁰³ How sweet your words taste to me; they are sweeter than honey.

¹⁰⁴ Your commandments give me understanding; no wonder I hate every false way of life.

¹⁰⁵ Your word is a lamp to guide my feet and a light for my path.

Psalm 119:75-80, 97-98, 101-105

May

Always Safe

*Y*ou are never out of God's sight or protection. It doesn't matter what's going on or what problems you have. God knows. He was watching over you yesterday. He is watching over you today. He will be watching over you tomorrow. Even if it seems you're having one problem after another, God knows and walks beside you offering strength and guidance.

[1] I look up to the mountains – does my help come from there?

[2] My help comes from the Lord, who made heaven and earth!

[3] He will not let you stumble; the one who watches over you will not slumber.

[4] Indeed, he who watches over Israel never slumbers or sleeps.

[5] The Lord himself watches over you! The Lord stands beside you as your protective shade.

[6] The sun will not harm you by day, nor the moon at night.

[7] The Lord keeps you from all harm and watches over your life.

[8] The Lord keeps watch over you as you come and go, both now and forever.

Psalm 121

Forever Thankful

*W*hen you think about what God does for you every single day, what's your response? One response should be a very thankful heart. Do you take for granted God's daily blessings? Do you expect them? Don't do that – stop and thank Him for His everyday blessings.

¹ Give thanks to the Lord, for he is good! His faithful love endures forever.

² Give thanks to the God of gods. His faithful love endures forever.

³ Give thanks to the Lord of lords. His faithful love endures forever.

⁴ Give thanks to him who alone does mighty miracles. His faithful love endures forever.

⁵ Give thanks to him who made the heavens so skillfully. His faithful love endures forever.

⁶ Give thanks to him who placed the earth among the waters. His faithful love endures forever.

⁷ Give thanks to him who made the heavenly lights – His faithful love endures forever.

²³ He remembered us in our weakness. His faithful love endures forever.

²⁴ He saved us from our enemies. His faithful love endures forever.

²⁵ He gives food to every living thing. His faithful love endures forever.

Psalm 136:1-7, 23-25

Everything Revealed

*A*re you willing for God to search your heart and know your thoughts? Have you been trying to hide things from Him? You can't, you know. Ask Him to reveal the things in your heart that keep you from knowing Him better.

¹ O Lord, you have examined my heart and know everything about me. ² You know when I sit down or stand up. You know my thoughts even when I'm far away.

⁴ You know what I am going to say even before I say it, Lord.

⁵ You go before me and follow me. You place your hand of blessing on my head.

¹³ You made all the delicate, inner parts of my body and knit me together in my mother's womb.

¹⁴ Thank you for making me so wonderfully complex! Your workmanship is marvelous – how well I know it.

¹⁵ You watched me as I was being formed in utter seclusion, as I was woven together in the dark of the womb. ¹⁶ You saw me before I was born. Every day of my life was recorded in your book. Every moment was laid out before a single day had passed.

¹⁷ How precious are your thoughts about me, O God. They cannot be numbered! ¹⁸ I can't even count them; they outnumber the grains of sand! And when I wake up, you are still with me!

²³ Search me, O God, and know my heart; test me and know my anxious thoughts.

²⁴ Point out anything in me that offends you, and lead me along the path of everlasting life.

Psalm 139:1-2, 4-5, 13-18, 23-24

Guard Your Words

*W*ow, your unguarded words can get you into trouble. Spouting angry words or unkind words leads you right down an evil path. Ask God to guard your words and help you speak in ways that will please Him.

[1] O Lord, I am calling to you. Please hurry! Listen when I cry to you for help!

[2] Accept my prayer as incense offered to you, and my upraised hands as an evening offering.

[3] Take control of what I say, O Lord, and guard my lips.

[4] Don't let me drift toward evil or take part in acts of wickedness. Don't let me share in the delicacies of those who do wrong.

[5] Let the godly strike me! It will be a kindness! If they correct me, it is soothing medicine. Don't let me refuse it.

But I pray constantly against the wicked and their deeds.

[6] When their leaders are thrown down from a cliff, the wicked will listen to my words and find them true.

[7] Like rocks brought up by a plow, the bones of the wicked will lie scattered without burial.

[8] I look to you for help, O Sovereign Lord. You are my refuge; don't let them kill me.

[9] Keep me from the traps they have set for me, from the snares of those who do wrong.

[10] Let the wicked fall into their own nets, but let me escape.

Psalm 141

May 4

Passing It On

*H*ow did you hear about God's love for you? Did your parents, grandparents or another adult share it with you? The psalmist said that one generation passes on the news to the next generation. Thank God today for the person who shared God's love with you.

⁴ Let each generation tell its children of your mighty acts; let them proclaim your power.

⁵ I will meditate on your majestic, glorious splendor and your wonderful miracles.

⁶ Your awe-inspiring deeds will be on every tongue; I will proclaim your greatness.

⁷ Everyone will share the story of your wonderful goodness; they will sing with joy about your righteousness.

⁸ The Lord is merciful and compassionate, slow to get angry and filled with unfailing love.

⁹ The Lord is good to everyone. He showers compassion on all his creation.

¹⁰ All of your works will thank you, Lord, and your faithful followers will praise you.

¹¹ They will speak of the glory of your kingdom; they will give examples of your power.

¹² They will tell about your mighty deeds and about the majesty and glory of your reign.

¹³ For your kingdom is an everlasting kingdom. You rule throughout all generations.

The Lord always keeps his promises; he is gracious in all he does.

Psalm 145:4-13

So Many Words

*T*hink of all the words you speak every day. How many of them should never be spoken? Many are unkind, critical or just plain old improper. Measure your words and don't use idle ones that will hurt others. Use a big quantity of your words to praise the Lord every day!

¹ Praise the Lord from the heavens! Praise him from the skies! ² Praise him, all his angels! Praise him, all the armies of heaven!

³ Praise him, sun and moon! Praise him, all you twinkling stars!

⁴ Praise him, skies above! Praise him, vapors high above the clouds!

⁵ Let every created thing give praise to the Lord, for he issued his command, and they came into being.

⁶ He set them in place forever and ever. His decree will never be revoked.

⁷ Praise the Lord from the earth, you creatures of the ocean depths, ⁸ fire and hail, snow and clouds, wind and weather that obey him, ⁹ mountains and all hills, fruit trees and all cedars, ¹⁰ wild animals and all livestock, small scurrying animals and birds, ¹¹ kings of the earth and all people, rulers and judges of the earth, ¹² young men and young women, old men and children.

¹³ Let them all praise the name of the Lord. For his name is very great; his glory towers over the earth and heaven!

¹⁴ Praise the Lord!

Psalm 148

Any Praise You Can

*H*ow do you praise God? Do you sing songs? Play an instrument? Dance a worship dance? Praise is your offering of worship so give it any way you can and with all the joy in your heart!

¹ Praise the Lord!

Praise God in his sanctuary; praise him in his mighty heaven!

² Praise him for his mighty works; praise his unequaled greatness!

³ Praise him with a blast of the ram's horn; praise him with the lyre and harp!

⁴ Praise him with the tambourine and dancing; praise him with strings and flutes!

⁵ Praise him with a clash of cymbals; praise him with loud clanging cymbals.

⁶ Let everything that breathes sing praises to the Lord!

Psalm 150

Becoming Smarter

*L*earning in school is important. Learning from your parents is, too. But it isn't always easy. Being corrected when you do something wrong is painful and difficult. But, being able to accept correction ... especially from God ... is how you learn. Accepting correction shows that knowledge is important to you.

[5]Let the wise listen to these proverbs and become even wiser. Let those with understanding receive guidance [6] by exploring the meaning in these proverbs and parables, the words of the wise and their riddles.

[7] Fear of the Lord is the foundation of true knowledge, but fools despise wisdom and discipline.

[8] My child, listen when your father corrects you. Don't neglect your mother's instruction.

[9] What you learn from them will crown you with grace and be a chain of honor around your neck.

[10] My child, if sinners entice you, turn your back on them!

[15] My child, don't go along with them! Stay far away from their paths.

Proverbs 1:5-10, 15

What Is Wisdom?

*T*here are two definitions of wisdom. One is the definition of those who do not care anything about God. The other is God's definition of wisdom. God's wisdom is taught in the Bible. Following God's wisdom will keep you close to Him.

² Tune your ears to wisdom, and concentrate on understanding.

³ Cry out for insight, and ask for understanding.

⁴ Search for them as you would for silver; seek them like hidden treasures.

⁵ Then you will understand what it means to fear the Lord, and you will gain knowledge of God.

⁶ For the Lord grants wisdom! From his mouth come knowledge and understanding.

⁷ He grants a treasure of common sense to the honest. He is a shield to those who walk with integrity.

⁸ He guards the paths of the just and protects those who are faithful to him.

⁹ Then you will understand what is right, just, and fair, and you will find the right way to go.

¹⁰ For wisdom will enter your heart, and knowledge will fill you with joy.

¹¹ Wise choices will watch over you. Understanding will keep you safe.

¹² Wisdom will save you from evil people, from those whose words are twisted.

Proverbs 2:2-12

Who Do You Trust?

*V*erses 5 and 6 of this proverb are famous verses on trusting God. They call for full, whole-hearted trust. When you give Him all your trust, He will lead and guide you.

⁵ Trust in the Lord with all your heart; do not depend on your own understanding.

⁶ Seek his will in all you do, and he will show you which path to take.

⁷ Don't be impressed with your own wisdom. Instead, fear the Lord and turn away from evil.

⁸ Then you will have healing for your body and strength for your bones.

⁹ Honor the Lord with your wealth and with the best part of everything you produce.

¹⁰ Then he will fill your barns with grain, and your vats will overflow with good wine.

¹¹ My child, don't reject the Lord's discipline, and don't be upset when he corrects you.

¹² For the Lord corrects those he loves, just as a father corrects a child in whom he delights.

²¹ My child, don't lose sight of common sense and discernment. Hang on to them, ²² for they will refresh your soul. They are like jewels on a necklace.

²³ They keep you safe on your way, and your feet will not stumble.

²⁴ You can go to bed without fear; you will lie down and sleep soundly.

²⁷ Do not withhold good from those who deserve it when it's in your power to help them.

Proverbs 3:5-12, 21-24, 27

Godly Words Are Helpful Words

*G*irls can get pretty snarky with their words sometimes. Some even do it on purpose – trying to hurt other girls by the words they speak. But a girl who serves and loves God will speak words that are helpful and encouraging to others – showing God's love to all.

¹⁹ Too much talk leads to sin. Be sensible and keep your mouth shut.

²⁰ The words of the godly are like sterling silver; the heart of a fool is worthless.

²¹ The words of the godly encourage many, but fools are destroyed by their lack of common sense.

²² The blessing of the Lord makes a person rich, and he adds no sorrow with it.

²³ Doing wrong is fun for a fool, but living wisely brings pleasure to the sensible.

²⁷ Fear of the Lord lengthens one's life, but the years of the wicked are cut short.

²⁸ The hopes of the godly result in happiness, but the expectations of the wicked come to nothing.

²⁹ The way of the Lord is a stronghold to those with integrity, but it destroys the wicked.

³⁰ The godly will never be disturbed, but the wicked will be removed from the land.

³¹ The mouth of the godly person gives wise advice, but the tongue that deceives will be cut off.

³² The lips of the godly speak helpful words, but the mouth of the wicked speaks perverse words.

Proverbs 10:19-23, 27-32

May 11

Good Guidelines

*T*reating other people kindly seems like it should be easy and just come naturally. Unfortunately it doesn't always. This proverb gives some basic reminders to be honest and generous. This behavior will please God and will give you good relationships with other people, too.

³ Honesty guides good people; dishonesty destroys treacherous people.

⁵ The godly are directed by honesty; the wicked fall beneath their load of sin.

⁶ The godliness of good people rescues them; the ambition of treacherous people traps them.

¹³ A gossip goes around telling secrets, but those who are trustworthy can keep a confidence.

²⁰ The Lord detests people with crooked hearts, but he delights in those with integrity.

²⁴ Give freely and become more wealthy; be stingy and lose everything.

²⁵ The generous will prosper; those who refresh others will themselves be refreshed.

²⁷ If you search for good, you will find favor; but if you search for evil, it will find you!

²⁸ Trust in your money and down you go! But the godly flourish like leaves in spring.

Proverbs 11:3, 5-6, 13, 20, 24-25, 27-28

Getting Along with Others

*G*etting along with others is not always easy. It takes some thought. It takes some self-control. It takes living for God and reading His Word. It's true that it's not easy to be kind and considerate to others. But, it is the right thing to do – the God thing to do.

¹ A gentle answer deflects anger, but harsh words make tempers flare.

² The tongue of the wise makes knowledge appealing, but the mouth of a fool belches out foolishness.

³ The Lord is watching everywhere, keeping his eye on both the evil and the good.

⁴ Gentle words are a tree of life; a deceitful tongue crushes the spirit.

⁷ The lips of the wise give good advice; the heart of a fool has none to give.

¹³ A glad heart makes a happy face; a broken heart crushes the spirit.

¹⁴ A wise person is hungry for knowledge, while the fool feeds on trash.

¹⁶ Better to have little, with fear for the Lord, than to have great treasure and inner turmoil.

¹⁷ A bowl of vegetables with someone you love is better than steak with someone you hate.

¹⁸ A hot-tempered person starts fights; a cool-tempered person stops them.

²³ Everyone enjoys a fitting reply; it is wonderful to say the right thing at the right time!

Proverbs 15:1-4, 7, 13-14, 16-18, 23

Actions Talk

*Y*ou can "say" whatever you want about loving God and living for Him. But, if your behavior doesn't back up your words ... save your breath. Words are cheap and behavior is not. If you have asked Jesus to be your Savior, He changes your heart and your behavior. It will show in how you treat others.

⁹ Who can say, "I have cleansed my heart; I am pure and free from sin"?

¹⁰ False weights and unequal measures – the Lord detests double standards of every kind.

¹¹ Even children are known by the way they act, whether their conduct is pure, and whether it is right.

²² Don't say, "I will get even for this wrong." Wait for the Lord to handle the matter.

²³ The Lord detests double standards; he is not pleased by dishonest scales.

²⁴ The Lord directs our steps, so why try to understand everything along the way?

²⁹ The glory of the young is their strength; the gray hair of experience is the splendor of the old.

Proverbs 20:9-11, 22-24, 29

Self Thoughts

*D*o you look at yourself and think you're doing pretty good? Do you compare yourself to other people and feel, "I'm not so bad." Remember that being prideful is sin. God sees everything – your thoughts, your actions, your words and He knows the true condition of your heart. Submit to Him, live for Him and let Him teach and guide you.

[1] The king's heart is like a stream of water directed by the Lord; he guides it wherever he pleases.

[2] People may be right in their own eyes, but the Lord examines their heart.

[3] The Lord is more pleased when we do what is right and just than when we offer him sacrifices.

[4] Haughty eyes, a proud heart, and evil actions are all sin.

[5] Good planning and hard work lead to prosperity, but hasty shortcuts lead to poverty.

[6] Wealth created by a lying tongue is a vanishing mist and a deadly trap.

[20] The wise have wealth and luxury, but fools spend whatever they get.

[21] Whoever pursues righteousness and unfailing love will find life, righteousness, and honor.

[25] Despite their desires, the lazy will come to ruin, for their hands refuse to work.

[26] Some people are always greedy for more, but the godly love to give!

Proverbs 21:1-6, 20-21, 25-26

How to Treat Others

*G*od is pretty clear on how you should treat other people. His Word instructs you to be honest and kind to others and to treat them with respect. He tells you to stay away from angry people so you don't become like them. Pay attention to God's teachings. It is the wise thing to do.

[17] Listen to the words of the wise; apply your heart to my instruction.

[18] For it is good to keep these sayings in your heart and always ready on your lips.

[19] I am teaching you today – yes, you – so you will trust in the Lord.

[20] I have written thirty sayings for you, filled with advice and knowledge.

[21] In this way, you may know the truth and take an accurate report to those who sent you.

[22] Don't rob the poor just because you can, or exploit the needy in court.

[23] For the Lord is their defender. He will ruin anyone who ruins them.

[24] Don't befriend angry people or associate with hot-tempered people, [25] or you will learn to be like them and endanger your soul.

[26] Don't agree to guarantee another person's debt or put up security for someone else.

[27] If you can't pay it, even your bed will be snatched from under you.

Proverbs 22:17-27

May 16

A Role Model

*T*he world may tell you that a woman of value is physically beautiful. But a true woman of value is honest, speaks wisely and cares for those around her. She is more precious than expensive jewels!

¹⁰ Who can find a virtuous and capable wife? She is more precious than rubies.

¹¹ Her husband can trust her, and she will greatly enrich his life.

¹² She brings him good, not harm, all the days of her life.

¹⁵ She gets up before dawn to prepare breakfast for her household and plan the day's work for her servant girls.

¹⁶ She goes to inspect a field and buys it; with her earnings she plants a vineyard.

¹⁷ She is energetic and strong, a hard worker.

¹⁸ She makes sure her dealings are profitable; her lamp burns late into the night.

¹⁹ Her hands are busy spinning thread, her fingers twisting fiber.

²⁰ She extends a helping hand to the poor and opens her arms to the needy.

²¹ She has no fear of winter for her household, for everyone has warm clothes.

²² She makes her own bedspreads. She dresses in fine linen and purple gowns.

²³ Her husband is well known at the city gates, where he sits with the other civic leaders.

²⁵ She is clothed with strength and dignity, and she laughs without fear of the future.

Proverbs 31:10-12, 15-23, 25

Everything in Its Time

Sometimes we get impatient with God because things don't happen as quickly as we want them to. But never fear – He knows what He is doing. Just as there are right times to plant crops and to harvest them, there are right times for everything else in life. Trusting God is the key to accepting that everything happens in the right time.

¹ For everything there is a season, a time for every activity under heaven.

² A time to be born and a time to die. A time to plant and a time to harvest.

³ A time to kill and a time to heal. A time to tear down and a time to build up.

⁴ A time to cry and a time to laugh. A time to grieve and a time to dance.

⁵ A time to scatter stones and a time to gather stones. A time to embrace and a time to turn away.

⁶ A time to search and a time to quit searching. A time to keep and a time to throw away.

⁷ A time to tear and a time to mend. A time to be quiet and a time to speak.

⁸ A time to love and a time to hate. A time for war and a time for peace.

Ecclesiastes 3:1-8

The Power of Friends

*T*here is so much power in friendship. A good friend becomes a partner who helps you become the best person you can be. A good friend encourages you when you are sad. She picks you up when you are down. She laughs with you, stands with you, prays with you. A good friend is one who encourages you to know God better and better. Together, you, your friend and God are the strongest team ever!

9 Two people are better off than one, for they can help each other succeed.

10 If one person falls, the other can reach out and help. But someone who falls alone is in real trouble.

11 Likewise, two people lying close together can keep each other warm. But how can one be warm alone?

12 A person standing alone can be attacked and defeated, but two can stand back-to-back and conquer. Three are even better, for a triple-braided cord is not easily broken.

Ecclesiastes 4:9-12

Empty Promises

Sometimes when a girl has a problem or is afraid, she is tempted to make all kinds of promises to God. These are often empty promises and ones that cannot be kept. Empty promises, like empty words are ... empty. Don't disrespect God in this way. When you make a promise to Him, intend to keep it and honor Him with your actions and your words.

[1] As you enter the house of God, keep your ears open and your mouth shut. It is evil to make mindless offerings to God.
[2] Don't make rash promises, and don't be hasty in bringing matters before God. After all, God is in heaven, and you are here on earth. So let your words be few.

[3] Too much activity gives you restless dreams; too many words make you a fool.

[4] When you make a promise to God, don't delay in following through, for God takes no pleasure in fools. Keep all the promises you make to him. [5] It is better to say nothing than to make a promise and not keep it. [6] Don't let your mouth make you sin. And don't defend yourself by telling the Temple messenger that the promise you made was a mistake. That would make God angry, and he might wipe out everything you have achieved.

[7] Talk is cheap, like daydreams and other useless activities. Fear God instead.

Ecclesiastes 5:1-7

Use Your Time Wisely

*I*t may be hard to understand while you're young but it matters how you spend your time – all your time. When you have work to do (including schoolwork) work hard at it. When it's time to trust God – trust Him. In other words, pay attention to what you're doing and what you're saying because ... it matters.

⁴ Farmers who wait for perfect weather never plant. If they watch every cloud, they never harvest.

⁵ Just as you cannot understand the path of the wind or the mystery of a tiny baby growing in its mother's womb, so you cannot understand the activity of God, who does all things.

⁶ Plant your seed in the morning and keep busy all afternoon, for you don't know if profit will come from one activity or another – or maybe both.

⁷ Light is sweet; how pleasant to see a new day dawning.

⁸ When people live to be very old, let them rejoice in every day of life. But let them also remember there will be many dark days. Everything still to come is meaningless.

⁹ Young people, it's wonderful to be young! Enjoy every minute of it. Do everything you want to do; take it all in. But remember that you must give an account to God for everything you do.

¹⁰ So refuse to worry, and keep your body healthy. But remember that youth, with a whole life before you, is meaningless.

Ecclesiastes 11:4-10

May 21

Starting Well

*G*etting off on the right foot means making good choices that get you off to a good start on a project or in a friendship – it means beginning well. Choosing at a young age to start living for God, obeying Him, trusting Him, loving Him and sharing all that with others is getting off on the right foot.

¹ Don't let the excitement of youth cause you to forget your Creator. Honor him in your youth before you grow old and say, "Life is not pleasant anymore." ² Remember him before the light of the sun, moon, and stars is dim to your old eyes, and rain clouds continually darken your sky.

³ Remember him before your legs – the guards of your house – start to tremble; and before your shoulders – the strong men – stoop. Remember him before your teeth – your few remaining servants – stop grinding; and before your eyes – the women looking through the windows – see dimly.

⁴ Remember him before the door to life's opportunities is closed and the sound of work fades. Now you rise at the first chirping of the birds, but then all their sounds will grow faint.

⁶ Yes, remember your Creator now while you are young, before the silver cord of life snaps and the golden bowl is broken. Don't wait until the water jar is smashed at the spring and the pulley is broken at the well.

¹³ That's the whole story. Here now is my final conclusion: Fear God and obey his commands, for this is everyone's duty. ¹⁴ God will judge us for everything we do, including every secret thing, whether good or bad.

Ecclesiastes 12:1-4, 6, 13-14

I'm Sorry

*D*o you think this is a good philosophy: I'll do whatever I want and apologize later if necessary? It isn't, is it? It's not a good way to treat people and it is definitely not a good way to treat God. It's best to come to Him with a repentant heart and ask Him to wash your sins away. He will ... because He loves you.

¹² When you come to worship me, who asked you to parade through my courts with all your ceremony?

¹³ Stop bringing me your meaningless gifts; the incense of your offerings disgusts me! As for your celebrations of the new moon and the Sabbath and your special days for fasting – they are all sinful and false. I want no more of your pious meetings.

¹⁴ I hate your new moon celebrations and your annual festivals. They are a burden to me. I cannot stand them!

¹⁶ Wash yourselves and be clean! Get your sins out of my sight. Give up your evil ways.

¹⁷ Learn to do good. Seek justice. Help the oppressed. Defend the cause of orphans. Fight for the rights of widows.

¹⁸ "Come now, let's settle this," says the Lord. "Though your sins are like scarlet, I will make them as white as snow. Though they are red like crimson, I will make them as white as wool."

Isaiah 1:12-14, 16-18

I Know for Certain

It is so cool that the Old Testament prophets knew that Jesus was coming. They even wrote about it. They knew that Jesus was coming and they even knew what names He would be known by. Just think, if God told the Old Testament prophets about Jesus, then you know that His coming was the plan all along. That's how much God loves you – He sent His only Son to earth to take care of your sins!

⁶ For a child is born to us, a son is given to us. The government will rest on his shoulders. And he will be called: Wonderful Counselor, Mighty God, Everlasting Father, Prince of Peace.

⁷ His government and its peace will never end. He will rule with fairness and justice from the throne of his ancestor David for all eternity.

Isaiah 9:6-7

Perfect Description

*R*ead these words that describe Jesus – His delight in obeying God. His fairness in judging people and His desire for justice for everyone. Jesus is love and His love is focused on you.

¹ Out of the stump of David's family will grow a shoot – yes, a new Branch bearing fruit from the old root.

² And the Spirit of the Lord will rest on him – the Spirit of wisdom and understanding, the Spirit of counsel and might, the Spirit of knowledge and the fear of the Lord.

³ He will delight in obeying the Lord. He will not judge by appearance nor make a decision based on hearsay.

⁴ He will give justice to the poor and make fair decisions for the exploited. The earth will shake at the force of his word, and one breath from his mouth will destroy the wicked.

⁵ He will wear righteousness like a belt and truth like an undergarment.

Isaiah 11:1-5

Tower of Refuge

*T*here are times when life gets stinky – your best friend is mad at you, some other girls are being incredibly unkind, school isn't going well, you aren't getting along with your parents ... and you just need to know that you're loved. You want to know that someone has your back and is looking out for you. Look no farther – God is your tower of refuge. He loves you. He will take care of you.

4 But you are a tower of refuge to the poor, O Lord, a tower of refuge to the needy in distress. You are a refuge from the storm and a shelter from the heat. For the oppressive acts of ruthless people are like a storm beating against a wall, 5 or like the relentless heat of the desert. But you silence the roar of foreign nations. As the shade of a cloud cools relentless heat, so the boastful songs of ruthless people are stilled.

6 In Jerusalem, the Lord of Heaven's Armies will spread a wonderful feast for all the people of the world. It will be a delicious banquet with clear, well-aged wine and choice meat.

7 There he will remove the cloud of gloom, the shadow of death that hangs over the earth.

8 He will swallow up death forever! The Sovereign Lord will wipe away all tears. He will remove forever all insults and mockery against his land and people. The Lord has spoken!

9 In that day the people will proclaim, "This is our God! We trusted in him, and he saved us! This is the Lord, in whom we trusted. Let us rejoice in the salvation he brings!"

Isaiah 25:4-9

Place of Peace

*W*hat's the most peaceful scene you can imagine? Resting beside a gentle mountain stream? Or maybe you like a quiet forest or a powerful waterfall. Peaceful places can certainly calm you, but real peace comes from inside. Peace that comes from God calms your worries and settles your heart.

³ You will keep in perfect peace all who trust in you, all whose thoughts are fixed on you!

⁴ Trust in the Lord always, for the Lord God is the eternal Rock.

⁷ But for those who are righteous, the way is not steep and rough. You are a God who does what is right, and you smooth out the path ahead of them.

⁸ Lord, we show our trust in you by obeying your laws; our heart's desire is to glorify your name.

⁹ All night long I search for you; in the morning I earnestly seek for God. For only when you come to judge the earth will people learn what is right.

¹² Lord, you will grant us peace; all we have accomplished is really from you.

¹⁹ But those who die in the Lord will live; their bodies will rise again! Those who sleep in the earth will rise up and sing for joy! For your life-giving light will fall like dew on your people in the place of the dead!

Isaiah 26:3-4, 7-9, 12, 19

May 27

God's Way vs. Man's Way

*W*hat does it look like when a girl has given her heart to God? It's not just obeying a bazillion rules that people have made up. Anyone can keep a list of rules but when a girl truly loves God and wants to live for Him, her heart turns to Him in obedience. She wants to obey Him more than anything!

13 And so the Lord says, "These people say they are mine. They honor me with their lips, but their hearts are far from me. And their worship of me is nothing but man-made rules learned by rote.

14 Because of this, I will once again astound these hypocrites with amazing wonders. The wisdom of the wise will pass away, and the intelligence of the intelligent will disappear."

15 What sorrow awaits those who try to hide their plans from the Lord, who do their evil deeds in the dark! "The Lord can't see us," they say. "He doesn't know what's going on!"

16 How foolish can you be? He is the Potter, and he is certainly greater than you, the clay! Should the created thing say of the one who made it, "He didn't make me"? Does a jar ever say, "The potter who made me is stupid"?

17 Soon – and it will not be very long – the forests of Lebanon will become a fertile field, and the fertile field will yield bountiful crops.

19 The humble will be filled with fresh joy from the Lord. The poor will rejoice in the Holy One of Israel.

Isaiah 29:13-17, 19

Make Your Choice

*E*veryone chooses to follow some-one or something. That's right. You may say to yourself, "Oh, I'll think about following Christ later – when I'm older." But that means you are following some-thing else right now. Don't push Christ off – follow Him now. Learn and about Him and love Him.

[15] This is what the Sovereign Lord, the Holy One of Israel, says: "Only in returning to me and resting in me will you be saved. In quietness and confidence is your strength. But you would have none of it.

[16] You said, 'No, we will get our help from Egypt. They will give us swift horses for riding into battle.' But the only swiftness you are going to see is the swiftness of your enemies chasing you!

[18] So the Lord must wait for you to come to him so he can show you his love and compassion. For the Lord is a faithful God. Blessed are those who wait for his help.

[19] O people of Zion, who live in Jerusalem, you will weep no more. He will be gracious if you ask for help. He will surely respond to the sound of your cries.

[21] Your own ears will hear him. Right behind you a voice will say, "This is the way you should go," whether to the right or to the left.

Isaiah 30:15-16, 18-19, 21

What Really Lasts

The prophet says that all things considered beautiful here on this earth will one day fade away. The only thing that will last forever and ever is God. And that shouldn't bother you because look at all He has done. His power and creativity can never be equaled.

¹ "Comfort, comfort my people," says your God.

³ Listen! It's the voice of someone shouting, "Clear the way through the wilderness for the Lord! Make a straight highway through the wasteland for our God!

⁶ A voice said, "Shout!" I asked, "What should I shout?" "Shout that people are like the grass. Their beauty fades as quickly as the flowers in a field.

⁷ The grass withers and the flowers fade beneath the breath of the Lord. And so it is with people.

⁸ The grass withers and the flowers fade, but the word of our God stands forever."

¹¹ He will feed his flock like a shepherd. He will carry the lambs in his arms, holding them close to his heart. He will gently lead the mother sheep with their young.

¹² Who else has held the oceans in his hand? Who has measured off the heavens with his fingers? Who else knows the weight of the earth or has weighed the mountains and hills on a scale?

¹⁵ No, for all the nations of the world are but a drop in the bucket. They are nothing more than dust on the scales. He picks up the whole earth as though it were a grain of sand.

Isaiah 40:1, 3, 6-8, 11-12, 15

He Knows. Yes, He Knows

Sometimes you hear people say, "God doesn't understand what my life is like. He doesn't know how hard things are for me." Well, that just isn't true. He knew everything that the Israelites faced. He knows everything you deal with, too. You can trust Him because He will support you and strengthen you!

27 O Jacob, how can you say the Lord does not see your troubles? O Israel, how can you say God ignores your rights?

28 Have you never heard? Have you never understood? The Lord is the everlasting God, the Creator of all the earth. He never grows weak or weary. No one can measure the depths of his understanding.

29 He gives power to the weak and strength to the powerless.

30 Even youths will become weak and tired, and young men will fall in exhaustion.

31 But those who trust in the Lord will find new strength. They will soar high on wings like eagles. They will run and not grow weary. They will walk and not faint.

Isaiah 40:27-31

June

Don't Be Afraid

*I*s there something that keeps you awake at night? Something you worry about that is always on your mind? Is there something that discourages you, making you think less of yourself? These things can only happen if you give them permission to take charge of your thoughts and feelings. It is better to recognize that God is always with you. You are never alone and He is watching out for you and loving you every minute of every day!

⁴ "Who has done such mighty deeds, summoning each new generation from the beginning of time? It is I, the Lord, the First and the Last. I alone am he."

¹⁰ "Don't be afraid, for I am with you. Don't be discouraged, for I am your God. I will strengthen you and help you. I will hold you up with my victorious right hand.

¹³ For I hold you by your right hand – I, the Lord your God. And I say to you, 'Don't be afraid. I am here to help you.'"

Isaiah 41:4, 10, 13

Don't Forget

*T*here is a little chorus that says, "My God is so big, so strong and so mighty. There's nothing my God cannot do!" Do you know it? It's worth learning so that when life throws you some tough things you can remember that God is the biggest and strongest. There is nothing He cannot do!

10 Sing a new song to the Lord! Sing his praises from the ends of the earth! Sing, all you who sail the seas, all you who live in distant coastlands.

11 Join in the chorus, you desert towns; let the villages of Kedar rejoice! Let the people of Sela sing for joy; shout praises from the mountaintops!

12 Let the whole world glorify the Lord; let it sing his praise.

13 The Lord will march forth like a mighty hero; he will come out like a warrior, full of fury. He will shout his battle cry and crush all his enemies.

14 He will say, "I have long been silent; yes, I have restrained myself. But now, like a woman in labor, I will cry and groan and pant.

15 I will level the mountains and hills and blight all their greenery. I will turn the rivers into dry land and will dry up all the pools.

16 I will lead blind Israel down a new path, guiding them along an unfamiliar way. I will brighten the darkness before them and smooth out the road ahead of them. Yes, I will indeed do these things; I will not forsake them.

17 But those who trust in idols, who say, 'You are our gods,' will be turned away in shame."

Isaiah 42:10-17

June 2

Forever and Ever

*R*ead verse 13 in this passage. Read it again. Read it again. Memorize this verse so that any time it feels like the bad guys in the world are winning, you can remember that God has said, "No one can snatch you from Him!" You are His. That's final.

[1] But now, O Jacob, listen to the Lord who created you. O Israel, the one who formed you says, "Do not be afraid, for I have ransomed you. I have called you by name; you are mine.

[2] When you go through deep waters, I will be with you. When you go through rivers of difficulty, you will not drown. When you walk through the fire of oppression, you will not be burned up; the flames will not consume you."

[5] "Do not be afraid, for I am with you. I will gather you and your children from east and west. [6] I will say to the north and south, 'Bring my sons and daughters back to Israel from the distant corners of the earth. [7] Bring all who claim me as their God, for I have made them for my glory. It was I who created them.'"

[11] "I, yes I, am the Lord, and there is no other Savior.

[13] From eternity to eternity I am God. No one can snatch anyone out of my hand. No one can undo what I have done."

Isaiah 43:1-2, 5-7, 11, 13

Family Traits

*D*o you look like other members of your family? Can people tell you are related? Are there other things you have in common, such as musical talent or athletic ability? There is usually some way to tell people are related. The same is true with your Christian roots. Remember the rock from which you were cut because you have the same DNA – God's!

[1]"Listen to me, all who hope for deliverance – all who seek the Lord! Consider the rock from which you were cut, the quarry from which you were mined.

[2] Yes, think about Abraham, your ancestor, and Sarah, who gave birth to your nation. Abraham was only one man when I called him. But when I blessed him, he became a great nation."

[11] Those who have been ransomed by the Lord will return. They will enter Jerusalem singing, crowned with everlasting joy. Sorrow and mourning will disappear, and they will be filled with joy and gladness.

[12] "I, yes I, am the one who comforts you. So why are you afraid of mere humans, who wither like the grass and disappear?"

[15] "For I am the Lord your God, who stirs up the sea, causing its waves to roar. My name is the Lord of Heaven's Armies.

[16] And I have put my words in your mouth and hidden you safely in my hand. I stretched out the sky like a canopy and laid the foundations of the earth. I am the one who says to Israel, 'You are my people!'"

Isaiah 51:1-2, 11-12, 15-16

Sacrifice

*Y*ou may know John 3:16 and the story of Jesus dying for your sins. But this passage from Isaiah gives a detailed explanation of what Jesus went through. Sin requires a sacrifice. Jesus' life is the sacrifice for you.

³ He was despised and rejected – a man of sorrows, acquainted with deepest grief. We turned our backs on him and looked the other way. He was despised, and we did not care.

⁴ Yet it was our weaknesses he carried; it was our sorrows that weighed him down. And we thought his troubles were a punishment from God, a punishment for his own sins!

⁵ But he was pierced for our rebellion, crushed for our sins. He was beaten so we could be whole. He was whipped so we could be healed.

⁶ All of us, like sheep, have strayed away. We have left God's paths to follow our own. Yet the Lord laid on him the sins of us all.

⁷ He was oppressed and treated harshly, yet he never said a word. He was led like a lamb to the slaughter. And as a sheep is silent before the shearers, he did not open his mouth.

⁹ He had done no wrong and had never deceived anyone. But he was buried like a criminal; he was put in a rich man's grave.

¹⁰ But it was the Lord's good plan to crush him and cause him grief. Yet when his life is made an offering for sin, he will have many descendants. He will enjoy a long life, and the Lord's good plan will prosper in his hands.

Isaiah 53:3-7, 9-10

Who Knows Best?

Some girls think they have all the answers. They think they know best for themselves and anyone else. But ... they are wrong. God's thoughts are higher. God's knowledge is greater. God's love is deeper. Don't be a know-it-all, trust God who does know all.

6 Seek the Lord while you can find him. Call on him now while he is near.

7 Let the wicked change their ways and banish the very thought of doing wrong. Let them turn to the Lord that he may have mercy on them. Yes, turn to our God, for he will forgive generously.

8 "My thoughts are nothing like your thoughts," says the Lord. "And my ways are far beyond anything you could imagine. 9 For just as the heavens are higher than the earth, so my ways are higher than your ways and my thoughts higher than your thoughts.

10 "The rain and snow come down from the heavens and stay on the ground to water the earth. They cause the grain to grow, producing seed for the farmer and bread for the hungry.

11 It is the same with my word. I send it out, and it always produces fruit. It will accomplish all I want it to, and it will prosper everywhere I send it.

12 You will live in joy and peace. The mountains and hills will burst into song, and the trees of the field will clap their hands!"

Isaiah 55:6-12

You Can't Outgive God

*B*e generous with all God gives you. Gladly help others, even when it's hard to do. God will guide you in who to help and He will bless you for following His guidance. Loving others shows your love for God.

⁷ Share your food with the hungry, and give shelter to the homeless. Give clothes to those who need them, and do not hide from relatives who need your help.

⁸ "Then your salvation will come like the dawn, and your wounds will quickly heal. Your godliness will lead you forward, and the glory of the Lord will protect you from behind."

¹⁰ "Feed the hungry, and help those in trouble. Then your light will shine out from the darkness, and the darkness around you will be as bright as noon.

¹¹ The Lord will guide you continually, giving you water when you are dry and restoring your strength. You will be like a well-watered garden, like an ever-flowing spring.

¹² Some of you will rebuild the deserted ruins of your cities. Then you will be known as a rebuilder of walls and a restorer of homes."

¹³ "Keep the Sabbath day holy. Don't pursue your own interests on that day, but enjoy the Sabbath and speak of it with delight as the Lord's holy day. Honor the Sabbath in everything you do on that day, and don't follow your own desires or talk idly.

¹⁴ Then the Lord will be your delight. I will give you great honor and satisfy you with the inheritance I promised to your ancestor Jacob. I, the Lord, have spoken!"

Isaiah 58:7-8, 10-14

Recognize Your Creator

*G*od created everything that is. The mountains you admire, the ocean you enjoy. There has never been anyone more powerful and there never will be. He made you, too. He made you exactly like He wants you to be. Thank Him for His power and creativity. Thank Him for His love.

3 When you came down long ago, you did awesome deeds beyond our highest expectations. And oh, how the mountains quaked!

4 For since the world began, no ear has heard and no eye has seen a God like you, who works for those who wait for him!

5 You welcome those who gladly do good, who follow godly ways. But you have been very angry with us, for we are not godly. We are constant sinners; how can people like us be saved?

6 We are all infected and impure with sin. When we display our righteous deeds, they are nothing but filthy rags. Like autumn leaves, we wither and fall, and our sins sweep us away like the wind.

7 Yet no one calls on your name or pleads with you for mercy. Therefore, you have turned away from us and turned us over to our sins.

8 And yet, O Lord, you are our Father. We are the clay, and you are the potter. We all are formed by your hand.

Isaiah 64:3-8

Pure Joy

*I*t's easy to get caught up in stuff that makes you happy; stuff that makes you feel like part of the crowd. Don't let anything distract you from staying close to God. Pure joy is found only in the peace that comes from knowing and serving Him.

¹ The Lord says, "I was ready to respond, but no one asked for help. I was ready to be found, but no one was looking for me. I said, 'Here I am, here I am!' to a nation that did not call on my name."

¹⁷ "Look! I am creating new heavens and a new earth, and no one will even think about the old ones anymore.

¹⁸ Be glad; rejoice forever in my creation! And look! I will create Jerusalem as a place of happiness. Her people will be a source of joy.

¹⁹ I will rejoice over Jerusalem and delight in my people. And the sound of weeping and crying will be heard in it no more.

²³ "They will not work in vain, and their children will not be doomed to misfortune. For they are people blessed by the Lord, and their children, too, will be blessed.

²⁴ I will answer them before they even call to me. While they are still talking about their needs, I will go ahead and answer their prayers! ²⁵ The wolf and the lamb will feed together. The lion will eat hay like a cow. But the snakes will eat dust. In those days no one will be hurt or destroyed on my holy mountain. I, the Lord, have spoken!"

Isaiah 65:1, 17-19, 23-25

All You Need

*G*od called Jeremiah to do a specific job for Him. Jeremiah wasn't sure he had the skill or knowledge but God said, "Don't worry. I'll give you what you need." Guess what? God has work for you to do, too. And guess what else? He'll help you get what you need to do it!

4 The Lord gave me this message: 5 "I knew you before I formed you in your mother's womb. Before you were born I set you apart and appointed you as my prophet to the nations."

6 "O Sovereign Lord," I said, "I can't speak for you! I'm too young!"

7 The Lord replied, "Don't say, 'I'm too young,' for you must go wherever I send you and say whatever I tell you.

8 And don't be afraid of the people, for I will be with you and will protect you. I, the Lord, have spoken!" 9 Then the Lord reached out and touched my mouth and said, "Look, I have put my words in your mouth!

10 Today I appoint you to stand up against nations and kingdoms. Some you must uproot and tear down, destroy and overthrow. Others you must build up and plant."

19 "They will fight you, but they will fail. For I am with you, and I will take care of you. I, the Lord, have spoken!"

Jeremiah 1:4-10, 19

Stay True

God pays attention to what you are doing. There's no fooling Him. If you have turned away from Him and are doing your own thing without thinking about obeying or serving Him ... He knows.

¹ The Lord gave me another message. He said, ² "Go and shout this message to Jerusalem. This is what the Lord says:

"I remember how eager you were to please me as a young bride long ago, how you loved me and followed me even through the barren wilderness.

³ In those days Israel was holy to the Lord, the first of his children. All who harmed his people were declared guilty, and disaster fell on them. I, the Lord, have spoken!"

¹³ "For my people have done two evil things: They have abandoned me – the fountain of living water. And they have dug for themselves cracked cisterns that can hold no water at all!

¹⁹ Your wickedness will bring its own punishment. Your turning from me will shame you. You will see what an evil, bitter thing it is to abandon the Lord your God and not to fear him. I, the Lord, the Lord of Heaven's Armies, have spoken!

²⁰ "Long ago I broke the yoke that oppressed you and tore away the chains of your slavery, but still you said, 'I will not serve you.' On every hill and under every green tree, you have prostituted yourselves by bowing down to idols.

²¹ But I was the one who planted you, choosing a vine of the purest stock – the very best. How did you grow into this corrupt wild vine?"

Jeremiah 2:1-3, 13, 19-21

No Fooling

*T*here are two powers at work in your world – the right one (God) and the one that promises you everything in the world but can't really deliver. Don't be fooled by that second one. Keep your focus on God and the truths of His Word.

³ This is what the Lord of Heaven's Armies, the God of Israel, says:

"'Even now, if you quit your evil ways, I will let you stay in your own land. ⁴ But don't be fooled by those who promise you safety simply because the Lord's Temple is here. They chant, "The Lord's Temple is here! The Lord's Temple is here!" ⁵ But I will be merciful only if you stop your evil thoughts and deeds and start treating each other with justice; ⁶ only if you stop exploiting foreigners, orphans, and widows; only if you stop your murdering; and only if you stop harming yourselves by worshiping idols. ⁷ Then I will let you stay in this land that I gave to your ancestors to keep forever.

⁸ "'Don't be fooled into thinking that you will never suffer because the Temple is here. It's a lie! ⁹ Do you really think you can steal, murder, commit adultery, lie, and burn incense to Baal and all those other new gods of yours, ¹⁰ and then come here and stand before me in my Temple and chant, "We are safe!" – only to go right back to all those evils again? ¹¹ Don't you yourselves admit that this Temple, which bears my name, has become a den of thieves? Surely I see all the evil going on there. I, the Lord, have spoken!'"

Jeremiah 7:3-11

Don't Boast

*T*he people who get the most attention in this world are the powerful and rich. They demand it and they get it. But from God's perspective they really have nothing to boast about. The only thing that is really worth anything in this world is knowing God, serving God, loving God. That's it. All the other things will fall away and only your relationship with God will last for eternity.

23 This is what the Lord says: "Don't let the wise boast in their wisdom, or the powerful boast in their power, or the rich boast in their riches.

24 But those who wish to boast should boast in this alone: that they truly know me and understand that I am the Lord who demonstrates unfailing love and who brings justice and righteousness to the earth, and that I delight in these things. I, the Lord, have spoken!"

25 "A time is coming," says the Lord, "when I will punish all those who are circumcised in body but not in spirit."

Jeremiah 9:23-25

Your Life

*O*K, you are a kid, right? You don't make decisions that affect world peace or national finance. So why should you think about big things like whether everyone in the world has the chance to know God? Or whether there are people who are starving or thirsty? Because God cares. So ask Him to make your heart sensitive to what He cares about.

7 Who would not fear you, O King of nations? That title belongs to you alone! Among all the wise people of the earth and in all the kingdoms of the world, there is no one like you.

10 But the Lord is the only true God. He is the living God and the everlasting King! The whole earth trembles at his anger. The nations cannot stand up to his wrath.

12 But God made the earth by his power, and he preserves it by his wisdom. With his own understanding he stretched out the heavens.

13 When he speaks in the thunder, the heavens roar with rain. He causes the clouds to rise over the earth. He sends the lightning with the rain and releases the wind from his storehouses.

14 The whole human race is foolish and has no knowledge! The craftsmen are disgraced by the idols they make, for their carefully shaped works are a fraud. These idols have no breath or power.

15 Idols are worthless; they are ridiculous lies! On the day of reckoning they will all be destroyed.

16 But the God of Israel is no idol! He is the Creator of everything that exists, including Israel, his own special possession. The Lord of Heaven's Armies is his name!

Jeremiah 10:7, 10, 12-16

Life Plans

Some of God's people were kicked out of their own countries. They left their homes, their work ... everything they knew. But they didn't leave God and He didn't leave them. He had plans for their lives ... plans that were good. If God had plans for the lives of these people who were in such a difficult situation, you can believe that He has plans for you, too. Get to know Him well and He will reveal those plans, one step at a time.

[11] "For I know the plans I have for you," says the Lord. "They are plans for good and not for disaster, to give you a future and a hope. [12] In those days when you pray, I will listen. [13] If you look for me wholeheartedly, you will find me. [14] I will be found by you," says the Lord. "I will end your captivity and restore your fortunes. I will gather you out of the nations where I sent you and will bring you home again to your own land."

Jeremiah 29:11-14

No Idols

*W*hy do people put their trust in anything other than God? Some do and it leads to problems. Remember that God is the Creator of all. God makes the rain fall, the wind blow. Nothing else can do that. Only God is worthy of your worship. Don't be fooled by anything else.

15 The Lord made the earth by his power, and he preserves it by his wisdom. With his own understanding he stretched out the heavens.

16 When he speaks in the thunder, the heavens are filled with water. He causes the clouds to rise over the earth. He sends the lightning with the rain and releases the wind from his storehouses.

17 The whole human race is foolish and has no knowledge! The craftsmen are disgraced by the idols they make, for their carefully shaped works are a fraud. These idols have no breath or power.

18 Idols are worthless; they are ridiculous lies! On the day of reckoning they will all be destroyed.

19 But the God of Israel is no idol! He is the Creator of everything that exists, including his people, his own special possession. The Lord of Heaven's Armies is his name!

Jeremiah 51:15-19

Endless Love

The message in the first verse of today's Scripture is so precious. God's love for YOU is faithful. That means it is constant. It never ends. Never. God loves you every minute of every day forever.

²² The faithful love of the Lord never ends! His mercies never cease.

²³ Great is his faithfulness; his mercies begin afresh each morning.

²⁴ I say to myself, "The Lord is my inheritance; therefore, I will hope in him!"

²⁵ The Lord is good to those who depend on him, to those who search for him.

²⁶ So it is good to wait quietly for salvation from the Lord.

²⁷ And it is good for people to submit at an early age to the yoke of his discipline:

²⁸ Let them sit alone in silence beneath the Lord's demands.

²⁹ Let them lie face down in the dust, for there may be hope at last.

³⁰ Let them turn the other cheek to those who strike them and accept the insults of their enemies.

³¹ For no one is abandoned by the Lord forever.

Lamentations 3:22-31

All Cleaned Up

*Y*ou may have heard the teasing comment, "You clean up well." Think about it like this – a girl who plays hard at a sport and doesn't mind getting hot, sweaty and even dirty. Afterward, she gets cleaned up and puts on nice clothes. She looks different.

In an even bigger picture, God cleans up your sinful heart, which is dirty and yucky. He makes it clean and presentable to Him. Pretty cool, huh?

[25] "Then I will sprinkle clean water on you, and you will be clean. Your filth will be washed away, and you will no longer worship idols.

[26] And I will give you a new heart, and I will put a new spirit in you. I will take out your stony, stubborn heart and give you a tender, responsive heart.

[27] And I will put my Spirit in you so that you will follow my decrees and be careful to obey my regulations."

Ezekiel 36:25-27

Standing Strong

If you had to choose between honoring God and anything else, what would you choose? Daniel had to make that choice. He stood strong for God!

³ Then the king ordered Ashpenaz, his chief of staff, to bring to the palace some of the young men of Judah's royal family and other noble families, who had been brought to Babylon as captives.

⁵ The king assigned them a daily ration of food and wine from his own kitchens. They were to be trained for three years, and then they would enter the royal service.

⁶ Daniel, Hananiah, Mishael, and Azariah were four of the young men chosen, all from the tribe of Judah. ⁷ The chief of staff renamed them with these Babylonian names: Daniel was called Belteshazzar. Hananiah was called Shadrach. Mishael was called Meshach. Azariah was called Abednego.

⁸ But Daniel was determined not to defile himself by eating the food and wine given to them by the king. He asked the chief of staff for permission not to eat these unacceptable foods.

¹² "Please test us for ten days on a diet of vegetables and water," Daniel said. ¹³ "At the end of the ten days, see how we look compared to the other young men who are eating the king's food. Then make your decision in light of what you see." ¹⁵ At the end of the ten days, Daniel and his three friends looked healthier and better nourished than the young men who had been eating the food assigned by the king.

Daniel 1:3, 5-8, 12-13, 15

Fearless

*T*hree boys were threatened with a horrible death if they didn't worship a statue instead of God. Did they stand strong and trust God or did they cave in to the pressure? Be fearless for God. He is fearless for you!

¹² There are some Jews – Shadrach, Meshach, and Abednego – whom you have put in charge of the province of Babylon. They pay no attention to you, Your Majesty. They refuse to serve your gods and do not worship the gold statue you have set up."

¹³ Then Nebuchadnezzar flew into a rage and ordered that Shadrach, Meshach, and Abednego be brought before him.

¹⁷ "If we are thrown into the blazing furnace, the God whom we serve is able to save us. He will rescue us from your power, Your Majesty. ¹⁸ But even if he doesn't, we want to make it clear to you, Your Majesty, that we will never serve your gods or worship the gold statue you have set up."

²³ So Shadrach, Meshach, and Abednego, securely tied, fell into the roaring flames. ²⁵ "Look!" Nebuchadnezzar shouted. "I see four men, unbound, walking around in the fire unharmed! And the fourth looks like a god!"

²⁶ Then Nebuchadnezzar shouted: "Shadrach, Meshach, and Abednego, servants of the Most High God, come out! Come here!"

²⁸ Then Nebuchadnezzar said, "Praise to the God of Shadrach, Meshach, and Abednego! He sent his angel to rescue his servants who trusted in him."

Daniel 3:12-13, 17-18, 23, 25-26, 28

God's Protection

*D*aniel chose to obey God and that put him in great danger. But God protected him. Choosing to obey God puts His bubble of protection around you.

⁶ So the administrators and high officers went to the king and said, ⁷ "Give orders that for the next thirty days any person who prays to anyone, divine or human – except to you, Your Majesty – will be thrown into the den of lions." ⁹ So King Darius signed the law.

¹⁰ But when Daniel learned that the law had been signed, he knelt down as usual in his upstairs room, with its windows open. He prayed three times a day, just as he had always done, giving thanks to his God. ¹¹ The officials went to Daniel's house and found him praying and asking for God's help.

¹³ Then they told the king, "That man Daniel ... is ignoring you and your law. He still prays to his God three times a day."

¹⁶ So at last the king gave orders for Daniel to be arrested and thrown into the den of lions. The king said to him, "May your God, whom you serve so faithfully, rescue you."

¹⁹ Very early the next morning, the king got up and hurried to the lions' den. ²⁰ When he got there, he called out in anguish, "Daniel, servant of the living God! Was your God, whom you serve so faithfully, able to rescue you from the lions?"

²² "My God sent his angel to shut the lions' mouths so that they would not hurt me, for I have been found innocent in his sight. And I have not wronged you, Your Majesty."

Daniel 6:6-7, 9-11, 13, 16, 19, 20, 22

Confession

*D*aniel knew his people had turned away from God. He prayed to God and confessed their failure and asked God's forgiveness. Confession is a good thing.

⁴ I prayed to the Lord my God and confessed:

"O Lord, you are a great and awesome God! You always fulfill your covenant and keep your promises of unfailing love to those who love you and obey your commands. ⁵ But we have sinned and done wrong. We have rebelled against you and scorned your commands and regulations. ⁶ We have refused to listen to your servants the prophets.

¹⁵ "O Lord our God, you brought lasting honor to your name by rescuing your people from Egypt in a great display of power. But we have sinned and are full of wickedness. ¹⁶ In view of all your faithful mercies, Lord, please turn your furious anger away from your city Jerusalem, your holy mountain.

¹⁷ "O our God, hear your servant's prayer! Listen as I plead. For your own sake, Lord, smile again on your desolate sanctuary.

¹⁸ "O my God, lean down and listen to me. Open your eyes and see our despair. See how your city – the city that bears your name – lies in ruins. We make this plea, not because we deserve help, but because of your mercy.

¹⁹ "O Lord, hear. O Lord, forgive. O Lord, listen and act! For your own sake, do not delay, O my God, for your people and your city bear your name."

Daniel 9:4-6, 15-19

June 22

No More Worry

*D*aniel was worried about his people so he prayed. God answered his prayer by sending an angel to tell him to stop worrying. God was taking care of things. Pray from a sincere heart and you can be sure that God will hear you, too.

²¹ As I was praying, Gabriel, whom I had seen in the earlier vision, came swiftly to me at the time of the evening sacrifice. ²² He explained to me, "Daniel, I have come here to give you insight and understanding."

10¹⁰ Just then a hand touched me and lifted me, still trembling, to my hands and knees. ¹¹ And the man said to me, "Daniel, you are very precious to God, so listen carefully to what I have to say to you. Stand up, for I have been sent to you." When he said this to me, I stood up, still trembling.

¹² Then he said, "Don't be afraid, Daniel. Since the first day you began to pray for understanding and to humble yourself before your God, your request has been heard in heaven. I have come in answer to your prayer.

¹⁴ Now I am here to explain what will happen to your people in the future, for this vision concerns a time yet to come."

¹⁸ Then the one who looked like a man touched me again, and I felt my strength returning. ¹⁹ "Don't be afraid," he said, "for you are very precious to God. Peace! Be encouraged! Be strong!"

As he spoke these words to me, I suddenly felt stronger and said to him, "Please speak to me, my lord, for you have strengthened me."

Daniel 9:21-22; 10:10-12, 14, 18-19

Come Back to God

When you have a disagreement with a friend, it may break your relationship – you don't hang out, you don't talk. The same kind of break happens with God when sin gets in the way. The message is to turn away from sin – stop sinning and come back to God.

[1] Return, O Israel, to the Lord your God, for your sins have brought you down.

[2] Bring your confessions, and return to the Lord. Say to him, "Forgive all our sins and graciously receive us, so that we may offer you our praises."

[4] The Lord says, "Then I will heal you of your faithlessness; my love will know no bounds, for my anger will be gone forever.

[5] I will be to Israel like a refreshing dew from heaven. Israel will blossom like the lily; it will send roots deep into the soil like the cedars in Lebanon.

[6] Its branches will spread out like beautiful olive trees, as fragrant as the cedars of Lebanon.

[7] My people will again live under my shade. They will flourish like grain and blossom like grapevines. They will be as fragrant as the wines of Lebanon.

[8] "O Israel, stay away from idols! I am the one who answers your prayers and cares for you. I am like a tree that is always green; all your fruit comes from me."

[9] Let those who are wise understand these things. Let those with discernment listen carefully. The paths of the Lord are true and right, and righteous people live by walking in them. But in those paths sinners stumble and fall.

Hosea 14:1-2, 4-9

True Sorrow

God asks you to turn away from sin-ning. He wants your obedience. But, beyond just changing your habits, thoughts or actions, be truly sorry for disobeying God. Let your heart be broken for its disobedience as it turns back to God.

¹² That is why the Lord says, "Turn to me now, while there is time. Give me your hearts. Come with fasting, weeping, and mourning.

¹³ Don't tear your clothing in your grief, but tear your hearts instead." Return to the Lord your God, for he is merciful and compassionate, slow to get angry and filled with unfailing love. He is eager to relent and not punish.

²³ Rejoice, you people of Jerusalem! Rejoice in the Lord your God! For the rain he sends demonstrates his faithfulness. Once more the autumn rains will come, as well as the rains of spring.

²⁴ The threshing floors will again be piled high with grain, and the presses will overflow with new wine and olive oil.

²⁷ Then you will know that I am among my people Israel, that I am the Lord your God, and there is no other. Never again will my people be disgraced.

²⁸ "Then, after doing all those things, I will pour out my Spirit upon all people. Your sons and daughters will prophesy. Your old men will dream dreams, and your young men will see visions.

²⁹ In those days I will pour out my Spirit even on servants – men and women alike.

Joel 2:12-13, 23-24, 27-29

Recognizing the Power

God didn't leave anything to chance. He told the Old Testament prophets His plans and they let the people know. So, read His Word, recognize His power and then what is left? Only to obey Him.

2 "From among all the families on the earth, I have been intimate with you alone. That is why I must punish you for all your sins."

3 Can two people walk together without agreeing on the direction?

4 Does a lion ever roar in a thicket without first finding a victim? Does a young lion growl in its den without first catching its prey?

5 Does a bird ever get caught in a trap that has no bait? Does a trap spring shut when there's nothing to catch?

6 When the ram's horn blows a warning, shouldn't the people be alarmed? Does disaster come to a city unless the Lord has planned it?

7 Indeed, the Sovereign Lord never does anything until he reveals his plans to his servants the prophets.

8 The lion has roared – so who isn't frightened? The Sovereign Lord has spoken – so who can refuse to proclaim his message?

Amos 3:2-8

Hide and Seek

*H*ave you ever disobeyed your folks then hidden from them to escape punishment? That doesn't usually work for long. The same is true with God. Jonah tried it. He chose to disobey but he couldn't hide from God.

¹ The Lord gave this message to Jonah son of Amittai: ² "Get up and go to the great city of Nineveh. Announce my judgment against it because I have seen how wicked its people are."

³ But Jonah got up and went in the opposite direction to get away from the Lord. He went down to the port of Joppa, where he found a ship leaving for Tarshish. He bought a ticket and went on board, hoping to escape from the Lord by sailing to Tarshish.

⁴ But the Lord hurled a powerful wind over the sea, causing a violent storm that threatened to break the ship apart. ⁵ Jonah was sound asleep down in the hold. ⁶ So the captain went down after him. "How can you sleep at a time like this?" he shouted. "Get up and pray to your god! Maybe he will pay attention to us and spare our lives."

⁹ Jonah answered, "I am a Hebrew, and I worship the Lord, the God of heaven, who made the sea and the land."

¹² "Throw me into the sea," Jonah said, "and it will become calm again. I know that this terrible storm is all my fault."

¹⁵ Then the sailors picked Jonah up and threw him into the raging sea, and the storm stopped at once!

¹⁷ Now the Lord had arranged for a great fish to swallow Jonah. And Jonah was inside the fish for three days and three nights.

Jonah 1:1-6, 9, 12, 15, 17

Do Over

You know what's cool? God wants you to succeed. He is not standing over you waiting for you to fail. He even gives "do over" chances to help you succeed. Jonah is a great example of that.

[1] Then Jonah prayed to the Lord his God from inside the fish. [2] He said, "I cried out to the Lord in my great trouble, and he answered me. I called to you from the land of the dead, and Lord, you heard me!

[3] You threw me into the ocean depths, and I sank down to the heart of the sea. The mighty waters engulfed me; I was buried beneath your wild and stormy waves.

[4] Then I said, 'O Lord, you have driven me from your presence. Yet I will look once more toward your holy Temple.'

[5] "I sank beneath the waves, and the waters closed over me. Seaweed wrapped itself around my head.

[6] I sank down to the very roots of the mountains. I was imprisoned in the earth, whose gates lock shut forever. But you, O Lord my God, snatched me from the jaws of death!

[7] As my life was slipping away, I remembered the Lord. And my earnest prayer went out to you in your holy Temple.

[8] Those who worship false gods turn their backs on all God's mercies.

[9] But I will offer sacrifices to you with songs of praise, and I will fulfill all my vows. For my salvation comes from the Lord alone."

[10] Then the Lord ordered the fish to spit Jonah out onto the beach.

Jonah 2:1-10

June 28

The Message Works

*J*onah got a second chance to do the work God asked him to do. He went to Nineveh and told the people to repent. They did and God forgave them. Doing the work God asks you to do will get results.

[1] Then the Lord spoke to Jonah a second time: [2] "Get up and go to the great city of Nineveh, and deliver the message I have given you."

[3] This time Jonah obeyed the Lord's command and went to Nineveh, a city so large that it took three days to see it all.

[4] On the day Jonah entered the city, he shouted to the crowds: "Forty days from now Nineveh will be destroyed!" [5] The people of Nineveh believed God's message, and from the greatest to the least, they declared a fast and put on burlap to show their sorrow.

[6] When the king of Nineveh heard what Jonah was saying, he stepped down from his throne and took off his royal robes. He dressed himself in burlap and sat on a heap of ashes. [7] Then the king and his nobles sent this decree throughout the city:

"No one, not even the animals from your herds and flocks, may eat or drink anything at all.

[8] People and animals alike must wear garments of mourning, and everyone must pray earnestly to God. They must turn from their evil ways and stop all their violence. [9] Who can tell? Perhaps even yet God will change his mind and hold back his fierce anger from destroying us."

Jonah 3:1-9

Compassion

*J*onah got angry because God forgave the people of Nineveh. But, God reminded him that God has compassion for all, because He loves all of us.

¹ This change of plans greatly upset Jonah, and he became very angry. ² So he complained to the Lord about it: "Didn't I say before I left home that you would do this, Lord? That is why I ran away to Tarshish! I knew that you are a merciful and compassionate God, slow to get angry and filled with unfailing love. You are eager to turn back from destroying people."

⁵ Then Jonah went out to the east side of the city and made a shelter to sit under as he waited to see what would happen to the city. ⁶ And the Lord God arranged for a leafy plant to grow there, and soon it spread its broad leaves over Jonah's head, shading him from the sun. This eased his discomfort, and Jonah was very grateful for the plant.

⁷ But God also arranged for a worm! The next morning at dawn the worm ate through the stem of the plant so that it withered away. ⁸ The sun beat down on his head until he grew faint and wished to die.

⁹ Then God said to Jonah, "Is it right for you to be angry because the plant died?"

"Yes," Jonah retorted, "even angry enough to die!"

¹⁰ Then the Lord said, "You feel sorry about the plant, though you did nothing to put it there. It came quickly and died quickly. ¹¹ But Nineveh has more than 120,000 people living in spiritual darkness, not to mention all the animals. Shouldn't I feel sorry for such a great city?"

Jonah 4:1-2, 5-11

July

Promise of Peace

*G*od had a plan from day one – a plan to bring peace and love and joy to the world. The Old Testament prophets spoke of this plan. It was Jesus ... the source of peace.

² But you, O Bethlehem Ephrathah, are only a small village among all the people of Judah. Yet a ruler of Israel will come from you, one whose origins are from the distant past.

³ The people of Israel will be abandoned to their enemies until the woman in labor gives birth. Then at last his fellow countrymen will return from exile to their own land.

⁴ And he will stand to lead his flock with the Lord's strength, in the majesty of the name of the Lord his God. Then his people will live there undisturbed, for he will be highly honored around the world.

⁵ And he will be the source of peace.

Micah 5:2-5

God Alone

*M*aybe you know some girls who think they can be God's girl AND fit in with a crowd who doesn't follow God. God won't put up with that. He doesn't allow a God AND ... anything else. Follow God and God alone.

2 The Lord is a jealous God, filled with vengeance and rage. He takes revenge on all who oppose him and continues to rage against his enemies!

3 The Lord is slow to get angry, but his power is great, and he never lets the guilty go unpunished. He displays his power in the whirlwind and the storm. The billowing clouds are the dust beneath his feet.

4 At his command the oceans dry up, and the rivers disappear. The lush pastures of Bashan and Carmel fade, and the green forests of Lebanon wither.

5 In his presence the mountains quake, and the hills melt away; the earth trembles, and its people are destroyed.

6 Who can stand before his fierce anger? Who can survive his burning fury? His rage blazes forth like fire, and the mountains crumble to dust in his presence.

7 The Lord is good, a strong refuge when trouble comes. He is close to those who trust in him.

8 But he will sweep away his enemies in an overwhelming flood. He will pursue his foes into the darkness of night.

Nahum 1:2-8

July 2

How Deep Is Your Trust?

*D*o you feel all warm and snuggly toward God when life is going well and everything is good? Sure you do. But what about when things are tough? Can you rejoice even in difficult times?

² I have heard all about you, Lord. I am filled with awe by your amazing works. In this time of our deep need, help us again as you did in years gone by. And in your anger, remember your mercy.

⁸ Was it in anger, Lord, that you struck the rivers and parted the sea? Were you displeased with them? No, you were sending your chariots of salvation!

⁹ You brandished your bow and your quiver of arrows. You split open the earth with flowing rivers.

¹⁰ The mountains watched and trembled. Onward swept the raging waters. The mighty deep cried out, lifting its hands to the Lord.

¹⁷ Even though the fig trees have no blossoms, and there are no grapes on the vines; even though the olive crop fails, and the fields lie empty and barren; even though the flocks die in the fields, and the cattle barns are empty, ¹⁸ yet I will rejoice in the Lord! I will be joyful in the God of my salvation!

¹⁹ The Sovereign Lord is my strength! He makes me as surefooted as a deer, able to tread upon the heights.

Habakkuk 3:2, 8-10, 17-19

July 3

God Among Us

*I*t wouldn't be easy to be friends with someone you never saw face to face, would it? If your friend wasn't approachable; for instance she felt she was too important to talk to you ... the friendship wouldn't go anywhere, would it? You don't have to worry about that with God. He came to live among people. He wants to be close to you!

14 Sing, O daughter of Zion; shout aloud, O Israel! Be glad and rejoice with all your heart, O daughter of Jerusalem!

15 For the Lord will remove his hand of judgment and will disperse the armies of your enemy. And the Lord himself, the King of Israel, will live among you! At last your troubles will be over, and you will never again fear disaster.

16 On that day the announcement to Jerusalem will be, "Cheer up, Zion! Don't be afraid!

17 For the Lord your God is living among you. He is a mighty savior. He will take delight in you with gladness. With his love, he will calm all your fears. He will rejoice over you with joyful songs."

Zephaniah 3:14-17

I'm Here

*D*o you like dark, stormy nights when thunder booms and lightning flashes? Perhaps when you were a little girl a night like this would make you call for your parents. Sometimes it just feels better knowing a grown-up is close by. Same with God, right? It just feels better knowing He is near.

¹² Then Zerubbabel son of Shealtiel, and Jeshua son of Jehozadak, the high priest, and the whole remnant of God's people began to obey the message from the Lord their God. When they heard the words of the prophet Haggai, whom the Lord their God had sent, the people feared the Lord. ¹³ Then Haggai, the Lord's messenger, gave the people this message from the Lord: "I am with you, says the Lord!"

¹⁴ So the Lord sparked the enthusiasm of Zerubbabel son of Shealtiel, governor of Judah, and the enthusiasm of Jeshua son of Jehozadak, the high priest, and the enthusiasm of the whole remnant of God's people. They began to work on the house of their God, the Lord of Heaven's Armies.

Haggai 1:12-14

It's Not Over!

*D*iscouragement can overtake your very soul when life gets tough – and stays that way for a while. It can feel as though God has walked away, maybe taken a vacation. But, it isn't so! In His time He will do His work. He will change everything. Trust Him and wait on Him!

¹ Then on October 17 of that same year, the Lord sent another message through the prophet Haggai. ² "Say this to Zerubbabel son of Shealtiel, governor of Judah, and to Jeshua son of Jehozadak, the high priest, and to the remnant of God's people there in the land: ³ 'Does anyone remember this house – this Temple – in its former splendor? How, in comparison, does it look to you now? It must seem like nothing at all!

⁴ But now the Lord says: Be strong, Zerubbabel. Be strong, Jeshua son of Jehozadak, the high priest. Be strong, all you people still left in the land. And now get to work, for I am with you, says the Lord of Heaven's Armies. ⁵ My Spirit remains among you, just as I promised when you came out of Egypt. So do not be afraid.'

⁶ "For this is what the Lord of Heaven's Armies says: In just a little while I will again shake the heavens and the earth, the oceans and the dry land.

⁷ I will shake all the nations, and the treasures of all the nations will be brought to this Temple. I will fill this place with glory, says the Lord of Heaven's Armies."

Haggai 2:1-7

One Lord

*E*ven before Jesus came to earth God proclaimed that He was king. He let everyone know that the day would come when Jesus alone would be worshiped. All other things that once seemed so important will fade away. Only one Lord will stand.

⁹ Rejoice, O people of Zion! Shout in triumph, O people of Jerusalem! Look, your king is coming to you. He is righteous and victorious, yet he is humble, riding on a donkey – riding on a donkey's colt.

¹⁰ I will remove the battle chariots from Israel and the warhorses from Jerusalem. I will destroy all the weapons used in battle, and your king will bring peace to the nations. His realm will stretch from sea to sea and from the Euphrates River to the ends of the earth.

10¹² "By my power I will make my people strong, and by my authority they will go wherever they wish. I, the Lord, have spoken!"

14⁹ And the Lord will be king over all the earth. On that day there will be one Lord – his name alone will be worshiped.

Zechariah 9:9-10; 10:12; 14:9

Cheating God

*T*aking something that rightfully belongs to one person and giving it to someone else cheats the person who should have gotten it. When you don't give God what rightfully should be His then you are cheating Him. What belongs to God? Your heart, time, money, talents ... everything.

[6] "I am the Lord, and I do not change. That is why you descendants of Jacob are not already destroyed. [7] Ever since the days of your ancestors, you have scorned my decrees and failed to obey them. Now return to me, and I will return to you," says the Lord of Heaven's Armies.

"But you ask, 'How can we return when we have never gone away?'

[8] "Should people cheat God? Yet you have cheated me!

"But you ask, 'What do you mean? When did we ever cheat you?'

"You have cheated me of the tithes and offerings due to me. [9] You are under a curse, for your whole nation has been cheating me. [10] Bring all the tithes into the storehouse so there will be enough food in my Temple. If you do," says the Lord of Heaven's Armies, "I will open the windows of heaven for you. I will pour out a blessing so great you won't have enough room to take it in! Try it! Put me to the test! [11] Your crops will be abundant, for I will guard them from insects and disease. Your grapes will not fall from the vine before they are ripe," says the Lord of Heaven's Armies. [12] "Then all nations will call you blessed, for your land will be such a delight," says the Lord of Heaven's Armies.

Malachi 3:6-12

Day of Judgment

*O*K, girl, be honest. Do you kind of feel that you are going to escape God's judgment? Do you think, "I'm so good and so important to God that He will overlook anything wrong I do"? Sorry to burst your bubble, but God says a day of judgment is coming – for everyone.

[1] The Lord of Heaven's Armies says, "The day of judgment is coming, burning like a furnace. On that day the arrogant and the wicked will be burned up like straw. They will be consumed – roots, branches, and all.

[2] "But for you who fear my name, the Sun of Righteousness will rise with healing in his wings. And you will go free, leaping with joy like calves let out to pasture."

Malachi 4:1-2

One of Us

*G*od's plan to send Jesus to earth was so that all people could have the opportunity to know God. The only way Jesus would be attractive to all people would be if He were one of us. So – His mother was an ordinary woman. Jesus became human – like you.

¹⁸ This is how Jesus the Messiah was born. His mother, Mary, was engaged to be married to Joseph. But before the marriage took place, while she was still a virgin, she became pregnant through the power of the Holy Spirit. ¹⁹ Joseph, her fiancé, was a good man and did not want to disgrace her publicly, so he decided to break the engagement quietly.

²⁰ As he considered this, an angel of the Lord appeared to him in a dream. "Joseph, son of David," the angel said, "do not be afraid to take Mary as your wife. For the child within her was conceived by the Holy Spirit. ²¹ And she will have a son, and you are to name him Jesus, for he will save his people from their sins."

²² All of this occurred to fulfill the Lord's message through his prophet:

²³ "Look! The virgin will conceive a child! She will give birth to a son, and they will call him Immanuel, which means 'God is with us.'"

²⁴ When Joseph woke up, he did as the angel of the Lord commanded and took Mary as his wife.

²⁵ But he did not have sexual relations with her until her son was born. And Joseph named him Jesus.

Matthew 1:18-25

July 10

Protection

*G*od protected the baby Jesus from a king who wanted to hurt Him. He made sure that His plan to offer salvation was not ruined. God's plans always stand!

¹ Jesus was born in Bethlehem in Judea, during the reign of King Herod. About that time some wise men from eastern lands arrived in Jerusalem, asking, ² "Where is the newborn king of the Jews? We saw his star as it rose, and we have come to worship him."

³ King Herod was deeply disturbed when he heard this, as was everyone in Jerusalem. ⁴ He called a meeting of the leading priests and teachers of religious law and asked, "Where is the Messiah supposed to be born?"

⁵ "In Bethlehem in Judea," they said, "for this is what the prophet wrote: ⁶ 'And you, O Bethlehem in the land of Judah, are not least among the ruling cities of Judah, for a ruler will come from you who will be the shepherd for my people Israel.'"

⁷ Then Herod called for a private meeting with the wise men, and he learned from them the time when the star first appeared.

⁹ After this interview the wise men went their way. And the star they had seen in the east guided them to Bethlehem. It went ahead of them and stopped over the place where the child was. ¹⁰ When they saw the star, they were filled with joy! ¹¹ They entered the house and saw the child with his mother, Mary, and they bowed down and worshiped him. Then they opened their treasure chests and gave him gifts of gold, frankincense, and myrrh.

Matthew 2:1-7, 9-11

Obedience

*G*od knew what He was doing when He chose Joseph and Mary to take care of His Son. Joseph's obedience was immediate when the angel told him Jesus was in trouble. He didn't ask questions. He didn't argue. He obeyed. Obedience isn't always easy. Do you want to challenge rules sometimes, whether it's God's rules or your parents?

¹³ After the wise men were gone, an angel of the Lord appeared to Joseph in a dream. "Get up! Flee to Egypt with the child and his mother," the angel said. "Stay there until I tell you to return, because Herod is going to search for the child to kill him."

¹⁴ That night Joseph left for Egypt with the child and Mary, his mother, ¹⁵ and they stayed there until Herod's death. This fulfilled what the Lord had spoken through the prophet: "I called my Son out of Egypt."

¹⁹ When Herod died, an angel of the Lord appeared in a dream to Joseph in Egypt. ²⁰ "Get up!" the angel said. "Take the child and his mother back to the land of Israel, because those who were trying to kill the child are dead."

²¹ So Joseph got up and returned to the land of Israel with Jesus and his mother. ²² But when he learned that the new ruler of Judea was Herod's son Archelaus, he was afraid to go there. Then, after being warned in a dream, he left for the region of Galilee. ²³ So the family went and lived in a town called Nazareth. This fulfilled what the prophets had said: "He will be called a Nazarene."

Matthew 2:13-15, 19-23

July 12

Do Your Job

There are no small jobs in God's kingdom. Everyone matters. John the Baptist understood that. His job was to announce that Jesus was coming. He was OK with that. He didn't have to be the "star". He was just fine with doing the job God had for him.

¹ In those days John the Baptist came to the Judean wilderness and began preaching. His message was, ² "Repent of your sins and turn to God, for the Kingdom of Heaven is near."

⁴ John's clothes were woven from coarse camel hair, and he wore a leather belt around his waist. For food he ate locusts and wild honey. ⁵ People from Jerusalem and from all of Judea and all over the Jordan Valley went out to see and hear John. ⁶ And when they confessed their sins, he baptized them in the Jordan River.

¹¹ "I baptize with water those who repent of their sins and turn to God. But someone is coming soon who is greater than I am – so much greater that I'm not worthy even to be his slave and carry his sandals. He will baptize you with the Holy Spirit and with fire."

Matthew 3:1-2, 4-6, 11

July 13

Fighting Temptation

*G*od knows how hard it is to struggle with temptation. Jesus faced intense temptation Himself – from the master tempter. He fought it off with Scripture. Sounds like a good reason to memorize all you can!

[1] Then Jesus was led by the Spirit into the wilderness to be tempted there by the devil. [2] For forty days and forty nights he fasted and became very hungry.

[3] During that time the devil came and said to him, "If you are the Son of God, tell these stones to become loaves of bread."

[4] But Jesus told him, "No! The Scriptures say, 'People do not live by bread alone, but by every word that comes from the mouth of God.'"

[5] Then the devil took him to the holy city, Jerusalem, to the highest point of the Temple, [6] and said, "If you are the Son of God, jump off! For the Scriptures say, 'He will order his angels to protect you. And they will hold you up with their hands so you won't even hurt your foot on a stone.'"

[7] Jesus responded, "The Scriptures also say, 'You must not test the Lord your God.'"

[8] Next the devil took him to the peak of a very high mountain and showed him all the kingdoms of the world and their glory. [9] "I will give it all to you," he said, "if you will kneel down and worship me."

[10] "Get out of here, Satan," Jesus told him. "For the Scriptures say, 'You must worship the Lord your God and serve only him.'"

[11] Then the devil went away, and angels came and took care of Jesus.

Matthew 4:1-11

July 14

Studying with the Master

*J*esus chose some men to spend time with Him, travel with Him, see how He related to people and listen to Him teach about God. These men got the chance to learn a lot about living for Him by spending time with Him. What an opportunity! How can you spend time with Jesus?

¹⁸ One day as Jesus was walking along the shore of the Sea of Galilee, he saw two brothers – Simon, also called Peter, and Andrew – throwing a net into the water, for they fished for a living. ¹⁹ Jesus called out to them, "Come, follow me, and I will show you how to fish for people!" ²⁰ And they left their nets at once and followed him.

²¹ A little farther up the shore he saw two other brothers, James and John, sitting in a boat with their father, Zebedee, repairing their nets. And he called them to come, too. ²² They immediately followed him, leaving the boat and their father behind.

²³ Jesus traveled throughout the region of Galilee, teaching in the synagogues and announcing the Good News about the Kingdom. And he healed every kind of disease and illness.

²⁴ News about him spread as far as Syria, and people soon began bringing to him all who were sick. And whatever their sickness or disease, or if they were demon possessed or epileptic or paralyzed – he healed them all. ²⁵ Large crowds followed him wherever he went – people from Galilee, the Ten Towns, Jerusalem, from all over Judea, and from east of the Jordan River.

Matthew 4:18-25

Blessings Abound

*J*esus sat down with a crowd of followers and began teaching them about living for God. Read His words and learn how dependence on God and complete surrender to Him will bring blessings on your life.

¹ One day as he saw the crowds gathering, Jesus went up on the mountainside and sat down. His disciples gathered around him, ² and he began to teach them.

³ "God blesses those who are poor and realize their need for him, for the Kingdom of Heaven is theirs.

⁴ God blesses those who mourn, for they will be comforted.

⁵ God blesses those who are humble, for they will inherit the whole earth.

⁶ God blesses those who hunger and thirst for justice, for they will be satisfied.

⁷ God blesses those who are merciful, for they will be shown mercy.

⁸ God blesses those whose hearts are pure, for they will see God.

⁹ God blesses those who work for peace, for they will be called the children of God.

¹⁰ God blesses those who are persecuted for doing right, for the Kingdom of Heaven is theirs.

¹¹ "God blesses you when people mock you and persecute you and lie about you and say all sorts of evil things against you because you are my followers.
¹² Be happy about it! Be very glad! For a great reward awaits you in heaven. And remember, the ancient prophets were persecuted in the same way."

Matthew 5:1-12

July 16

Salt and Light

*F*ollowers of Jesus make a difference in the world ... if you are following Him and serving Him. If you compromise your beliefs and standards in order to "fit in" with a crowd, then you lose your saltiness and light. Be salt. Be light. Make a difference.

[13] "You are the salt of the earth. But what good is salt if it has lost its flavor? Can you make it salty again? It will be thrown out and trampled underfoot as worthless.

[14] "You are the light of the world – like a city on a hilltop that cannot be hidden.

[15] No one lights a lamp and then puts it under a basket. Instead, a lamp is placed on a stand, where it gives light to everyone in the house.

[16] In the same way, let your good deeds shine out for all to see, so that everyone will praise your heavenly Father."

Matthew 5:13-16

Watch Your Words

*I*t's so easy when you get mad at a friend to spout off words that are hurtful and filled with judgment and criticism. Does it matter? After all, you go back later and apologize. Yes, it matters. God hears your words. He sees your lack of control. Pay attention to your words.

21 "You have heard that our ancestors were told, 'You must not murder. If you commit murder, you are subject to judgment.' 22 But I say, if you are even angry with someone, you are subject to judgment! If you call someone an idiot, you are in danger of being brought before the court. And if you curse someone, you are in danger of the fires of hell.

23 "So if you are presenting a sacrifice at the altar in the Temple and you suddenly remember that someone has something against you, 24 leave your sacrifice there at the altar. Go and be reconciled to that person. Then come and offer your sacrifice to God.

25 "When you are on the way to court with your adversary, settle your differences quickly. Otherwise, your accuser may hand you over to the judge, who will hand you over to an officer, and you will be thrown into prison. 26 And if that happens, you surely won't be free again until you have paid the last penny."

Matthew 5:21-26

Love Your Enemies

*G*etting even" is such a temptation, isn't it? When someone hurts you, you want to hurt her back ... harder! But what does God say about that? What does He say about getting along with others? What does He say about loving your friends but hating your enemies? He doesn't agree with what most of the world says, that's for sure!

38 "You have heard the law that says the punishment must match the injury: 'An eye for an eye, and a tooth for a tooth.' 39 But I say, do not resist an evil person! If someone slaps you on the right cheek, offer the other cheek also. 40 If you are sued in court and your shirt is taken from you, give your coat, too. 41 If a soldier demands that you carry his gear for a mile, carry it two miles. 42 Give to those who ask, and don't turn away from those who want to borrow.

43 "You have heard the law that says, 'Love your neighbor' and hate your enemy. 44 But I say, love your enemies! Pray for those who persecute you! 45 In that way, you will be acting as true children of your Father in heaven. For he gives his sunlight to both the evil and the good, and he sends rain on the just and the unjust alike. 46 If you love only those who love you, what reward is there for that? Even corrupt tax collectors do that much. 47 If you are kind only to your friends, how are you different from anyone else? Even pagans do that. 48 But you are to be perfect, even as your Father in heaven is perfect."

Matthew 5:38-48

Humble Giving

Some people do nice things for others and hope that everyone notices. They long for that pat on the back that says, "You're a good person!" But that motivation won't win you any prizes from God. He says to do nice things quietly, privately so that no one really knows except you and Him.

[1] "Watch out! Don't do your good deeds publicly, to be admired by others, for you will lose the reward from your Father in heaven.

[2] "When you give to someone in need, don't do as the hypocrites do – blowing trumpets in the synagogues and streets to call attention to their acts of charity! I tell you the truth, they have received all the reward they will ever get.

[3] "But when you give to someone in need, don't let your left hand know what your right hand is doing.

[4] "Give your gifts in private, and your Father, who sees everything, will reward you."

Matthew 6:1-4

Prayer Lesson

*A*re you too shy to pray in public? Does it scare you to pray out loud? That's okay. Some people who grab the chance to pray in public are doing so hoping that others will think they are super spiritual. Praying just for "show" does not please God. Jesus gave a gentle, simple, direct example of how your prayers should be.

[6] "But when you pray, go away by yourself, shut the door behind you, and pray to your Father in private. Then your Father, who sees everything, will reward you.

[7] "When you pray, don't babble on and on as people of other religions do. They think their prayers are answered merely by repeating their words again and again. [8] Don't be like them, for your Father knows exactly what you need even before you ask him! [9] Pray like this:

Our Father in heaven, may your name be kept holy.

[10] May your Kingdom come soon. May your will be done on earth, as it is in heaven.

[11] Give us today the food we need, [12] and forgive us our sins, as we have forgiven those who sin against us.

[13] And don't let us yield to temptation, but rescue us from the evil one.

[14] "If you forgive those who sin against you, your heavenly Father will forgive you. [15] But if you refuse to forgive others, your Father will not forgive your sins."

Matthew 6:6-15

Where's Your Priority?

*Y*ou may say that you care about serving God. But, if you spend your time hanging with friends and doing things that do not honor God then you are just fooling yourself ... or trying to. Where you put your time, effort and energy shows what you truly consider important.

[19] "Don't store up treasures here on earth, where moths eat them and rust destroys them, and where thieves break in and steal. [20] Store your treasures in heaven, where moths and rust cannot destroy, and thieves do not break in and steal.

[21] Wherever your treasure is, there the desires of your heart will also be.

[22] "Your eye is a lamp that provides light for your body. When your eye is good, your whole body is filled with light. [23] But when your eye is bad, your whole body is filled with darkness. And if the light you think you have is actually darkness, how deep that darkness is!

[24] "No one can serve two masters. For you will hate one and love the other; you will be devoted to one and despise the other. You cannot serve both God and money."

Matthew 6:19-24

What's Fair?

*N*o one likes to be judged unfairly. First impressions that are way off base are frustrating. Being judged due to situations that appear to be one thing but are really something else is unfair. So ... don't judge others. Take care of your own behavior.

¹ "Do not judge others, and you will not be judged. ² For you will be treated as you treat others. The standard you use in judging is the standard by which you will be judged.

³ "And why worry about a speck in your friend's eye when you have a log in your own? ⁴ How can you think of saying to your friend, 'Let me help you get rid of that speck in your eye,' when you can't see past the log in your own eye?

⁵ Hypocrite! First get rid of the log in your own eye; then you will see well enough to deal with the speck in your friend's eye.

⁶ "Don't waste what is holy on people who are unholy. Don't throw your pearls to pigs! They will trample the pearls, then turn and attack you.

¹² "Do to others whatever you would like them to do to you. This is the essence of all that is taught in the law and the prophets."

Matthew 7:1-6, 12

Faith in Action

*P*raying for Jesus to do something and truly believing that He is answering your prayers shows your true faith. In Matthew we see an example of faith so strong that even Jesus was amazed!

⁵ When Jesus returned to Capernaum, a Roman officer came and pleaded with him, ⁶ "Lord, my young servant lies in bed, paralyzed and in terrible pain."

⁷ Jesus said, "I will come and heal him."

⁸ But the officer said, "Lord, I am not worthy to have you come into my home. Just say the word from where you are, and my servant will be healed. ⁹ I know this because I am under the authority of my superior officers, and I have authority over my soldiers. I only need to say, 'Go,' and they go, or 'Come,' and they come. And if I say to my slaves, 'Do this,' they do it."

¹⁰ When Jesus heard this, he was amazed. Turning to those who were following him, he said, "I tell you the truth, I haven't seen faith like this in all Israel! ¹¹ And I tell you this, that many Gentiles will come from all over the world – from east and west – and sit down with Abraham, Isaac, and Jacob at the feast in the Kingdom of Heaven. ¹² But many Israelites – those for whom the Kingdom was prepared – will be thrown into outer darkness, where there will be weeping and gnashing of teeth."

¹³ Then Jesus said to the Roman officer, "Go back home. Because you believed, it has happened." And the young servant was healed that same hour.

Matthew 8:5-13

July 24

Power Over Everything

Jesus' followers got into a boat with Him for the purpose of crossing the lake. They had seen Him do miracles. They had heard Him teaching about God. They had heard His prayers. But, when they saw Him quiet a storm and make the wind stop blowing, they were still amazed.

[23] Then Jesus got into the boat and started across the lake with his disciples. [24] Suddenly, a fierce storm struck the lake, with waves breaking into the boat. But Jesus was sleeping. [25] The disciples went and woke him up, shouting, "Lord, save us! We're going to drown!"

[26] Jesus responded, "Why are you afraid? You have so little faith!" Then he got up and rebuked the wind and waves, and suddenly there was a great calm.

[27] The disciples were amazed. "Who is this man?" they asked. "Even the winds and waves obey him!"

Matthew 8:23-27

Anyone Can Serve

*M*atthew was an unlikely follower of Jesus. He was a tax collector and no one liked them! They were usually dishonest and didn't care at all about other people. Jesus saw Matthew's heart though. He knew that Matthew could become a good follower of God. Jesus sees more than people see. Even a girl who appears to have nothing to offer God can become a devoted servant.

9 As Jesus was walking along, he saw a man named Matthew sitting at his tax collector's booth. "Follow me and be my disciple," Jesus said to him. So Matthew got up and followed him.

10 Later, Matthew invited Jesus and his disciples to his home as dinner guests, along with many tax collectors and other disreputable sinners. 11 But when the Pharisees saw this, they asked his disciples, "Why does your teacher eat with such scum?"

12 When Jesus heard this, he said, "Healthy people don't need a doctor – sick people do." 13 Then he added, "Now go and learn the meaning of this Scripture: 'I want you to show mercy, not offer sacrifices.' For I have come to call not those who think they are righteous, but those who know they are sinners."

Matthew 9:9-13

Rest Like You Wouldn't Believe

*E*veryone has problems. But maybe you sometimes feel that your problems are bigger than anyone else's. Maybe they are. There is only one place to get rest and peace in the middle of your troubles. Only one place.

25 At that time Jesus prayed this prayer: "O Father, Lord of heaven and earth, thank you for hiding these things from those who think themselves wise and clever, and for revealing them to the childlike. 26 Yes, Father, it pleased you to do it this way!

27 "My Father has entrusted everything to me. No one truly knows the Son except the Father, and no one truly knows the Father except the Son and those to whom the Son chooses to reveal him."

28 Then Jesus said, "Come to me, all of you who are weary and carry heavy burdens, and I will give you rest. 29 Take my yoke upon you. Let me teach you, because I am humble and gentle at heart, and you will find rest for your souls. 30 For my yoke is easy to bear, and the burden I give you is light."

Matthew 11:25-30

He Cares About Your Every Need

*D*oes Jesus only care about how well you pray or how often you read the Bible? No, He cares about your every need – even hunger. He cares.

²⁹ Jesus returned to the Sea of Galilee and climbed a hill and sat down. ³⁰ A vast crowd brought to him people who were lame, blind, crippled, those who couldn't speak, and many others. They laid them before Jesus, and he healed them all. ³¹ The crowd was amazed! Those who hadn't been able to speak were talking, the crippled were made well, the lame were walking, and the blind could see again! And they praised the God of Israel.

³² Then Jesus called his disciples and told them, "I feel sorry for these people. They have been here with me for three days, and they have nothing left to eat. I don't want to send them away hungry, or they will faint along the way."

³³ The disciples replied, "Where would we get enough food here in the wilderness for such a huge crowd?"

³⁴ Jesus asked, "How much bread do you have?"
They replied, "Seven loaves, and a few small fish."

³⁵ So Jesus told all the people to sit down on the ground. ³⁶ Then he took the seven loaves and the fish, thanked God for them, and broke them into pieces. He gave them to the disciples, who distributed the food to the crowd.

³⁷ They all ate as much as they wanted. Afterward, the disciples picked up seven large baskets of leftover food. ³⁸ There were 4,000 men who were fed that day, in addition to all the women and children. ³⁹ Then Jesus sent the people home, and he got into a boat and crossed over to the region of Magadan.

Matthew 15:29-39

July 28

What Are You Hanging On To?

Jesus expects full devotion. It's just not possible to "sort of" be a follower of Jesus but also hang on to your old life. You must give Him everything.

²¹ From then on Jesus began to tell his disciples plainly that it was necessary for him to go to Jerusalem, and that he would suffer many terrible things at the hands of the elders, the leading priests, and the teachers of religious law. He would be killed, but on the third day he would be raised from the dead.

²² But Peter took him aside and began to reprimand him for saying such things. "Heaven forbid, Lord," he said. "This will never happen to you!"

²³ Jesus turned to Peter and said, "Get away from me, Satan! You are a dangerous trap to me. You are seeing things merely from a human point of view, not from God's."

²⁴ Then Jesus said to his disciples, "If any of you wants to be my follower, you must turn from your selfish ways, take up your cross, and follow me. ²⁵ If you try to hang on to your life, you will lose it. But if you give up your life for my sake, you will save it. ²⁶ And what do you benefit if you gain the whole world but lose your own soul? Is anything worth more than your soul? ²⁷ For the Son of Man will come with his angels in the glory of his Father and will judge all people according to their deeds.

²⁸ And I tell you the truth, some standing here right now will not die before they see the Son of Man coming in his Kingdom."

Matthew 16:21-28

Have Faith

*J*esus did amazing miracles. He said that if His followers had enough faith they could also do amazing miracles. Learn to trust Jesus more and more. Ask Him to make your faith stronger.

14 At the foot of the mountain, a large crowd was waiting for them. A man came and knelt before Jesus and said, 15 "Lord, have mercy on my son. He has seizures and suffers terribly. He often falls into the fire or into the water. 16 So I brought him to your disciples, but they couldn't heal him."

17 Jesus said, "You faithless and corrupt people! How long must I be with you? How long must I put up with you? Bring the boy here to me." 18 Then Jesus rebuked the demon in the boy, and it left him. From that moment the boy was well.

19 Afterward the disciples asked Jesus privately, "Why couldn't we cast out that demon?"

20 "You don't have enough faith," Jesus told them. "I tell you the truth, if you had faith even as small as a mustard seed, you could say to this mountain, 'Move from here to there,' and it would move. Nothing would be impossible."

Matthew 17:14-20

Forgiving Others

*F*orgiveness is tough, isn't it? You want to BE forgiven, but forgiving others is not always easy. Jesus says you must forgive if you want to be forgiven.

²¹ Then Peter came to him and asked, "Lord, how often should I forgive someone who sins against me? Seven times?" ²² "No, not seven times," Jesus replied, "but seventy times seven! ²³ "Therefore, the Kingdom of Heaven can be compared to a king who decided to bring his accounts up to date with servants who had borrowed money from him. ²⁴ In the process, one of his debtors was brought in who owed him millions of dollars. ²⁵ He couldn't pay, so his master ordered that he be sold – along with his wife, his children, and everything he owned – to pay the debt. ²⁶ But the man fell down before his master and begged him, 'Please, be patient with me, and I will pay it all.' ²⁷ Then his master was filled with pity for him, and he released him and forgave his debt. ²⁸ "But when the man left the king, he went to a fellow servant who owed him a few thousand dollars. He grabbed him by the throat and demanded instant payment.

²⁹ "His fellow servant fell down before him and begged for a little more time. 'Be patient with me, and I will pay it,' he pleaded. ³⁰ But his creditor wouldn't wait. He had the man arrested and put in prison until the debt could be paid in full.

³² Then the king called in the man he had forgiven and said, 'You evil servant! I forgave you that tremendous debt because you pleaded with me. ³³ Shouldn't you have mercy on your fellow servant, just as I had mercy on you?'"

Matthew 18:21-30, 32-33

August

Fair Is Fair

Some look at others and wonder, "Why does she have more talent than me?" or "Why does she have more stuff than me?" Don't do that. Just be thankful for whatever God gives you. It's all His to give. That's fair.

¹ "The Kingdom of Heaven is like the landowner who went out early one morning to hire workers for his vineyard. ² He agreed to pay the normal daily wage and sent them out to work. ³ "At nine o'clock in the morning he was passing through the marketplace and saw some people standing around doing nothing. ⁴ So he hired them. ⁵ So they went to work in the vineyard. At noon and again at three o'clock he did the same thing.

⁶ "At five o'clock that afternoon he was in town again and saw some more people standing around. He asked them, 'Why haven't you been working today?'

⁷ "They replied, 'Because no one hired us.'

"The landowner told them, 'Then go out and join the others in my vineyard.'

⁹ When those hired at five o'clock were paid, each received a full day's wage. ¹⁰ When those hired first came to get their pay, they assumed they would receive more. But they, too, were paid a day's wage. ¹¹ When they received their pay, they protested to the owner, ¹² 'Those people worked only one hour, and yet you've paid them just as much as you paid us who worked all day in the scorching heat.'

¹³ "He answered one of them, 'Friend, I haven't been unfair! Didn't you agree to work all day for the usual wage?

¹⁵ Is it against the law for me to do what I want with my money?'"

Matthew 20:1-7, 9-13, 15

Serving Others

Serving God means serving others. You can't serve God without caring for others. A servant is not a ruler who lords her power over others. She truly puts the needs of others first.

20 Then the mother of James and John, the sons of Zebedee, came to Jesus with her sons. She knelt respectfully to ask a favor. 21 "What is your request?" he asked.

She replied, "In your Kingdom, please let my two sons sit in places of honor next to you, one on your right and the other on your left."

22 But Jesus answered by saying to them, "You don't know what you are asking! Are you able to drink from the bitter cup of suffering I am about to drink?"

"Oh yes," they replied, "we are able!"

23 Jesus told them, "You will indeed drink from my bitter cup. But I have no right to say who will sit on my right or my left. My Father has prepared those places for the ones he has chosen."

24 When the ten other disciples heard what James and John had asked, they were indignant. 25 But Jesus called them together and said, "You know that the rulers in this world lord it over their people, and officials flaunt their authority over those under them. 26 But among you it will be different. Whoever wants to be a leader among you must be your servant,

27 and whoever wants to be first among you must become your slave. 28 For even the Son of Man came not to be served but to serve others and to give his life as a ransom for many."

Matthew 20:20-28

August 2

The Most Important Rule

*F*ollowing rules gets old, doesn't it? Some rules are important though. They help you learn to get along with others. They help you live within the law. They help you serve God. But, what's the most important rule of all? Jesus pointed out the most important one (and the second one). Obey these and you will be just fine.

[34] But when the Pharisees heard that he had silenced the Sadducees with his reply, they met together to question him again. [35] One of them, an expert in religious law, tried to trap him with this question: [36] "Teacher, which is the most important commandment in the law of Moses?"

[37] Jesus replied, "'You must love the Lord your God with all your heart, all your soul, and all your mind.' [38] This is the first and greatest commandment. [39] A second is equally important: 'Love your neighbor as yourself.' [40] The entire law and all the demands of the prophets are based on these two commandments."

Matthew 22:34-40

How Is Your Humility?

*D*on't be spouting all kinds of self-righteous "do's" and "don'ts" about living for Jesus if your life doesn't match what you say. This is truly an example of "Actions speak louder than words." Live it if you're going to speak it.

¹ Then Jesus said to the crowds and to his disciples, ² "The teachers of religious law and the Pharisees are the official interpreters of the law of Moses. ³ So practice and obey whatever they tell you, but don't follow their example. For they don't practice what they teach. ⁴ They crush people with unbearable religious demands and never lift a finger to ease the burden.

⁵ "Everything they do is for show. On their arms they wear extra wide prayer boxes with Scripture verses inside, and they wear robes with extra long tassels. ⁶ And they love to sit at the head table at banquets and in the seats of honor in the synagogues. ⁷ They love to receive respectful greetings as they walk in the marketplaces, and to be called 'Rabbi.'

⁸ "Don't let anyone call you 'Rabbi,' for you have only one teacher, and all of you are equal as brothers and sisters. ⁹ And don't address anyone here on earth as 'Father,' for only God in heaven is your spiritual Father. ¹⁰ And don't let anyone call you 'Teacher,' for you have only one teacher, the Messiah. ¹¹ The greatest among you must be a servant. ¹² But those who exalt themselves will be humbled, and those who humble themselves will be exalted."

Matthew 23:1-12

Look Around

*W*ow, it's so easy to get caught up in your own life and own problems, isn't it? But, Jesus says to pay attention to other people – and help whenever you can.

35 For I was hungry, and you fed me. I was thirsty, and you gave me a drink. I was a stranger, and you invited me into your home. 36 I was naked, and you gave me clothing. I was sick, and you cared for me. I was in prison, and you visited me.'

37 "Then these righteous ones will reply, 'Lord, when did we ever see you hungry and feed you? Or thirsty and give you something to drink? 38 Or a stranger and show you hospitality? Or naked and give you clothing? 39 When did we ever see you sick or in prison and visit you?'

40 "And the King will say, 'I tell you the truth, when you did it to one of the least of these my brothers and sisters, you were doing it to me!'

41 "Then the King will turn to those on the left and say, 'Away with you, you cursed ones, into the eternal fire. 42 For I was hungry, and you didn't feed me. I was thirsty, and you didn't give me a drink. 43 I was a stranger, and you didn't invite me into your home. I was naked, and you didn't give me clothing. I was sick and in prison, and you didn't visit me.'

44 "Then they will reply, 'Lord, when did we ever see you hungry or thirsty or a stranger or naked or sick or in prison, and not help you?'

45 "And he will answer, 'I tell you the truth, when you refused to help the least of these my brothers and sisters, you were refusing to help me.'"

Matthew 25:35-45

The Last Supper

*W*hen Communion is served at your church, it is a time to remember the incredible gift of love Jesus shared when He died for your sins.

²⁰ When it was evening, Jesus sat down at the table with the twelve disciples. ²¹ While they were eating, he said, "I tell you the truth, one of you will betray me."

²² Greatly distressed, each one asked in turn, "Am I the one, Lord?"

²³ He replied, "One of you who has just eaten from this bowl with me will betray me. ²⁴ For the Son of Man must die, as the Scriptures declared long ago. But how terrible it will be for the one who betrays him. It would be far better for that man if he had never been born!"

²⁵ Judas, the one who would betray him, also asked, "Rabbi, am I the one?"

And Jesus told him, "You have said it."

²⁶ As they were eating, Jesus took some bread and blessed it. Then he broke it in pieces and gave it to the disciples, saying, "Take this and eat it, for this is my body."

²⁷ And he took a cup of wine and gave thanks to God for it. He gave it to them and said, "Each of you drink from it, ²⁸ for this is my blood, which confirms the covenant between God and his people. It is poured out as a sacrifice to forgive the sins of many."

Matthew 26:20-28

August 6

Peter's Denial

*P*eter is criticized for speaking without thinking and making promises he can't keep. Before you criticize Peter, think about your words and actions. Do you ever deny Jesus by the words you speak before thinking or actions done without considering their results?

³¹ Jesus told them, "Tonight all of you will desert me."

³³ Peter declared, "Even if everyone else deserts you, I will never desert you."

³⁴ Jesus replied, "I tell you the truth, Peter – this very night, before the rooster crows, you will deny three times that you even know me." ³⁵ "No!" Peter insisted. "Even if I have to die with you, I will never deny you!"

⁶⁹ Meanwhile, Peter was sitting outside in the courtyard. A servant girl came over and said to him, "You were one of those with Jesus the Galilean."

⁷⁰ But Peter denied it in front of everyone. "I don't know what you're talking about," he said.

⁷¹ Later, out by the gate, another servant girl noticed him and said to those standing around, "This man was with Jesus of Nazareth."

⁷² Again Peter denied it, this time with an oath. "I don't even know the man," he said.

⁷³ A little later some of the other bystanders came over to Peter and said, "You must be one of them; we can tell by your Galilean accent."

⁷⁴ Peter swore, "A curse on me if I'm lying – I don't know the man!" And immediately the rooster crowed.

Matthew 26:31, 33-35, 69-74

Complete Surrender

*J*esus was tortured and crucified because He was surrendered to God's will. He went through incredible pain and agony ... for you ... because of His love for you and His love for God. Completely surrendered.

³⁶ Then Jesus went with them to the olive grove called Gethsemane, and he said, "Sit here while I go over there to pray." ³⁷ He took Peter and Zebedee's two sons, James and John, and he became anguished and distressed.

³⁸ He told them, "My soul is crushed with grief to the point of death. Stay here and keep watch with me."

³⁹ He went on a little farther and bowed with his face to the ground, praying, "My Father! If it is possible, let this cup of suffering be taken away from me. Yet I want your will to be done, not mine."

⁴⁰ Then he returned to the disciples and found them asleep. He said to Peter, "Couldn't you watch with me even one hour?

⁴¹ Keep watch and pray, so that you will not give in to temptation. For the spirit is willing, but the body is weak!"

⁴² Then Jesus left them a second time and prayed, "My Father! If this cup cannot be taken away unless I drink it, your will be done." ⁴³ When he returned to them again, he found them sleeping, for they couldn't keep their eyes open.

⁴⁴ So he went to pray a third time, saying the same things again. ⁴⁵ Then he came to the disciples and said, "Go ahead and sleep. Have your rest. But look – the time has come. The Son of Man is betrayed into the hands of sinners.

⁴⁶ Up, let's be going. Look, my betrayer is here!"

Matthew 26:36-46

August 8

Jesus' Death

*J*esus was tortured and murdered. He could have called angels to rescue Him. God could have whisked Him away from this horrible scene. But, He didn't. It was God's plan for Him to go through this agony ... for you. That's how much He loves you.

32 Along the way, they came across a man named Simon, who was from Cyrene, and the soldiers forced him to carry Jesus' cross. 33 And they went out to a place called Golgotha (which means "Place of the Skull"). 34 The soldiers gave him wine mixed with bitter gall, but when he had tasted it, he refused to drink it. 35 After they had nailed him to the cross, the soldiers gambled for his clothes by throwing dice. 36 Then they sat around and kept guard as he hung there. 37 A sign was fastened above Jesus' head, announcing the charge against him. It read: "This is Jesus, the King of the Jews." 38 Two revolutionaries were crucified with him, one on his right and one on his left.

39 The people passing by shouted abuse, shaking their heads in mockery. 40 "Look at you now!" they yelled at him. "You said you were going to destroy the Temple and rebuild it in three days. Well then, if you are the Son of God, save yourself and come down from the cross!"

41 The leading priests, the teachers of religious law, and the elders also mocked Jesus. 42 "He saved others," they scoffed, "but he can't save himself! So he is the King of Israel, is he? Let him come down from the cross right now, and we will believe in him! 43 He trusted God, so let God rescue him now if he wants him! For he said, 'I am the Son of God.'"

Matthew 27:32-43

The Loneliest Moment

*E*ven though people denied and abandoned Jesus. Even though they tortured Him, He still had God. Until that one moment when even God turned away as Jesus took on Himself the sins of all mankind. He paid the penalty for your sin so that you would never have to.

⁴⁵ At noon, darkness fell across the whole land until three o'clock. ⁴⁶ At about three o'clock, Jesus called out with a loud voice, *"Eli, Eli, lema sabachthani?"* which means "My God, my God, why have you abandoned me?"

⁴⁷ Some of the bystanders misunderstood and thought he was calling for the prophet Elijah. ⁴⁸ One of them ran and filled a sponge with sour wine, holding it up to him on a reed stick so he could drink. ⁴⁹ But the rest said, "Wait! Let's see whether Elijah comes to save him."

⁵⁰ Then Jesus shouted out again, and he released his spirit.

⁵¹ At that moment the curtain in the sanctuary of the Temple was torn in two, from top to bottom. The earth shook, rocks split apart, ⁵² and tombs opened. The bodies of many godly men and women who had died were raised from the dead. ⁵³ They left the cemetery after Jesus' resurrection, went into the holy city of Jerusalem, and appeared to many people.

⁵⁴ The Roman officer and the other soldiers at the crucifixion were terrified by the earthquake and all that had happened. They said, "This man truly was the Son of God!"

⁵⁵ And many women who had come from Galilee with Jesus to care for him were watching from a distance.

Matthew 27:45-55

It's Not Over!

Satan probably thought he had won – Jesus, the Son of God was dead. But, he didn't know the end of the story. God raised Jesus back to life. He had the victory! Jesus lives today, loving you and taking care of you and because He had victory over death, so will you!

¹ Early on Sunday morning, as the new day was dawning, Mary Magdalene and the other Mary went out to visit the tomb.

² Suddenly there was a great earthquake! For an angel of the Lord came down from heaven, rolled aside the stone, and sat on it. ³ His face shone like lightning, and his clothing was as white as snow. ⁴ The guards shook with fear when they saw him, and they fell into a dead faint.

⁵ Then the angel spoke to the women. "Don't be afraid!" he said. "I know you are looking for Jesus, who was crucified.

⁶ He isn't here! He is risen from the dead, just as he said would happen. Come, see where his body was lying. ⁷ And now, go quickly and tell his disciples that he has risen from the dead, and he is going ahead of you to Galilee. You will see him there. Remember what I have told you."

⁸ The women ran quickly from the tomb. They were very frightened but also filled with great joy, and they rushed to give the disciples the angel's message. ⁹ And as they went, Jesus met them and greeted them. And they ran to him, grasped his feet, and worshiped him. ¹⁰ Then Jesus said to them, "Don't be afraid! Go tell my brothers to leave for Galilee, and they will see me there."

Matthew 28:1-10

You Have a Job to Do!

After Jesus was resurrected back to life, He sat down with His followers and told them they had a job to do. He asked them to share His love and care with others. He asked them to make disciples. This is your job to do for Him, too. How can you do it?

[16] Then the eleven disciples left for Galilee, going to the mountain where Jesus had told them to go. [17] When they saw him, they worshiped him – but some of them doubted!

[18] Jesus came and told his disciples, "I have been given all authority in heaven and on earth. [19] Therefore, go and make disciples of all the nations, baptizing them in the name of the Father and the Son and the Holy Spirit. [20] Teach these new disciples to obey all the commands I have given you. And be sure of this: I am with you always, even to the end of the age."

Matthew 28:16-20

Living with Purpose

*N*otice two things about how Jesus lived. One – He got up early and had a private prayer time. It must be important, if Jesus did it. Second – when a man needed to be healed from a highly contagious disease, Jesus touched him. He was willing to get His hands "dirty" to serve God and others.

35 Before daybreak the next morning, Jesus got up and went out to an isolated place to pray. 36 Later Simon and the others went out to find him. 37 When they found him, they said, "Everyone is looking for you."

38 But Jesus replied, "We must go on to other towns as well, and I will preach to them, too. That is why I came." 39 So he traveled throughout the region of Galilee, preaching in the synagogues and casting out demons.

40 A man with leprosy came and knelt in front of Jesus, begging to be healed. "If you are willing, you can heal me and make me clean," he said.

41 Moved with compassion, Jesus reached out and touched him. "I am willing," he said. "Be healed!" 42 Instantly the leprosy disappeared, and the man was healed. 43 Then Jesus sent him on his way with a stern warning: 44 "Don't tell anyone about this. Instead, go to the priest and let him examine you. Take along the offering required in the law of Moses for those who have been healed of leprosy. This will be a public testimony that you have been cleansed."

Mark 1:35-44

True Friendship

*F*our friends wanted to help their sick friend. It wasn't easy. There were obstacles to what they wanted to do but they didn't give up. They got creative and found a way to get their friend to Jesus. They were committed to helping their friend … no matter what.

¹ When Jesus returned to Capernaum several days later, the news spread quickly that he was back home. ² Soon the house where he was staying was so packed with visitors that there was no more room, even outside the door. While he was preaching God's word to them, ³ four men arrived carrying a paralyzed man on a mat. ⁴ They couldn't bring him to Jesus because of the crowd, so they dug a hole through the roof above his head. Then they lowered the man on his mat, right down in front of Jesus. ⁵ Seeing their faith, Jesus said to the paralyzed man, "My child, your sins are forgiven."

⁶ But some of the teachers of religious law who were sitting there thought to themselves, ⁷ "What is he saying? This is blasphemy! Only God can forgive sins!"

⁸ Jesus knew immediately what they were thinking, so he asked them, "Why do you question this in your hearts? ⁹ Is it easier to say to the paralyzed man 'Your sins are forgiven,' or 'Stand up, pick up your mat, and walk'? ¹⁰ So I will prove to you that the Son of Man has the authority on earth to forgive sins." Then Jesus turned to the paralyzed man and said, ¹¹ "Stand up, pick up your mat, and go home!"

¹² And the man jumped up, grabbed his mat, and walked out through the stunned onlookers. They were all amazed and praised God, exclaiming, "We've never seen anything like this before!"

August 14

Mark 2:1-12

What Kind of Soil Are You?

When you first heard God's Word did you let it take root in your heart and grow? Are you growing stronger in your faith and doing God's work now?

³ "A farmer went out to plant some seed. ⁴ As he scattered it across his field, some of the seed fell on a footpath, and the birds came and ate it. ⁵ Other seed fell on shallow soil with underlying rock. The seed sprouted quickly because the soil was shallow. ⁶ But the plant soon wilted under the hot sun, and since it didn't have deep roots, it died. ⁷ Other seed fell among thorns that grew up and choked out the tender plants so they produced no grain. ⁸ Still other seeds fell on fertile soil, and they sprouted, grew, and produced a crop that was thirty, sixty, and even a hundred times as much as had been planted!"

¹³ Then Jesus said to them ... ¹⁵ "The seed that fell on the footpath represents those who hear the message, only to have Satan come at once and take it away. ¹⁶ The seed on the rocky soil represents those who hear the message and immediately receive it with joy. ¹⁷ But since they don't have deep roots, they don't last long. They fall away as soon as they have problems or are persecuted for believing God's word. ¹⁸ The seed that fell among the thorns represents others who hear God's word, ¹⁹ but all too quickly the message is crowded out by the worries of this life, the lure of wealth, and the desire for other things, so no fruit is produced. ²⁰ And the seed that fell on good soil represents those who hear and accept God's word and produce a harvest of thirty, sixty, or even a hundred times as much as had been planted!"

Mark 4:3-8, 13, 15-20

August 15

Believe Him

Jesus made a simple statement to His disciples. He said, "Let's cross to the other side of the lake." But when the trip got scary they doubted His plan. He had to stop a storm to show them His power. Do you sometimes doubt His plans, too?

[35] As evening came, Jesus said to his disciples, "Let's cross to the other side of the lake." [36] So they took Jesus in the boat and started out, leaving the crowds behind (although other boats followed). [37] But soon a fierce storm came up. High waves were breaking into the boat, and it began to fill with water.

[38] Jesus was sleeping at the back of the boat with his head on a cushion. The disciples woke him up, shouting, "Teacher, don't you care that we're going to drown?"

[39] When Jesus woke up, he rebuked the wind and said to the waves, "Silence! Be still!" Suddenly the wind stopped, and there was a great calm. [40] Then he asked them, "Why are you afraid? Do you still have no faith?"

[41] The disciples were absolutely terrified. "Who is this man?" they asked each other. "Even the wind and waves obey him!"

Mark 4:35-41

Don't Be Afraid

The disciples had seen Jesus do amazing miracles. They had heard Him teach, but they still didn't understand who He was. They didn't trust Him. They didn't truly believe Him. How are you doing in the areas of trust and belief?

⁴⁵ Immediately after this, Jesus insisted that his disciples get back into the boat and head across the lake to Bethsaida, while he sent the people home. ⁴⁶ After telling everyone goodbye, he went up into the hills by himself to pray.

⁴⁷ Late that night, the disciples were in their boat in the middle of the lake, and Jesus was alone on land. ⁴⁸ He saw that they were in serious trouble, rowing hard and struggling against the wind and waves. About three o'clock in the morning Jesus came toward them, walking on the water. He intended to go past them, ⁴⁹ but when they saw him walking on the water, they cried out in terror, thinking he was a ghost. ⁵⁰ They were all terrified when they saw him.

But Jesus spoke to them at once. "Don't be afraid," he said. "Take courage! I am here!" ⁵¹ Then he climbed into the boat, and the wind stopped. They were totally amazed, ⁵² for they still didn't understand the significance of the miracle of the loaves. Their hearts were too hard to take it in.

Mark 6:45-52

Faith for Everyone

*J*esus' message of God's love was not only for the Jewish people. It is for anyone. Can you think of someone who you feel would never be interested in knowing God? Don't rule that person out – anyone can come to faith!

²⁴ Then Jesus left Galilee and went north to the region of Tyre. He didn't want anyone to know which house he was staying in, but he couldn't keep it a secret. ²⁵ Right away a woman who had heard about him came and fell at his feet. Her little girl was possessed by an evil spirit, ²⁶ and she begged him to cast out the demon from her daughter.

Since she was a Gentile, born in Syrian Phoenicia, ²⁷ Jesus told her, "First I should feed the children – my own family, the Jews. It isn't right to take food from the children and throw it to the dogs."

²⁸ She replied, "That's true, Lord, but even the dogs under the table are allowed to eat the scraps from the children's plates."

²⁹ "Good answer!" he said. "Now go home, for the demon has left your daughter." ³⁰ And when she arrived home, she found her little girl lying quietly in bed, and the demon was gone.

Mark 7:24-30

The Last Shall Be First

*T*here's no room for pride in the Christian life. True followers of Jesus don't feel that they are better than others or that they deserve more. A follower of Jesus is a servant who values even the person who seems unimportant.

[33] After they arrived at Capernaum and settled in a house, Jesus asked his disciples, "What were you discussing out on the road?" [34] But they didn't answer, because they had been arguing about which of them was the greatest. [35] He sat down, called the twelve disciples over to him, and said, "Whoever wants to be first must take last place and be the servant of everyone else."

[36] Then he put a little child among them. Taking the child in his arms, he said to them, [37] "Anyone who welcomes a little child like this on my behalf welcomes me, and anyone who welcomes me welcomes not only me but also my Father who sent me."

Mark 9:33-37

Hold On to Nothing

*T*he Ten Commandments give a basic outline of how to live in obedience to God. But a true follower holds on to nothing – not money, not time, not talent. Everything belongs to God.

¹⁷ As Jesus was starting out on his way to Jerusalem, a man came running up to him, knelt down, and asked, "Good Teacher, what must I do to inherit eternal life?"

¹⁸ "Why do you call me good?" Jesus asked. "Only God is truly good. ¹⁹ But to answer your question, you know the commandments: 'You must not murder. You must not commit adultery. You must not steal. You must not testify falsely. You must not cheat anyone. Honor your father and mother.'"

²⁰ "Teacher," the man replied, "I've obeyed all these commandments since I was young."

²¹ Looking at the man, Jesus felt genuine love for him. "There is still one thing you haven't done," he told him. "Go and sell all your possessions and give the money to the poor, and you will have treasure in heaven. Then come, follow me."

²² At this the man's face fell, and he went away sad, for he had many possessions.

²³ Jesus looked around and said to his disciples, "How hard it is for the rich to enter the Kingdom of God!" ²⁴ This amazed them. But Jesus said again, "Dear children, it is very hard to enter the Kingdom of God."

²⁶ The disciples were astounded. "Then who in the world can be saved?" they asked.

²⁷ Jesus looked at them intently and said, "Humanly speaking, it is impossible. But not with God. Everything is possible with God."

Mark 10:17-24, 26-27

Faith that Gets Results

A blind man who heard that Jesus was passing by believed so deeply in Jesus' power that he asked for healing – and he got it. How strong is your faith? When you pray, do you believe that God can (and will) answer?

⁴⁶ Then they reached Jericho, and as Jesus and his disciples left town, a large crowd followed him. A blind beggar named Bartimaeus (son of Timaeus) was sitting beside the road.

⁴⁷ When Bartimaeus heard that Jesus of Nazareth was nearby, he began to shout, "Jesus, Son of David, have mercy on me!"

⁴⁸ "Be quiet!" many of the people yelled at him.

But he only shouted louder, "Son of David, have mercy on me!"

⁴⁹ When Jesus heard him, he stopped and said, "Tell him to come here."

So they called the blind man. "Cheer up," they said. "Come on, he's calling you!" ⁵⁰ Bartimaeus threw aside his coat, jumped up, and came to Jesus.

⁵¹ "What do you want me to do for you?" Jesus asked.

"My rabbi," the blind man said, "I want to see!"

⁵² And Jesus said to him, "Go, for your faith has healed you." Instantly the man could see, and he followed Jesus down the road.

Mark 10:46-52

Respecting God's House

*H*ow do you feel about church? Seriously, how do you feel? It's just a building, right? Well, yes, except that it's a building set aside to worship God. So what happens in that building should be honoring to God. That means what happens in the services as well as your own behavior.

¹⁵ When they arrived back in Jerusalem, Jesus entered the Temple and began to drive out the people buying and selling animals for sacrifices. He knocked over the tables of the money changers and the chairs of those selling doves, ¹⁶ and he stopped everyone from using the Temple as a marketplace. ¹⁷ He said to them, "The Scriptures declare, 'My Temple will be called a house of prayer for all nations,' but you have turned it into a den of thieves."

¹⁸ When the leading priests and teachers of religious law heard what Jesus had done, they began planning how to kill him. But they were afraid of him because the people were so amazed at his teaching.

¹⁹ That evening Jesus and the disciples left the city.

Mark 11:15-19

Real Understanding

*O*ver and over Jesus teaches that loving God and loving others is the most important. A follower of Jesus will be known by her love for others. That means putting aside silly little differences. It means not being jealous but being able to celebrate others' successes. It means being there for others when they need you.

28 One of the teachers of religious law was standing there listening to the debate. He realized that Jesus had answered well, so he asked, "Of all the commandments, which is the most important?"

29 Jesus replied, "The most important commandment is this: 'Listen, O Israel! The Lord our God is the one and only Lord. 30 And you must love the Lord your God with all your heart, all your soul, all your mind, and all your strength.' 31 The second is equally important: 'Love your neighbor as yourself.' No other commandment is greater than these."

32 The teacher of religious law replied, "Well said, Teacher. You have spoken the truth by saying that there is only one God and no other. 33 And I know it is important to love him with all my heart and all my understanding and all my strength, and to love my neighbor as myself. This is more important than to offer all of the burnt offerings and sacrifices required in the law."

34 Realizing how much the man understood, Jesus said to him, "You are not far from the Kingdom of God." And after that, no one dared to ask him any more questions.

Mark 12:28-34

Answered Prayer

When it seems that it takes a long time for God to answer prayer, maybe it's because He wants you to know that what's happening is completely because of Him – nothing else. Keep trusting.

⁶ Zechariah and Elizabeth were righteous in God's eyes, careful to obey all of the Lord's commandments and regulations. ⁷ They had no children because Elizabeth was unable to conceive, and they were both very old. ⁸ One day Zechariah was serving God in the Temple.
¹¹ While Zechariah was in the sanctuary, an angel of the Lord appeared to him, standing to the right of the incense altar. ¹³ The angel said, "Don't be afraid, Zechariah! God has heard your prayer. Your wife, Elizabeth, will give you a son, and you are to name him John. ¹⁵ He will be great in the eyes of the Lord. ¹⁷ He will be a man with the spirit and power of Elijah. He will prepare the people for the coming of the Lord. He will turn the hearts of the fathers to their children, and he will cause those who are rebellious to accept the wisdom of the godly."

¹⁸ Zechariah said to the angel, "How can I be sure this will happen? I'm an old man now, and my wife is also well along in years." ¹⁹ Then the angel said, "I am Gabriel! I stand in the very presence of God. It was he who sent me to bring you this good news!

²⁰ But now, since you didn't believe what I said, you will be silent and unable to speak until the child is born. For my words will certainly be fulfilled at the proper time."

²⁴ Soon afterward his wife, Elizabeth, became pregnant and went into seclusion for five months.

Luke 1:6-8, 11, 13, 15, 17-20, 24

"I Am the Lord's Servant"

*I*magine being Mary for a moment. She was a young, unmarried girl who was suddenly pregnant. There was probably gossip about her. She probably knew that would happen. But, when the angel told her what God wanted to do, she was completely willing. She trusted God with all her heart.

²⁶ God sent the angel Gabriel to Nazareth, a village in Galilee, ²⁷ to a virgin named Mary. She was engaged to be married to a man named Joseph, a descendant of King David. ²⁸ Gabriel appeared to her and said, "Greetings, favored woman! The Lord is with you!"

²⁹ Confused and disturbed, Mary tried to think what the angel could mean. ³⁰ "Don't be afraid, Mary," the angel told her, "for you have found favor with God! ³¹ You will conceive and give birth to a son, and you will name him Jesus. ³² He will be very great and will be called the Son of the Most High. The Lord God will give him the throne of his ancestor David. ³³ And he will reign over Israel forever; his Kingdom will never end!"

³⁴ Mary asked the angel, "But how can this happen? I am a virgin."

³⁵ The angel replied, "The Holy Spirit will come upon you, and the power of the Most High will overshadow you. So the baby to be born will be holy, and he will be called the Son of God. ³⁶ What's more, your relative Elizabeth has become pregnant in her old age! ³⁷ For nothing is impossible with God."

³⁸ Mary responded, "I am the Lord's servant. May everything you have said about me come true."

Luke 1:26-38

Zechariah's Obedience

*G*od took away Zechariah's voice when he doubted the angel's message. So, for nine long months he could not speak. His act of obedience, which went against family norms, gave him his voice back. Obedience rules, even when others question it.

57 When it was time for Elizabeth's baby to be born, she gave birth to a son. 58 And when her neighbors and relatives heard that the Lord had been very merciful to her, everyone rejoiced with her.

59 When the baby was eight days old, they all came for the circumcision ceremony. They wanted to name him Zechariah, after his father. 60 But Elizabeth said, "No! His name is John!"

61 "What?" they exclaimed. "There is no one in all your family by that name." 62 So they used gestures to ask the baby's father what he wanted to name him. 63 He motioned for a writing tablet, and to everyone's surprise he wrote, "His name is John." 64 Instantly Zechariah could speak again, and he began praising God.

65 Awe fell upon the whole neighborhood, and the news of what had happened spread throughout the Judean hills. 66 Everyone who heard about it reflected on these events and asked, "What will this child turn out to be?" For the hand of the Lord was surely upon him in a special way.

Luke 1:57-66

The Miracle Begins

Jesus is born. We've celebrated this Christmas miracle for years and years. His birth was an amazing gift from God. His Son. His only Son.

[1] At that time the Roman emperor, Augustus, decreed that a census should be taken throughout the Roman Empire. [3] All returned to their own ancestral towns to register for this census. [4] And because Joseph was a descendant of King David, he had to go to Bethlehem in Judea, David's ancient home. He traveled there from the village of Nazareth in Galilee. [5] He took with him Mary, his fiancée, who was now obviously pregnant.

[6] And while they were there, the time came for her baby to be born. [7] She gave birth to her first child, a son. She wrapped him snugly in strips of cloth and laid him in a manger, because there was no lodging available for them.

Luke 2:1, 3-7

The First Celebration

*A*s soon as Jesus was born angels appeared in the sky to ordinary shepherds – not kings or government officials – plain old shepherds. The angels were filled with joy and sang praises to God about Jesus' birth. Celebrate! Jesus is born!

8 There were shepherds staying in the fields nearby, guarding their flocks of sheep. 9 Suddenly, an angel of the Lord appeared among them, and the radiance of the Lord's glory surrounded them. They were terrified, 10 but the angel reassured them. "Don't be afraid!" he said. "I bring you good news that will bring great joy to all people. 11 The Savior – yes, the Messiah, the Lord – has been born today in Bethlehem, the city of David! 12 And you will recognize him by this sign: You will find a baby wrapped snugly in strips of cloth, lying in a manger."

13 Suddenly, the angel was joined by a vast host of others – the armies of heaven – praising God and saying,

14 "Glory to God in highest heaven, and peace on earth to those with whom God is pleased."

15 When the angels had returned to heaven, the shepherds said to each other, "Let's go to Bethlehem! Let's see this thing that has happened, which the Lord has told us about."

16 They hurried to the village and found Mary and Joseph. And there was the baby, lying in the manger. 17 After seeing him, the shepherds told everyone what had happened and what the angel had said to them about this child. 20 The shepherds went back to their flocks, glorifying and praising God for all they had heard and seen. It was just as the angel had told them.

Luke 2:8-17, 20

August 28

Listening to God

*M*ary and Joseph took their new son, Jesus, to the temple to be dedicated. Two people there – a man and a woman – were so in tune with God that they knew Jesus was the Messiah as soon as they saw Him. How in tune are you with God?

²⁵ Simeon was righteous and devout and was eagerly waiting for the Messiah to come and rescue Israel. The Holy Spirit was upon him ²⁶ and had revealed to him that he would not die until he had seen the Lord's Messiah. ²⁷ That day the Spirit led him to the Temple. So when Mary and Joseph came to present the baby Jesus to the Lord as the law required, ²⁸ Simeon was there. He took the child in his arms and praised God, saying,

³⁰ "I have seen your salvation, ³¹ which you have prepared for all people. ³² He is a light to reveal God to the nations, and he is the glory of your people Israel!"

³⁴ Then Simeon said to Mary, the baby's mother, "This child is destined to cause many in Israel to fall, but he will be a joy to many others. He has been sent as a sign from God, but many will oppose him."

³⁶ Anna, a prophet, was also there in the Temple. Her husband died when they had been married only seven years. ³⁷ She never left the Temple but stayed there day and night, worshiping God with fasting and prayer. ³⁸ She came along just as Simeon was talking with Mary and Joseph, and she began praising God. She talked about the child to everyone who had been waiting expectantly for God to rescue Jerusalem.

Luke 2:25-28, 30-32, 34, 36-38

My Father's Business

Jesus knew from a young age that He had work to do. He didn't have to wait until He was an adult. He could get busy serving God right away.

⁴¹ Every year Jesus' parents went to Jerusalem for the Passover festival. ⁴² When Jesus was twelve years old, they attended the festival as usual. ⁴³ After the celebration was over, they started home to Nazareth, but Jesus stayed behind in Jerusalem. His parents didn't miss him at first, ⁴⁴ because they assumed he was among the other travelers. But when he didn't show up that evening, they started looking for him among their relatives and friends.

⁴⁵ When they couldn't find him, they went back to Jerusalem to search for him there. ⁴⁶ Three days later they finally discovered him in the Temple, sitting among the religious teachers, listening to them and asking questions. ⁴⁷ All who heard him were amazed at his understanding and his answers.

⁴⁸ His parents didn't know what to think. "Son," his mother said to him, "why have you done this to us? Your father and I have been frantic, searching for you everywhere."

⁴⁹ "But why did you need to search?" he asked. "Didn't you know that I must be in my Father's house?" ⁵⁰ But they didn't understand what he meant.

⁵¹ Then he returned to Nazareth with them and was obedient to them. And his mother stored all these things in her heart.

⁵² Jesus grew in wisdom and in stature and in favor with God and all the people.

Luke 2:41-52

Recognizing Sin

One woman understood how much Jesus' forgiveness meant. She worshiped Him with all her heart and wept because she loved Him so much. Have you allowed the reality of your sin to break your heart and make you truly grateful to Jesus for salvation?

36 One of the Pharisees asked Jesus to have dinner with him, so Jesus went to his home and sat down to eat. 37 When a certain immoral woman from that city heard he was eating there, she brought a beautiful alabaster jar filled with expensive perfume. 38 Then she knelt behind him at his feet, weeping. Her tears fell on his feet, and she wiped them off with her hair. Then she kept kissing his feet and putting perfume on them.

39 When the Pharisee who had invited him saw this, he said to himself, "If this man were a prophet, he would know what kind of woman is touching him. She's a sinner!"

41 Then Jesus told him this story: "A man loaned money to two people – 500 pieces of silver to one and 50 pieces to the other. 42 But neither of them could repay him, so he kindly forgave them both, canceling their debts. Who do you suppose loved him more after that?"

43 Simon answered, "I suppose the one for whom he canceled the larger debt."

"That's right," Jesus said. 47 "I tell you, her sins – and they are many – have been forgiven, so she has shown me much love. But a person who is forgiven little shows only little love." 48 Then Jesus said to the woman, "Your sins are forgiven."

Luke 7:36-39, 41-43, 47-48

September

Faith and Love

Two stories of people with great faith in Jesus' ability to help them – one woman only needed to touch His robe and a father who wanted his daughter to be well. Both people saw Jesus' love and power in action.

[41] A man named Jairus, a leader of the local synagogue, came and fell at Jesus' feet. [42] His only daughter, who was about twelve years old, was dying.

As Jesus went with him, he was surrounded by the crowds. [43] A woman in the crowd had suffered for twelve years with constant bleeding. [44] Coming up behind Jesus, she touched the fringe of his robe. Immediately, the bleeding stopped.

[45] "Who touched me?" Jesus asked.

Everyone denied it, and Peter said, "Master, this whole crowd is pressing up against you."

[46] But Jesus said, "Someone deliberately touched me, for I felt healing power go out from me." [47] When the woman realized that she could not stay hidden, she began to tremble and fell to her knees in front of him. [48] "Daughter," he said to her, "your faith has made you well. Go in peace."

[49] While he was still speaking to her, a messenger arrived from the home of Jairus, the leader of the synagogue. He told him, "Your daughter is dead. There's no use troubling the Teacher now."

[50] But when Jesus heard what had happened, he said to Jairus, "Don't be afraid. Just have faith, and she will be healed."

[54] Then Jesus took her by the hand and said in a loud voice, "My child, get up!" [55] And at that moment her life returned, and she immediately stood up!

Luke 8:41-50, 54-55

The Good Samaritan

*I*t's easy to be nice to your friends or to people who are a lot like you. But, what about people who aren't your friends or who are super different from you? Do you have to be nice to them? Jesus had an answer.

³⁰ Jesus replied with a story: "A Jewish man was traveling from Jerusalem down to Jericho, and he was attacked by bandits. They stripped him of his clothes, beat him up, and left him half dead beside the road.

³¹ "By chance a priest came along. But when he saw the man lying there, he crossed to the other side of the road and passed him by. ³² A Temple assistant walked over and looked at him lying there, but he also passed by on the other side.

³³ "Then a despised Samaritan came along, and when he saw the man, he felt compassion for him. ³⁴ Going over to him, the Samaritan soothed his wounds with olive oil and wine and bandaged them. Then he put the man on his own donkey and took him to an inn, where he took care of him. ³⁵ The next day he handed the innkeeper two silver coins, telling him, 'Take care of this man. If his bill runs higher than this, I'll pay you the next time I'm here.'

³⁶ "Now which of these three would you say was a neighbor to the man who was attacked by bandits?" Jesus asked.

³⁷ The man replied, "The one who showed him mercy."

Then Jesus said, "Yes, now go and do the same."

Luke 10:30-37

What Really Matters

*M*artha was a "doer." She was busy, busy, busy. That's fine, except she thought her sister should be just as busy. What Martha didn't get is that sometimes her busyness made her miss the thing that was really most important. Her sister knew – spending time with Jesus is most important.

³⁸ As Jesus and the disciples continued on their way to Jerusalem, they came to a certain village where a woman named Martha welcomed him into her home. ³⁹ Her sister, Mary, sat at the Lord's feet, listening to what he taught. ⁴⁰ But Martha was distracted by the big dinner she was preparing. She came to Jesus and said, "Lord, doesn't it seem unfair to you that my sister just sits here while I do all the work? Tell her to come and help me."

⁴¹ But the Lord said to her, "My dear Martha, you are worried and upset over all these details! ⁴² There is only one thing worth being concerned about. Mary has discovered it, and it will not be taken away from her."

Luke 10:38-42

Finding the Lost

*E*ver wonder if YOU matter to God? Little old you? Well, wonder no more. You DO matter to God. He celebrates every person who comes to faith in Him.

³ So Jesus told them this story: ⁴ "If a man has a hundred sheep and one of them gets lost, what will he do? Won't he leave the ninety-nine others in the wilderness and go to search for the one that is lost until he finds it? ⁵ And when he has found it, he will joyfully carry it home on his shoulders. ⁶ When he arrives, he will call together his friends and neighbors, saying, 'Rejoice with me because I have found my lost sheep.' ⁷ In the same way, there is more joy in heaven over one lost sinner who repents and returns to God than over ninety-nine others who are righteous and haven't stray-ed away!

⁸ "Or suppose a woman has ten silver coins and loses one. Won't she light a lamp and sweep the entire house and search carefully until she finds it? ⁹ And when she finds it, she will call in her friends and neighbors and say, 'Rejoice with me because I have found my lost coin.' ¹⁰ In the same way, there is joy in the presence of God's angels when even one sinner repents."

Luke 15:3-10

Let the Party Begin!

*D*oes God forget about you if you disobey Him? No, He runs to meet you and throws a party to celebrate your return!

¹¹ To illustrate the point further, Jesus told them this story: "A man had two sons. ¹² The younger son told his father, 'I want my share of your estate now before you die.' So his father agreed to divide his wealth between his sons.

¹³ "A few days later this younger son packed all his belongings and moved to a distant land, and there he wasted all his money in wild living. ¹⁴ About the time his money ran out, a great famine swept over the land, and he began to starve. ¹⁵ He persuaded a local farmer to hire him, and the man sent him into his fields to feed the pigs. ¹⁶ The young man became so hungry that even the pods he was feeding the pigs looked good to him. But no one gave him anything.

¹⁸ "I will go home to my father and say, 'Father, I have sinned against both heaven and you, ¹⁹ and I am no longer worthy of being called your son. Please take me on as a hired servant.'

²⁰ "So he returned home to his father. And while he was still a long way off, his father saw him coming. Filled with love and compassion, he ran to his son, embraced him, and kissed him. ²² "His father said to the servants, 'Quick! Bring the finest robe in the house and put it on him. Get a ring for his finger and sandals for his feet. ²³ And kill the calf we have been fattening. We must celebrate with a feast, ²⁴ for this son of mine was dead and has now returned to life. He was lost, but now he is found.' So the party began."

Luke 15:11-16, 18-20, 22-24

Honesty Is the Best Policy

*I*t's hard to be honest if your heart is most interested in ... you. Whether it's in a job or in relationships it is important to be focused on serving them and serving God. If you're most concerned about yourself, then honesty will not be your focus.

[10] "If you are faithful in little things, you will be faithful in large ones. But if you are dishonest in little things, you won't be honest with greater responsibilities. [11] And if you are untrustworthy about worldly wealth, who will trust you with the true riches of heaven? [12] And if you are not faithful with other people's things, why should you be trusted with things of your own?

[13] "No one can serve two masters. For you will hate one and love the other; you will be devoted to one and despise the other. You cannot serve both God and money."

Luke 16:10-13

Persistent Prayer

*P*raying about something for a long time gets tiring. Do you wonder if God is paying attention? Do you wonder if He even cares or if He will ever answer? It pays to continually bring requests to God and believe that He will answer at the time He feels is right.

¹ One day Jesus told his disciples a story to show that they should always pray and never give up. ² "There was a judge in a certain city," he said, "who neither feared God nor cared about people. ³ A widow of that city came to him repeatedly, saying, 'Give me justice in this dispute with my enemy.' ⁴ The judge ignored her for a while, but finally he said to himself, 'I don't fear God or care about people, ⁵ but this woman is driving me crazy. I'm going to see that she gets justice, because she is wearing me out with her constant requests!'"

⁶ Then the Lord said, "Learn a lesson from this unjust judge. ⁷ Even he rendered a just decision in the end. So don't you think God will surely give justice to his chosen people who cry out to him day and night? Will he keep putting them off? ⁸ I tell you, he will grant justice to them quickly! But when the Son of Man returns, how many will he find on the earth who have faith?"

Luke 18:1-8

Children Are Important

*J*esus' disciples knew how busy He was. He was an important man who many people wanted to see. So, when some parents brought their children for Jesus to bless, His followers tried to shoo them away. But, Jesus didn't let them. He cared about the children and their simple trust in Him.

¹⁵ One day some parents brought their little children to Jesus so he could touch and bless them. But when the disciples saw this, they scolded the parents for bothering him.

¹⁶ Then Jesus called for the children and said to the disciples, "Let the children come to me. Don't stop them! For the Kingdom of God belongs to those who are like these children. ¹⁷ I tell you the truth, anyone who doesn't receive the Kingdom of God like a child will never enter it."

Luke 18:15-17

Zacchaeus Meets Jesus

*W*hoa, that girl is so rotten that she would never want to know Jesus!" Have you ever thought that about someone? Well, it's dangerous to make that kind of conclusion. You never know when a person's heart may turn to Jesus. You never know.

¹ Jesus entered Jericho and made his way through the town. ² There was a man there named Zacchaeus. He was the chief tax collector in the region, and he had become very rich. ³ He tried to get a look at Jesus, but he was too short to see over the crowd. ⁴ So he ran ahead and climbed a sycamore-fig tree beside the road, for Jesus was going to pass that way.

⁵ When Jesus came by, he looked up at Zacchaeus and called him by name. "Zacchaeus!" he said. "Quick, come down! I must be a guest in your home today."

⁶ Zacchaeus quickly climbed down and took Jesus to his house in great excitement and joy. ⁷ But the people were displeased. "He has gone to be the guest of a notorious sinner," they grumbled.

⁸ Meanwhile, Zacchaeus stood before the Lord and said, "I will give half my wealth to the poor, Lord, and if I have cheated people on their taxes, I will give them back four times as much!"

⁹ Jesus responded, "Salvation has come to this home today, for this man has shown himself to be a true son of Abraham. ¹⁰ For the Son of Man came to seek and save those who are lost."

Luke 19:1-10

September 9

Get Busy

*O*ne day Jesus will come back and take His children to heaven. Until then you are trusted to be doing His work here. It's a big responsibility.

[12] Jesus said, "A nobleman was called away to a distant empire to be crowned king and then return. [13] Before he left, he called together ten of his servants and divided among them ten pounds of silver, saying, 'Invest this for me while I am gone.'

[15] "After he was crowned king, he returned and called in the servants to whom he had given the money. He wanted to find out what their profits were. [16] The first servant reported, 'Master, I invested your money and made ten times the original amount!'

[17] "'Well done!' the king exclaimed. 'You are a good servant. You have been faithful with the little I entrusted to you, so you will be governor of ten cities as your reward.'

[18] "The next servant reported, 'Master, I invested your money and made five times the original amount.'

[19] "'Well done!' the king said. 'You will be governor over five cities.'

[20] "But the third servant brought back only the original amount of money and said, 'Master, I hid your money and kept it safe. [21] I was afraid because you are a hard man to deal with.'

[24] "Then, turning to the others standing nearby, the king ordered, 'Take the money from this servant, and give it to the one who has ten pounds.'

[26] "'To those who use well what they are given, even more will be given. But from those who do nothing, even what little they have will be taken away.'"

Luke 19:12-13, 15-21, 24, 26

A Generous Heart

*H*ow much money a person has is not all that important to Jesus. What matters more is how generous you are. When a girl is willing to give generously which means time or money that she could use (not left over) then Jesus notices.

¹ While Jesus was in the Temple, he watched the rich people dropping their gifts in the collection box. ² Then a poor widow came by and dropped in two small coins.

³ "I tell you the truth," Jesus said, "this poor widow has given more than all the rest of them. ⁴ For they have given a tiny part of their surplus, but she, poor as she is, has given everything she has."

Luke 21:1-4

Understanding Hearts

Jesus' followers were with Him for over three years. Yet, they still didn't believe what He taught. How about you? Do you believe what Jesus taught?

¹³ That same day two of Jesus' followers were walking to the village of Emmaus, seven miles from Jerusalem. ¹⁵ Jesus himself suddenly came and began walking with them. ¹⁶ But God kept them from recognizing him.

¹⁷ He asked them, "What are you discussing so intently as you walk along?"

They stopped short, sadness written across their faces. ¹⁸ Then one of them, Cleopas, replied, "You must be the only person in Jerusalem who hasn't heard about all the things that have happened there the last few days."

¹⁹ "What things?" Jesus asked.

"The things that happened to Jesus, the man from Nazareth," they said. "He was a prophet who did powerful miracles, and he was a mighty teacher in the eyes of God andall the people. ²⁰ But our leading priests and other religious leaders handed him over to be condemned to death, and they crucified him." ²⁵ Then Jesus said to them, "You foolish people! You find it so hard to believe all that the prophets wrote in the Scriptures. ²⁶ Wasn't it clearly predicted that the Messiah would have to suffer all these things before entering his glory?"

³⁰ As they sat down to eat, he took the bread and blessed it. Then he broke it and gave it to them. ³¹ Suddenly, their eyes were opened, and they recognized him.

Luke 24:13, 15-20, 25-26, 30-31

Jesus Is the Word

*G*od's amazing love for you was shown in the gift of Jesus. Have you opened your heart to receive this gift?

¹ In the beginning the Word already existed. The Word was with God, and the Word was God.

² He existed in the beginning with God.

³ God created everything through him, and nothing was created except through him.

⁴ The Word gave life to everything that was created, and his life brought light to everyone.

⁵ The light shines in the darkness, and the darkness can never extinguish it.

⁹ The one who is the true light, who gives light to everyone, was coming into the world.

¹⁰ He came into the very world he created, but the world didn't recognize him. ¹¹ He came to his own people, and even they rejected him. ¹² But to all who believed him and accepted him, he gave the right to become children of God. ¹³ They are reborn – not with a physical birth resulting from human passion or plan, but a birth that comes from God.

¹⁴ So the Word became human and made his home among us. He was full of unfailing love and faithfulness. And we have seen his glory, the glory of the Father's one and only Son.

¹⁶ From his abundance we have all received one gracious blessing after another. ¹⁷ For the law was given through Moses, but God's unfailing love and faithfulness came through Jesus Christ. ¹⁸ No one has ever seen God. But the unique One, who is himself God, is near to the Father's heart. He has revealed God to us.

John 1:1-5, 9-14, 16-18

The Beginning

*J*esus was an ordinary guest at a wedding. He had not yet begun any kind of ministry. But, His mother knew something that no one else knew yet – she knew that He was God's Son. So, she opened the door for everyone to begin to see His power. Amazing power. What does His power mean to you?

¹ The next day there was a wedding celebration in the village of Cana in Galilee. Jesus' mother was there, ² and Jesus and his disciples were also invited to the celebration. ³ The wine supply ran out during the festivities, so Jesus' mother told him, "They have no more wine."

⁴ "Dear woman, that's not our problem," Jesus replied.

⁵ But his mother told the servants, "Do whatever he tells you."

⁶ Standing nearby were six stone water jars, used for Jewish ceremonial washing. Each could hold twenty to thirty gallons. ⁷ Jesus told the servants, "Fill the jars with water." When the jars had been filled, ⁸ he said, "Now dip some out, and take it to the master of ceremonies." So the servants followed his instructions.

⁹ When the master of ceremonies tasted the water that was now wine, not knowing where it had come from (though, of course, the servants knew), he called the bridegroom over. ¹⁰ "A host always serves the best wine first," he said. "Then, when everyone has had a lot to drink, he brings out the less expensive wine. But you have kept the best until now!"

¹¹ This miraculous sign at Cana in Galilee was the first time Jesus revealed his glory. And his disciples believed in him.

John 2:1-11

Gift of Eternal Life

*P*robably the most famous verse in the Bible is John 3:16. It simply explains the foundational message of the Bible. God loved you so much that He gave His only Son. That's a lot of love!

³ Jesus replied, "I tell you the truth, unless you are born again, you cannot see the Kingdom of God."

⁴ "What do you mean?" exclaimed Nicodemus. "How can an old man go back into his mother's womb and be born again?"

⁵ Jesus replied, "I assure you, no one can enter the Kingdom of God without being born of water and the Spirit. ⁶ Humans can reproduce only human life, but the Holy Spirit gives birth to spiritual life. ⁷ So don't be surprised when I say, 'You must be born again.' ⁸ The wind blows wherever it wants. Just as you can hear the wind but can't tell where it comes from or where it is going, so you can't explain how people are born of the Spirit."

⁹ "How are these things possible?" Nicodemus asked.

¹⁶ "For God loved the world so much that he gave his one and only Son, so that everyone who believes in him will not perish but have eternal life. ¹⁷ God sent his Son into the world not to judge the world, but to save the world through him."

John 3:3-9, 16-17

Supporting Cast

*J*ohn the Baptist knew from the beginning that he was not the "star" but was the supporting player to Jesus. He was just fine with that. It was his job. The supporting cast is just as important as any other part. Just do your part.

[23] John the Baptist was baptizing at Aenon, near Salim, because there was plenty of water there; and people kept coming to him for baptism. [25] A debate broke out between John's disciples and a certain Jew over ceremonial cleansing. [26] So John's disciples came to him and said, "Rabbi, the man you met on the other side of the Jordan River, the one you identified as the Messiah, is also baptizing people. And everybody is going to him instead of coming to us."

[27] John replied, "No one can receive anything unless God gives it from heaven. [28] You yourselves know how plainly I told you, 'I am not the Messiah. I am only here to prepare the way for him.' [29] It is the bridegroom who marries the bride, and the best man is simply glad to stand with him and hear his vows. Therefore, I am filled with joy at his success. [30] He must become greater and greater, and I must become less and less.

[34] For he is sent by God. He speaks God's words, for God gives him the Spirit without limit. [35] The Father loves his Son and has put everything into his hands. [36] And anyone who believes in God's Son has eternal life. Anyone who doesn't obey the Son will never experience eternal life but remains under God's angry judgment."

John 3:23, 25-30, 34-36

The Woman at the Well

A woman who lived a less than perfect life met Jesus. She listened to Him and her heart was opened to know that He was the Messiah. What was her reaction? Telling EVERYONE!

⁷ Soon a Samaritan woman came to draw water, and Jesus said to her, "Please give me a drink."

⁹ The woman was surprised, for Jews refuse to have anything to do with Samaritans. She said to Jesus, "You are a Jew, and I am a Samaritan woman. Why are you asking me for a drink?"

¹⁰ Jesus replied, "If you only knew the gift God has for you and who you are speaking to, you would ask me, and I would give you living water."

¹¹ "But sir, you don't have a rope or a bucket," she said, "and this well is very deep. Where would you get this living water?

¹³ Jesus replied, "Anyone who drinks this water will soon become thirsty again. ¹⁴ But those who drink the water I give will never be thirsty again. It becomes a fresh, bubbling spring within them, giving them eternal life."

¹⁵ "Please, sir," the woman said, "give me this water! Then I'll never be thirsty again, and I won't have to come here to get water."

¹⁶ "Go and get your husband," Jesus told her.

¹⁷ "I don't have a husband," the woman replied.

Jesus said, "You're right! You don't have a husband."

²⁶ Then Jesus told her, "I Aᴍ the Messiah!"

²⁸ The woman left her water jar beside the well and ran back to the village, telling everyone, ²⁹ "Come and see a man who told me everything I ever did! Could he possibly be the Messiah?"

John 4:7, 9-11, 13-17, 26, 28-29

The Feeding of the Five Thousand

*O*K, be honest. If you saw a miracle right in front of your eyes, what would you do? How would you react? Would it push you to believe in the miracle-worker's power?

¹ After this, Jesus crossed over to the far side of the Sea of Galilee, also known as the Sea of Tiberias. ² A huge crowd kept following him wherever he went, because they saw his miraculous signs as he healed the sick. ³ Then Jesus climbed a hill and sat down with his disciples around him. ⁴ (It was nearly time for the Jewish Passover celebration.) ⁵ Jesus soon saw a huge crowd of people coming to look for him. Turning to Philip, he asked, "Where can we buy bread to feed all these people?" ⁶ He was testing Philip, for he already knew what he was going to do.

⁷ Philip replied, "Even if we worked for months, we wouldn't have enough money to feed them!"

⁸ Then Andrew, Simon Peter's brother, spoke up. ⁹ "There's a young boy here with five barley loaves and two fish. But what good is that with this huge crowd?"

¹⁰ "Tell everyone to sit down," Jesus said. So they all sat down on the grassy slopes. (The men alone numbered about 5,000.) ¹¹ Then Jesus took the loaves, gave thanks to God, and distributed them to the people. Afterward he did the same with the fish. And they all ate as much as they wanted. ¹² After everyone was full, Jesus told his disciples, "Now gather the leftovers, so that nothing is wasted." ¹³ So they picked up the pieces and filled twelve baskets with scraps left by the people who had eaten from the five barley loaves.

September 18

John 6:1-13

Lazarus, Come Out!

*J*esus has power over death. He raised Lazarus so people would witness His power and believe. When you read about His miracles does your faith increase?

¹ A man named Lazarus was sick.

⁴ When Jesus heard about it he said, "Lazarus's sickness will not end in death. No, it happened for the glory of God so that the Son of God will receive glory from this." ¹¹ Then he said, "Our friend Lazarus has fallen asleep, but now I will go and wake him up."

²¹ Martha said to Jesus, "Lord, if only you had been here, my brother would not have died." ²⁵ Jesus told her, "I am the resurrection and the life. Anyone who believes in me will live, even after dying. ²⁶ Everyone who lives in me and believes in me will never ever die. Do you believe this, Martha?"

²⁷ "Yes, Lord," she told him. "I have always believed you are the Messiah, the Son of God, the one who has come into the world from God." ³⁴ "Where have you put him?" he asked them.

They told him, "Lord, come and see." ³⁵ Then Jesus wept. ³⁹ "Roll the stone aside," Jesus told them.

But Martha, the dead man's sister, protested, "Lord, he has been dead for four days. The smell will be terrible."

⁴⁰ Jesus responded, "Didn't I tell you that you would see God's glory if you believe?" ⁴¹ So they rolled the stone aside. Then Jesus looked up to heaven and said, "Father, thank you for hearing me." ⁴³ Then Jesus shouted, "Lazarus, come out!" ⁴⁴ And the dead man came out, his hands and feet bound in graveclothes, his face wrapped in a headcloth. Jesus told them, "Unwrap him and let him go!"

John 11:1, 4, 11, 21, 25-27, 34-35, 39-41, 43-44

Worshiping Your Way

*W*orship comes from your heart. It's your response to God for His love and power. Worship is shown in many ways. As long as it is from your heart it will please God.

¹ Six days before the Passover celebration began, Jesus arrived in Bethany, the home of Lazarus – the man he had raised from the dead. ² A dinner was prepared in Jesus' honor. Martha served, and Lazarus was among those who ate with him. ³ Then Mary took a twelve-ounce jar of expensive perfume made from essence of nard, and she anointed Jesus' feet with it, wiping his feet with her hair. The house was filled with the fragrance.

⁴ But Judas Iscariot, the disciple who would soon betray him, said, ⁵ "That perfume was worth a year's wages. It should have been sold and the money given to the poor." ⁶ Not that he cared for the poor – he was a thief, and since he was in charge of the disciples' money, he often stole some for himself.

⁷ Jesus replied, "Leave her alone. She did this in preparation for my burial. ⁸ You will always have the poor among you, but you will not always have me."

John 12:1-8

Praise Jesus!

Going to Jerusalem was the beginning of "the end" for Jesus. He entered Jerusalem to the sounds of praise from all who saw Him. What would happen to those praises in a few days?

¹² The next day, the news that Jesus was on the way to Jerusalem swept through the city. A large crowd of Passover visitors ¹³ took palm branches and went down the road to meet him. They shouted,

"Praise God! Blessings on the one who comes in the name of the Lord! Hail to the King of Israel!"

¹⁴ Jesus found a young donkey and rode on it, fulfilling the prophecy that said:

¹⁵ "Don't be afraid, people of Jerusalem. Look, your King is coming, riding on a donkey's colt."

¹⁶ His disciples didn't understand at the time that this was a fulfillment of prophecy. But after Jesus entered into his glory, they remembered what had happened and realized that these things had been written about him.

¹⁷ Many in the crowd had seen Jesus call Lazarus from the tomb, raising him from the dead, and they were telling others about it. ¹⁸ That was the reason so many went out to meet him – because they had heard about this miraculous sign. ¹⁹ Then the Pharisees said to each other, "There's nothing we can do. Look, everyone has gone after him!"

John 12:12-19

Example of Serving

*I*magine washing someone else's feet. Yeah, you probably wouldn't do that, would you? Jesus did. He gave an example of serving others in ways that might not be pleasant but would surely be appreciated. It's real servanthood.

³ Jesus knew that the Father had given him authority over everything and that he had come from God and would return to God. ⁴ So he got up from the table, took off his robe, wrapped a towel around his waist, ⁵ and poured water into a basin. Then he began to wash the disciples' feet, drying them with the towel he had around him.

⁶ When Jesus came to Simon Peter, Peter said to him, "Lord, are you going to wash my feet?"

⁷ Jesus replied, "You don't understand now what I am doing, but someday you will."

⁸ "No," Peter protested, "you will never ever wash my feet!"

Jesus replied, "Unless I wash you, you won't belong to me."

⁹ Simon Peter exclaimed, "Then wash my hands and head as well, Lord, not just my feet!"

¹⁰ Jesus replied, "A person who has bathed all over does not need to wash, except for the feet, to be entirely clean. And you disciples are clean, but not all of you." ¹² After washing their feet, he put on his robe again and sat down and asked, "Do you understand what I was doing? ¹³ You call me 'Teacher' and 'Lord,' and you are right, because that's what I am. ¹⁴ And since I, your Lord and Teacher, have washed your feet, you ought to wash each other's feet. ¹⁵ I have given you an example to follow. Do as I have done to you."

John 13:3-10, 12-15

The Way, Truth and Life

*T*here is only one way to God. One way to heaven. The only path is through belief in Jesus. Others may try to convince you there are other ways. They are fooling themselves and trying to fool you. There is only ONE WAY.

[1] "Don't let your hearts be troubled. Trust in God, and trust also in me. [2] There is more than enough room in my Father's home. If this were not so, would I have told you that I am going to prepare a place for you? [3] When everything is ready, I will come and get you, so that you will always be with me where I am. [4] And you know the way to where I am going."

[5] "No, we don't know, Lord," Thomas said. "We have no idea where you are going, so how can we know the way?"

[6] Jesus told him, "I am the way, the truth, and the life. No one can come to the Father except through me. [7] If you had really known me, you would know who my Father is. From now on, you do know him and have seen him!"

[8] Philip said, "Lord, show us the Father, and we will be satisfied."

[9] Jesus replied, "Have I been with you all this time, Philip, and yet you still don't know who I am? Anyone who has seen me has seen the Father! So why are you asking me to show him to you? [10] Don't you believe that I am in the Father and the Father is in me? The words I speak are not my own, but my Father who lives in me does his work through me. [11] Just believe that I am in the Father and the Father is in me. Or at least believe because of the work you have seen me do."

John 14:1-11

The True Vine

*A*re you serious about serving God? You can say you are, but if you don't stay connected to Him by reading His Word and praying then you're just kidding yourself.

[1] "I am the true grapevine, and my Father is the gardener. [2] He cuts off every branch of mine that doesn't produce fruit, and he prunes the branches that do bear fruit so they will produce even more. [4] Remain in me, and I will remain in you. For a branch cannot produce fruit if it is severed from the vine, and you cannot be fruitful unless you remain in me.

[5] "Yes, I am the vine; you are the branches. Those who remain in me, and I in them, will produce much fruit. For apart from me you can do nothing. [6] Anyone who does not remain in me is thrown away like a useless branch and withers. Such branches are gathered into a pile to be burned. [7] But if you remain in me and my words remain in you, you may ask for anything you want, and it will be granted!

[9] "I have loved you even as the Father has loved me. Remain in my love. [10] When you obey my commandments, you remain in my love, just as I obey my Father's commandments and remain in his love. [11] I have told you these things so that you will be filled with my joy. Yes, your joy will overflow! [12] This is my commandment: Love each other in the same way I have loved you. [13] There is no greater love than to lay down one's life for one's friends. [14] You are my friends if you do what I command. [17] This is my command: Love each other."

John 15:1-2, 4-7, 9-14, 17

September 24

Action over Words

It's easy to say the words you think people want you to say like, "Sure, Jesus, I love You." But if actions don't match the words then you're just fooling yourself ... but you're not fooling God!

¹⁵ After breakfast Jesus asked Simon Peter, "Simon son of John, do you love me more than these?"

"Yes, Lord," Peter replied, "you know I love you."

"Then feed my lambs," Jesus told him.

¹⁶ Jesus repeated the question: "Simon son of John, do you love me?"

"Yes, Lord," Peter said, "you know I love you."

"Then take care of my sheep," Jesus said.

¹⁷ A third time he asked him, "Simon son of John, do you love me?"

Peter was hurt that Jesus asked the question a third time. He said, "Lord, you know everything. You know that I love you."

Jesus said, "Then feed my sheep."

John 21:15-17

The Promise

*J*esus had promised to send the Holy Spirit to believers after He left the earth. The Holy Spirit lives in your heart and helps you stay close to God. What an incredible gift!

[1] On the day of Pentecost all the believers were meeting together in one place. [2] Suddenly, there was a sound from heaven like the roaring of a mighty windstorm, and it filled the house where they were sitting. [3] Then, what looked like flames or tongues of fire appeared and settled on each of them. [4] And everyone present was filled with the Holy Spirit and began speaking in other languages, as the Holy Spirit gave them this ability.

[14] Then Peter stepped forward with the eleven other apostles and shouted to the crowd, "Listen carefully, all of you, fellow Jews and residents of Jerusalem! Make no mistake about this.

[22] "People of Israel, listen! God publicly endorsed Jesus the Nazarene by doing powerful miracles, wonders, and signs through him, as you well know.

[32] "God raised Jesus from the dead, and we are all witnesses of this. [33] Now he is exalted to the place of highest honor in heaven, at God's right hand. And the Father, as he had promised, gave him the Holy Spirit to pour out upon us, just as you see and hear today."

[38] Peter replied, "Each of you must repent of your sins and turn to God, and be baptized in the name of Jesus Christ for the forgiveness of your sins. Then you will receive the gift of the Holy Spirit."

Acts 2:1-4, 14, 22, 32-33, 38

September 26

Devotion

What are you devoted to? Friends? Hobbies? The first Christians devoted themselves to studying the Bible and to prayer. That was what was important to them.

42 All the believers devoted themselves to the apostles' teaching, and to fellowship, and to sharing in meals (including the Lord's Supper), and to prayer.

43 A deep sense of awe came over them all, and the apostles performed many miraculous signs and wonders. 44 And all the believers met together in one place and shared everything they had. 45 They sold their property and possessions and shared the money with those in need. 46 They worshiped together at the Temple each day, met in homes for the Lord's Supper, and shared their meals with great joy and generosity – 47 all the while praising God and enjoying the goodwill of all the people. And each day the Lord added to their fellowship those who were being saved.

Acts 2:42-47

The Best Gift

*W*hat do you consider the best gift you've ever been given? One man thought money was just what he needed. Peter and John knew better. They had something way better than money to give him.

¹ Peter and John went to the Temple one afternoon to take part in the three o'clock prayer service. ² As they approached the Temple, a man lame from birth was being carried in. Each day he was put beside the Temple gate, the one called the Beautiful Gate, so he could beg from the people going into the Temple. ³ When he saw Peter and John about to enter, he asked them for some money.

⁴ Peter and John looked at him intently, and Peter said, "Look at us!" ⁵ The lame man looked at them eagerly, expecting some money. ⁶ But Peter said, "I don't have any silver or gold for you. But I'll give you what I have. In the name of Jesus Christ the Nazarene, get up and walk!"

⁷ Then Peter took the lame man by the right hand and helped him up. And as he did, the man's feet and ankles were instantly healed and strengthened. ⁸ He jumped up, stood on his feet, and began to walk! Then, walking, leaping, and praising God, he went into the Temple with them.

⁹ All the people saw him walking and heard him praising God. ¹⁰ When they realized he was the lame beggar they had seen so often at the Beautiful Gate, they were absolutely astounded! ¹¹ They all rushed out in amazement to Solomon's Colonnade, where the man was holding tightly to Peter and John.

Acts 3:1-11

Stay Focused

*T*here is only one way to salvation. That's what Peter and John taught. That got them in trouble but they didn't back down. They knew they were right – there was only way.

¹ While Peter and John were speaking to the people, they were confronted by the priests, the captain of the Temple guard, and some of the Sadducees. ² These leaders were very disturbed that Peter and John were teaching the people that through Jesus there is a resurrection of the dead. ³ They arrested them and, since it was already evening, put them in jail until morning. ⁴ But many of the people who heard their message believed it, so the number of believers now totaled about 5,000 men, not counting women and children.

⁵ The next day the council of all the rulers and elders and teachers of religious law met in Jerusalem. ⁶ Annas the high priest was there, along with Caiaphas, John, Alexander, and other relatives of the high priest. ⁷ They brought in the two disciples and demanded, "By what power, or in whose name, have you done this?"

⁸ Then Peter, filled with the Holy Spirit, said to them, "Rulers and elders of our people ... ¹⁰ Let me clearly state to all of you and to all the people of Israel that he was healed by the powerful name of Jesus Christ the Nazarene, the man you crucified but whom God raised from the dead. ¹¹ For Jesus is the one referred to in the Scriptures, where it says, 'The stone that you builders rejected has now become the cornerstone.'

¹² There is salvation in no one else! God has given no other name under heaven by which we must be saved."

Acts 4:1-8, 10-12

Sharing Unselfishly

The first Christians shared everything they had with one another. So when one person had two pieces of bread and another person had none – the first person shared hers. Life wasn't all about getting more than anyone else, it was about helping one another. There's a good lesson in that!

32 All the believers were united in heart and mind. And they felt that what they owned was not their own, so they shared everything they had. 33 The apostles testified powerfully to the resurrection of the Lord Jesus, and God's great blessing was upon them all. 34 There were no needy people among them, because those who owned land or houses would sell them 35 and bring the money to the apostles to give to those in need.

36 For instance, there was Joseph, the one the apostles nicknamed Barnabas (which means "Son of Encouragement"). He was from the tribe of Levi and came from the island of Cyprus. 37 He sold a field he owned and brought the money to the apostles.

Acts 4:32-37

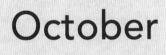

October

Be Honest

*B*ig talk and little action will lead to punishment. Don't brag about your devotion to God just to impress people. God knows your heart. You don't fool Him.

¹ But there was a certain man named Ananias who, with his wife, Sapphira, sold some property. ² He brought part of the money to the apostles, claiming it was the full amount. With his wife's consent, he kept the rest.

³ Then Peter said, "Ananias, why have you let Satan fill your heart? You lied to the Holy Spirit, and you kept some of the money for yourself. ⁴ The property was yours to sell or not sell, as you wished. And after selling it, the money was also yours to give away. How could you do a thing like this? You weren't lying to us but to God!"

⁵ As soon as Ananias heard these words, he fell to the floor and died. Everyone who heard about it was terrified.

⁷ About three hours later his wife came in, not knowing what had happened. ⁸ Peter asked her, "Was this the price you and your husband received for your land?"

"Yes," she replied, "that was the price."

⁹ And Peter said, "How could the two of you even think of conspiring to test the Spirit of the Lord like this?"

¹⁰ Instantly, she fell to the floor and died.

¹¹ Great fear gripped the entire church and everyone else who heard what had happened.

Acts 5:1-5, 7-11

Available and Willing

*I*f you knew God was telling you to do something, would you do it even if you didn't understand why? Philip did. He was told to go to a specific place and he didn't know why. But, his willingness to obey had a cool result!

26 As for Philip, an angel of the Lord said to him, "Go south down the desert road that runs from Jerusalem to Gaza." 27 So he started out, and he met the treasurer of Ethiopia, a eunuch of great authority under the Kandake, the queen of Ethiopia. 28 He was reading aloud from the book of the prophet Isaiah. 29 The Holy Spirit said to Philip, "Go over and walk along beside the carriage."

30 Philip ran over and heard the man reading from the prophet Isaiah. Philip asked, "Do you understand what you are reading?"

31 The man replied, "How can I, unless someone instructs me?"

32 The passage of Scripture he had been reading was this: "He was led like a sheep to the slaughter. And as a lamb is silent before the shearers, he did not open his mouth. 33 He was humiliated and received no justice. Who can speak of his descendants? For his life was taken from the earth."

34 The eunuch asked Philip, "Tell me, was the prophet talking about himself or someone else?" 35 So beginning with this same Scripture, Philip told him the Good News about Jesus.

36 As they rode along, they came to some water, and the eunuch said, "Look! There's some water! Why can't I be baptized?" 38 He ordered the carriage to stop, and they went down into the water, and Philip baptized him.

Acts 8:26-36, 38

God Gets Your Attention

Some people try to totally ignore God. Some are dead set against Him and make no bones about it. But, when God wants to get their attention, He has ways of doing it. He wants a chance to be heard.

[1] Meanwhile, Saul was uttering threats with every breath and was eager to kill the Lord's followers. So he went to the high priest. [2] He requested letters addressed to the synagogues in Damascus, asking for their cooperation in the arrest of any followers of the Way he found there. He wanted to bring them – both men and women – back to Jerusalem in chains.

[3] As he was approaching Damascus on this mission, a light from heaven suddenly shone down around him. [4] He fell to the ground and heard a voice saying to him, "Saul! Saul! Why are you persecuting me?"

[5] "Who are you, lord?" Saul asked.

And the voice replied, "I am Jesus, the one you are persecuting! [6] Now get up and go into the city, and you will be told what you must do."

[7] The men with Saul stood speechless, for they heard the sound of someone's voice but saw no one! [8] Saul picked himself up off the ground, but when he opened his eyes he was blind. So his companions led him by the hand to Damascus. [9] He remained there blind for three days and did not eat or drink.

Acts 9:1-9

Trusting in Danger

*U*se your common sense. Stay out of dangerous situations," your parents say. But what do you do when it seems that God is leading you INTO a dangerous situation. If you're sure it's God leading – then trust Him. He knows what He's doing.

¹⁰ Now there was a believer in Damascus named Ananias. The Lord spoke to him in a vision, calling, "Ananias!"

"Yes, Lord!" he replied.

¹¹ The Lord said, "Go over to Straight Street, to the house of Judas. When you get there, ask for a man from Tarsus named Saul. He is praying to me right now. ¹² I have shown him a vision of a man named Ananias coming in and laying hands on him so he can see again."

¹³ "But Lord," exclaimed Ananias, "I've heard many people talk about the terrible things this man has done to the believers in Jerusalem! ¹⁴ And he is authorized by the leading priests to arrest everyone who calls upon your name."

¹⁵ But the Lord said, "Go, for Saul is my chosen instrument to take my message to the Gentiles and to kings, as well as to the people of Israel. ¹⁶ And I will show him how much he must suffer for my name's sake."

¹⁷ So Ananias went and found Saul. He laid his hands on him and said, "Brother Saul, the Lord Jesus, who appeared to you on the road, has sent me so that you might regain your sight and be filled with the Holy Spirit." ¹⁸ Instantly something like scales fell from Saul's eyes, and he regained his sight. Then he got up and was baptized. ¹⁹ Afterward he ate some food and regained his strength.

Acts 9:10-19

October 4

A Heart Can Change

*C*an a mean person become a loving person? Sure. Saul did. He persecuted Christians. Then became a Christian and his old friends persecuted him. His heart changed when he believed in Jesus.

[20] And immediately he began preaching about Jesus in the synagogues, saying, "He is indeed the Son of God!"

[21] All who heard him were amazed. "Isn't this the same man who caused such devastation among Jesus' followers in Jerusalem?" they asked. "And didn't he come here to arrest them and take them in chains to the leading priests?"

[22] Saul's preaching became more and more powerful, and the Jews in Damascus couldn't refute his proofs that Jesus was indeed the Messiah. [23] After a while some of the Jews plotted together to kill him. [24] But Saul was told about their plot. [25] So during the night, some of the other believers lowered him in a large basket through an opening in the city wall.

[26] When Saul arrived in Jerusalem, he tried to meet with the believers, but they were all afraid of him. They did not believe he had truly become a believer! [27] Then Barnabas brought him to the apostles and told them how Saul had seen the Lord on the way to Damascus and how the Lord had spoken to Saul. He also told them that Saul had preached boldly in the name of Jesus in Damascus.

[28] So Saul stayed with the apostles and went all around Jerusalem with them, preaching boldly in the name of the Lord.

Acts 9:20-28

Helping Others

Dorcas was known for helping people – even people who were super poor. She helped because she could and she knew they needed it. Those people she helped ended up helping her, too. Help others whenever you can.

³⁶ There was a believer in Joppa named Tabitha (which in Greek is Dorcas). She was always doing kind things for others and helping the poor. ³⁷ About this time she became ill and died. Her body was washed for burial and laid in an upstairs room. ³⁸ But the believers had heard that Peter was nearby at Lydda, so they sent two men to beg him, "Please come as soon as possible!"

³⁹ So Peter returned with them; and as soon as he arrived, they took him to the upstairs room. The room was filled with widows who were weeping and showing him the coats and other clothes Dorcas had made for them. ⁴⁰ But Peter asked them all to leave the room; then he knelt and prayed. Turning to the body he said, "Get up, Tabitha." And she opened her eyes! When she saw Peter, she sat up! ⁴¹ He gave her his hand and helped her up. Then he called in the widows and all the believers, and he presented her to them alive.

⁴² The news spread through the whole town, and many believed in the Lord.

Acts 9:36-42

Power of Prayer

*N*o matter how hopeless a situation seems to be, pray. The power of prayer is greater than anything else.

[4] Herod intended to bring Peter out for public trial after the Passover. [5] But while Peter was in prison, the church prayed very earnestly for him.

[6] The night before Peter was to be placed on trial, he was asleep, fastened with two chains between two soldiers. Others stood guard at the prison gate. [7] Suddenly, there was a bright light in the cell, and an angel of the Lord stood before Peter. The angel struck him on the side to awaken him and said, "Quick! Get up!" And the chains fell off his wrists. [8] Then the angel told him, "Get dressed and put on your sandals." And he did. "Now put on your coat and follow me," the angel ordered.

[9] So Peter left the cell, following the angel. But all the time he thought it was a vision. He didn't realize it was actually happening. [10] They passed the first and second guard posts and came to the iron gate leading to the city, and this opened for them all by itself. So they passed through and started walking down the street, and then the angel suddenly left him.

[12] When he realized this, he went to the home of Mary, the mother of John Mark, where many were gathered for prayer. [13] He knocked at the door in the gate, and a servant girl named Rhoda came to open it. [14] When she recognized Peter's voice, she was so overjoyed that, instead of opening the door, she ran back inside and told everyone, "Peter is standing at the door!" [16] When they finally opened the door and saw him, they were amazed.

Acts 12:4-10, 12-14, 16

Representing Jesus

*A*lways remember you are representing Jesus in everything you do. Do the right thing and others will be drawn to Jesus, too!

²² A mob quickly formed against Paul and Silas, and the city officials ordered them stripped and beaten with wooden rods. ²³ They were severely beaten, and then they were thrown into prison. The jailer was ordered to make sure they didn't escape. ²⁴ So the jailer put them into the inner dungeon and clamped their feet in the stocks.

²⁵ Around midnight Paul and Silas were praying and singing hymns to God, and the other prisoners were listening. ²⁶ Suddenly, there was a massive earthquake, and the prison was shaken to its foundations. All the doors immediately flew open, and the chains of every prisoner fell off! ²⁷ The jailer woke up to see the prison doors wide open. He assumed the prisoners had escaped, so he drew his sword to kill himself. ²⁸ But Paul shouted to him, "Stop! Don't kill yourself! We are all here!"

²⁹ The jailer called for lights and ran to the dungeon and fell down trembling before Paul and Silas. ³⁰ Then he brought them out and asked, "Sirs, what must I do to be saved?"

³¹ They replied, "Believe in the Lord Jesus and you will be saved, along with everyone in your household." ³² And they shared the word of the Lord with him and with all who lived in his household. ³³ Even at that hour of the night, the jailer cared for them and washed their wounds. Then he and everyone in his household were immediately baptized. ³⁴ He brought them into his house and set a meal before them, and he and his entire household rejoiced because they all believed in God.

Acts 16:22-34

Know What You Believe

You never know when you'll get a chance to quickly share your faith. Knowing what you believe and being able to express it is very important.

²² So Paul, standing before the council, addressed them as follows: "Men of Athens, I notice that you are very religious in every way, ²³ for as I was walking along I saw your many shrines. And one of your altars had this inscription on it: 'To an Unknown God.' This God, whom you worship without knowing, is the one I'm telling you about.

²⁴ "He is the God who made the world and everything in it. Since he is Lord of heaven and earth, he doesn't live in man-made temples, ²⁵ and human hands can't serve his needs – for he has no needs. He himself gives life and breath to everything, and he satisfies every need. ²⁶ From one man he created all the nations throughout the whole earth. He decided beforehand when they should rise and fall, and he determined their boundaries.

²⁷ "His purpose was for the nations to seek after God and perhaps feel their way toward him and find him – though he is not far from any one of us. ²⁸ For in him we live and move and exist. As some of your own poets have said, 'We are his offspring.' ²⁹ And since this is true, we shouldn't think of God as an idol designed by craftsmen from gold or silver or stone."

Acts 17:22-29

A Clear Conscience

*P*aul knew he had done everything he could to share the message of God's love. He was 100% devoted to doing God's work. Can you say that, too?

22 "And now I am bound by the Spirit to go to Jerusalem. I don't know what awaits me, 23 except that the Holy Spirit tells me in city after city that jail and suffering lie ahead. 24 But my life is worth nothing to me unless I use it for finishing the work assigned me by the Lord Jesus – the work of telling others the Good News about the wonderful grace of God.

25 "And now I know that none of you to whom I have preached the Kingdom will ever see me again. 26 I declare today that I have been faithful. If anyone suffers eternal death, it's not my fault, 27 for I didn't shrink from declaring all that God wants you to know.

28 "So guard yourselves and God's people. Feed and shepherd God's flock – his church, purchased with his own blood – over which the Holy Spirit has appointed you as elders. 29 I know that false teachers, like vicious wolves, will come in among you after I leave, not sparing the flock. 30 Even some men from your own group will rise up and distort the truth in order to draw a following. 31 Watch out! Remember the three years I was with you – my constant watch and care over you night and day, and my many tears for you.

32 "And now I entrust you to God and the message of his grace that is able to build you up and give you an inheritance with all those he has set apart for himself."

Acts 20:22-32

A Courageous Thing

*S*ometimes it takes courage to serve God. The young man in this story may have been afraid of getting in trouble – but his courage saved Paul's life!

¹² The next morning a group of Jews got together and bound themselves with an oath not to eat or drink until they had killed Paul. ¹⁴ They went to the leading priests and elders and told them, "We have bound ourselves with an oath to eat nothing until we have killed Paul. ¹⁵ So you and the high council should ask the commander to bring Paul back to the council again. Pretend you want to examine his case more fully. We will kill him on the way."

¹⁶ But Paul's nephew – his sister's son – heard of their plan and went to the fortress and told Paul. ¹⁷ Paul called for one of the Roman officers and said, "Take this young man to the commander. He has something important to tell him."

¹⁸ So the officer did. ¹⁹ The commander took his hand, led him aside, and asked, "What is it you want to tell me?"

²⁰ Paul's nephew told him, "Some Jews are going to ask you to bring Paul before the high council tomorrow, pretending they want to get some more information. ²¹ But don't do it! There are more than forty men hiding along the way ready to ambush him. They have vowed not to eat or drink anything until they have killed him. They are ready now, just waiting for your consent."

²² "Don't let anyone know you told me this," the commander warned the young man.

Acts 23:12, 14-22

Don't Be Ashamed

*T*here may be times when you're tempted to keep your faith quiet because you don't want anyone to think you're weird. Ask God for the courage to stand strong and to be proud of your faith. Remember, Jesus died for you and He wasn't ashamed to do it!

[1] This letter is from Paul, a slave of Christ Jesus, chosen by God to be an apostle and sent out to preach his Good News. [2] God promised this Good News long ago through his prophets in the holy Scriptures. [3] The Good News is about his Son. In his earthly life he was born into King David's family line, [4] and he was shown to be the Son of God when he was raised from the dead by the power of the Holy Spirit. He is Jesus Christ our Lord.

[16] For I am not ashamed of this Good News about Christ. It is the power of God at work, saving everyone who believes – the Jew first and also the Gentile. [17] This Good News tells us how God makes us right in his sight. This is accomplished from start to finish by faith. As the Scriptures say, "It is through faith that a righteous person has life."

Romans 1:1-4, 16-17

Everyone Sins

*Y*ou probably are a good person – try to be nice to others; try not to gossip or cheat or anything else. But no matter how hard you try, you still sin. Everyone does. There is only one way for the punishment for sin to be paid – believe in Jesus. You can't do anything to fix it – except believe.

21 But now God has shown us a way to be made right with him without keeping the requirements of the law, as was promised in the writings of Moses and the prophets long ago. 22 We are made right with God by placing our faith in Jesus Christ. And this is true for everyone who believes, no matter who we are.

23 For everyone has sinned; we all fall short of God's glorious standard. 24 Yet God, with undeserved kindness, declares that we are righteous. He did this through Christ Jesus when he freed us from the penalty for our sins. 25 For God presented Jesus as the sacrifice for sin. People are made right with God when they believe that Jesus sacrificed his life, shedding his blood. This sacrifice shows that God was being fair when he held back and did not punish those who sinned in times past, 26 for he was looking ahead and including them in what he would do in this present time. God did this to demonstrate his righteousness, for he himself is fair and just, and he declares sinners to be right in his sight when they believe in Jesus.

27 Can we boast, then, that we have done anything to be accepted by God? No, because our acquittal is not based on obeying the law. It is based on faith. 28 So we are made right with God through faith and not by obeying the law.

Romans 3:21-28

Building Character

*I*t's no fun to have problems. Most people pray like crazy for God to take them away. But, if you lean on God and trust Him you will grow a lot stronger because of them.

¹ Therefore, since we have been made right in God's sight by faith, we have peace with God because of what Jesus Christ our Lord has done for us. ² Because of our faith, Christ has brought us into this place of undeserved privilege where we now stand, and we confidently and joyfully look forward to sharing God's glory.

³ We can rejoice, too, when we run into problems and trials, for we know that they help us develop endurance. ⁴ And endurance develops strength of character, and character strengthens our confident hope of salvation. ⁵ And this hope will not lead to disappointment. For we know how dearly God loves us, because he has given us the Holy Spirit to fill our hearts with his love.

⁶ When we were utterly helpless, Christ came at just the right time and died for us sinners. ⁷ Now, most people would not be willing to die for an upright person, though someone might perhaps be willing to die for a person who is especially good. ⁸ But God showed his great love for us by sending Christ to die for us while we were still sinners. ⁹ And since we have been made right in God's sight by the blood of Christ, he will certainly save us from God's condemnation. ¹⁰ For since our friendship with God was restored by the death of his Son while we were still his enemies, we will certainly be saved through the life of his Son.

October 14

Romans 5:1-10

Your Choice

*W*hatever you choose to serve – that means where you put your time and energy – the thing that's most important to you – you become a slave to. You may not realize it or even want to admit it, but it's true.

¹⁵ Well then, since God's grace has set us free from the law, does that mean we can go on sinning? Of course not! ¹⁶ Don't you realize that you become the slave of whatever you choose to obey? You can be a slave to sin, which leads to death, or you can choose to obey God, which leads to righteous living. ¹⁷ Thank God! Once you were slaves of sin, but now you wholeheartedly obey this teaching we have given you.

¹⁹ Because of the weakness of your human nature, I am using the illustration of slavery to help you understand all this. Previously, you let yourselves be slaves to impurity and lawlessness, which led ever deeper into sin. Now you must give yourselves to be slaves to righteous living so that you will become holy.

²⁰ When you were slaves to sin, you were free from the obligation to do right. ²¹ And what was the result? You are now ashamed of the things you used to do, things that end in eternal doom. ²² But now you are free from the power of sin and have become slaves of God. Now you do those things that lead to holiness and result in eternal life. ²³ For the wages of sin is death, but the free gift of God is eternal life through Christ Jesus our Lord.

Romans 6:15-17, 19-23

I WANT to Do Right

*I*t's frustrating. As hard as you try to do what's right and as much as you want to obey God's Word, sometimes you just don't. It's sin. Ask God to help you to be truly sorry for your sin so that more and more, through His strength, you can turn away from it.

[18] And I know that nothing good lives in me, that is, in my sinful nature. I want to do what is right, but I can't. [19] I want to do what is good, but I don't. I don't want to do what is wrong, but I do it anyway. [20] But if I do what I don't want to do, I am not really the one doing wrong; it is sin living in me that does it.

[21] I have discovered this principle of life – that when I want to do what is right, I inevitably do what is wrong. [22] I love God's law with all my heart. [23] But there is another power within me that is at war with my mind. This power makes me a slave to the sin that is still within me. [24] Oh, what a miserable person I am! Who will free me from this life that is dominated by sin and death? [25] Thank God! The answer is in Jesus Christ our Lord. So you see how it is: In my mind I really want to obey God's law, but because of my sinful nature I am a slave to sin.

Romans 7:18-25

The Holy Spirit

*A*t times when it feels as though God is far away, remember that the Holy Spirit is living in you. Ask Him for help with obeying, with making decisions, with growing to be a strong woman of God.

⁵ Those who are dominated by the sinful nature think about sinful things, but those who are controlled by the Holy Spirit think about things that please the Spirit. ⁶ So letting your sinful nature control your mind leads to death. But letting the Spirit control your mind leads to life and peace. ⁷ For the sinful nature is always hostile to God. It never did obey God's laws, and it never will. ⁸ That's why those who are still under the control of their sinful nature can never please God.

⁹ But you are not controlled by your sinful nature. You are controlled by the Spirit if you have the Spirit of God living in you. (And remember that those who do not have the Spirit of Christ living in them do not belong to him at all.) ¹⁰ And Christ lives within you, so even though your body will die because of sin, the Spirit gives you life because you have been made right with God. ¹¹ The Spirit of God, who raised Jesus from the dead, lives in you. And just as God raised Christ Jesus from the dead, he will give life to your mortal bodies by this same Spirit living within you.

Romans 8:5-11

Part of the Family

*B*eing a member of a family has privileges. You belong to each other. Family cares for one another. Children inherit talents, abilities and skills from parents. They may also inherit the parents' estate one day. Guess what? You're God's child – a member of HIS family and all those things apply to that relationship, too. Cool, huh?

[12] Therefore, dear brothers and sisters, you have no obligation to do what your sinful nature urges you to do. [13] For if you live by its dictates, you will die. But if through the power of the Spirit you put to death the deeds of your sinful nature, you will live. [14] For all who are led by the Spirit of God are children of God.

[15] So you have not received a spirit that makes you fearful slaves. Instead, you received God's Spirit when he adopted you as his own children. Now we call him, "Abba, Father." [16] For his Spirit joins with our spirit to affirm that we are God's children. [17] And since we are his children, we are his heirs. In fact, together with Christ we are heirs of God's glory. But if we are to share his glory, we must also share his suffering.

Romans 8:12-17

God's Purposes

*T*he Holy Spirit prays for you. When you don't know what to pray or can't find the words to say what's in your heart, He takes over. God listens to Him, too. Then, God works things out in the end. Sometimes you have to wait a while for it to be "the end." But, it comes.

26 And the Holy Spirit helps us in our weakness. For example, we don't know what God wants us to pray for. But the Holy Spirit prays for us with groanings that cannot be expressed in words. 27 And the Father who knows all hearts knows what the Spirit is saying, for the Spirit pleads for us believers in harmony with God's own will. 28 And we know that God causes everything to work together for the good of those who love God and are called according to his purpose for them.

Romans 8:26-28

No Separation

*D*id you know that absolutely nothing can separate you from God's love. When you have trouble it doesn't mean He has turned away. If you can't "feel" Him it doesn't mean He has turned away. He promised that nothing can separate you from His love.

³¹ What shall we say about such wonderful things as these? If God is for us, who can ever be against us? ³² Since he did not spare even his own Son but gave him up for us all, won't he also give us everything else? ³³ Who dares accuse us whom God has chosen for his own? No one – for God himself has given us right standing with himself. ³⁴ Who then will condemn us? No one – for Christ Jesus died for us and was raised to life for us, and he is sitting in the place of honor at God's right hand, pleading for us.

³⁵ Can anything ever separate us from Christ's love? Does it mean he no longer loves us if we have trouble or calamity, or are persecuted, or hungry, or destitute, or in danger, or threatened with death? ³⁶ (As the Scriptures say, "For your sake we are killed every day; we are being slaughtered like sheep.") ³⁷ No, despite all these things, overwhelming victory is ours through Christ, who loved us.

³⁸ And I am convinced that nothing can ever separate us from God's love. Neither death nor life, neither angels nor demons, neither our fears for today nor our worries about tomorrow – not even the powers of hell can separate us from God's love. ³⁹ No power in the sky above or in the earth below – indeed, nothing in all creation will ever be able to separate us from the love of God that is revealed in Christ Jesus our Lord.

Romans 8:31-39

Nothing Held Back

Give everything you have – time, talent, energy, thoughts, service – everything to God. It's all valuable to His work on this earth.

[1] And so, dear brothers and sisters, I plead with you to give your bodies to God because of all he has done for you. Let them be a living and holy sacrifice – the kind he will find acceptable. This is truly the way to worship him. [2] Don't copy the behavior and customs of this world, but let God transform you into a new person by changing the way you think. Then you will learn to know God's will for you, which is good and pleasing and perfect.

[3] Because of the privilege and authority God has given me, I give each of you this warning: Don't think you are better than you really are. Be honest in your evaluation of yourselves, measuring yourselves by the faith God has given us. [4] Just as our bodies have many parts and each part has a special function, [5] so it is with Christ's body. We are many parts of one body, and we all belong to each other.

[6] In his grace, God has given us different gifts for doing certain things well. So if God has given you the ability to prophesy, speak out with as much faith as God has given you. [7] If your gift is serving others, serve them well. If you are a teacher, teach well. [8] If your gift is to encourage others, be encouraging. If it is giving, give generously. If God has given you leadership ability, take the responsibility seriously. And if you have a gift for showing kindness to others, do it gladly.

Romans 12:1-8

The Greatest Commandment

*R*emember that Jesus said the greatest commandment is to love others as you love yourself. It's not always easy to do, is it? But, it's the way you serve God and show His love to others.

9 Don't just pretend to love others. Really love them. Hate what is wrong. Hold tightly to what is good. 10 Love each other with genuine affection, and take delight in honoring each other. 11 Never be lazy, but work hard and serve the Lord enthusiastically. 12 Rejoice in our confident hope. Be patient in trouble, and keep on praying. 13 When God's people are in need, be ready to help them. Always be eager to practice hospitality.

14 Bless those who persecute you. Don't curse them; pray that God will bless them. 15 Be happy with those who are happy, and weep with those who weep. 16 Live in harmony with each other. Don't be too proud to enjoy the company of ordinary people. And don't think you know it all!

17 Never pay back evil with more evil. Do things in such a way that everyone can see you are honorable. 18 Do all that you can to live in peace with everyone.

19 Dear friends, never take revenge. Leave that to the righteous anger of God. For the Scriptures say,

"I will take revenge; I will pay them back," says the Lord.

20 Instead, "If your enemies are hungry, feed them. If they are thirsty, give them something to drink. In doing this, you will heap burning coals of shame on their heads."

21 Don't let evil conquer you, but conquer evil by doing good.

Romans 12:9-21

October 22

Being the Better Person

When a friend is being unkind the temptation is to strike back. Don't give in to that temptation, though. Be the better person by being kind and forgiving. Be patient and loving. If that's hard to do, ask God to help you do it.

[1] We who are strong must be considerate of those who are sensitive about things like this. We must not just please ourselves. [2] We should help others do what is right and build them up in the Lord. [3] For even Christ didn't live to please himself. As the Scriptures say, "The insults of those who insult you, O God, have fallen on me." [4] Such things were written in the Scriptures long ago to teach us. And the Scriptures give us hope and encouragement as we wait patiently for God's promises to be fulfilled.

[5] May God, who gives this patience and encouragement, help you live in complete harmony with each other, as is fitting for followers of Christ Jesus. [6] Then all of you can join together with one voice, giving praise and glory to God, the Father of our Lord Jesus Christ.

[7] Therefore, accept each other just as Christ has accepted you so that God will be given glory.

Romans 15:1-7

Getting Rid of Jealousy

Jealousy is not a good thing. Wishing you had some-one else's look or talent or money or anything can only lead to problems. Every person is unique. Every person and every talent is important and necessary to God. So, don't be jealous of what you don't have – thank God for what you do have!

³ You are still controlled by your sinful nature. You are jealous of one another and quarrel with each other. Doesn't that prove you are controlled by your sinful nature? Aren't you living like people of the world? ⁴ When one of you says, "I am a follower of Paul," and another says, "I follow Apollos," aren't you acting just like people of the world?

⁵ After all, who is Apollos? Who is Paul? We are only God's servants through whom you believed the Good News. Each of us did the work the Lord gave us. ⁶ I planted the seed in your hearts, and Apollos watered it, but it was God who made it grow. ⁷ It's not important who does the planting, or who does the watering. What's important is that God makes the seed grow. ⁸ The one who plants and the one who waters work together with the same purpose. And both will be rewarded for their own hard work. ⁹ For we are both God's workers. And you are God's field. You are God's building.

¹⁰ Because of God's grace to me, I have laid the foundation like an expert builder. Now others are building on it. But whoever is building on this foundation must be very careful. ¹¹ For no one can lay any foundation other than the one we already have – Jesus Christ.

1 Corinthians 3:3-11

October 24

Real Wisdom

*E*verything around you is trying to tell you what truly matters. From television, to movies, the internet, magazines, social media, friends – it's all trying to push the world's values on you. Remember, you belong to God. So, your values should be different from any of those other ones.

[16] Don't you realize that all of you together are the temple of God and that the Spirit of God lives in you? [17] God will destroy anyone who destroys this temple. For God's temple is holy, and you are that temple.

[18] Stop deceiving yourselves. If you think you are wise by this world's standards, you need to become a fool to be truly wise. [19] For the wisdom of this world is foolishness to God. As the Scriptures say,

"He traps the wise in the snare of their own cleverness."

[20] And again,

"The Lord knows the thoughts of the wise; he knows they are worthless."

[21] So don't boast about following a particular human leader. For everything belongs to you – [22] whether Paul or Apollos or Peter, or the world, or life and death, or the present and the future. Everything belongs to you, [23] and you belong to Christ, and Christ belongs to God.

1 Corinthians 3:16-23

Spiritual Gifts

*T*he Holy Spirit gives special gifts to each person to be used in God's work. You may not know yet what your gift is but as you stay close to God and do the work He gives you to do, you will discover it.

[7] A spiritual gift is given to each of us so we can help each other. [8] To one person the Spirit gives the ability to give wise advice; to another the same Spirit gives a message of special knowledge. [9] The same Spirit gives great faith to another, and to someone else the one Spirit gives the gift of healing. [10] He gives one person the power to perform miracles, and another the ability to prophesy. He gives someone else the ability to discern whether a message is from the Spirit of God or from another spirit. Still another person is given the ability to speak in unknown languages, while another is given the ability to interpret what is being said. [11] It is the one and only Spirit who distributes all these gifts. He alone decides which gift each person should have.

1 Corinthians 12:7-11

The Body

It seems as though there are some "stars" in life; even among Christians. That's OK. But remember that in God's eyes every person and every job is important.

¹² The human body has many parts, but the many parts make up one whole body. So it is with the body of Christ. ¹⁴ Yes, the body has many different parts, not just one part. ¹⁵ If the foot says, "I am not a part of the body because I am not a hand," that does not make it any less a part of the body. ¹⁶ And if the ear says, "I am not part of the body because I am not an eye," would that make it any less a part of the body? ¹⁷ If the whole body were an eye, how would you hear? Or if your whole body were an ear, how would you smell anything?

¹⁸ But our bodies have many parts, and God has put each part just where he wants it. ¹⁹ How strange a body would be if it had only one part! ²⁰ Yes, there are many parts, but only one body. ²¹ The eye can never say to the hand, "I don't need you." The head can't say to the feet, "I don't need you."

²² In fact, some parts of the body that seem weakest and least important are actually the most necessary. ²³ And the parts we regard as less honorable are those we clothe with the greatest care. So we carefully protect those parts that should not be seen. ²⁵ This makes for harmony among the members, so that all the members care for each other. ²⁶ If one part suffers, all the parts suffer with it, and if one part is honored, all the parts are glad.

²⁷ All of you together are Christ's body, and each of you is a part of it.

1 Corinthians 12:12, 14-23, 25-27

True Love

*Y*ou know you're supposed to love others – all the time – and not just your friends. What does true love look like? God answered that question with a nice description of love.

[1] If I could speak all the languages of earth and of angels, but didn't love others, I would only be a noisy gong or a clanging cymbal. [2] If I had the gift of prophecy, and if I understood all of God's secret plans and possessed all knowledge, and if I had such faith that I could move mountains, but didn't love others, I would be nothing. [3] If I gave everything I have to the poor and even sacrificed my body, I could boast about it; but if I didn't love others, I would have gained nothing.

[4] Love is patient and kind. Love is not jealous or boastful or proud [5] or rude. It does not demand its own way. It is not irritable, and it keeps no record of being wronged. [6] It does not rejoice about injustice but rejoices whenever the truth wins out. [7] Love never gives up, never loses faith, is always hopeful, and endures through every circumstance.

[8] Prophecy and speaking in unknown languages and special knowledge will become useless. But love will last forever!

[13] Three things will last forever – faith, hope, and love – and the greatest of these is love.

1 Corinthians 13:1-8, 13

October 28

Helping Others

When someone you know has troubles, how can you help? Pray. Lift others up to the Lord in prayer every day. Then you become a partner in their work and ministry, and they become a partner with you.

³ All praise to God, the Father of our Lord Jesus Christ. God is our merciful Father and the source of all comfort. ⁴ He comforts us in all our troubles so that we can comfort others. When they are troubled, we will be able to give them the same comfort God has given us. ⁵ For the more we suffer for Christ, the more God will shower us with his comfort through Christ. ⁶ Even when we are weighed down with troubles, it is for your comfort and salvation! For when we ourselves are comforted, we will certainly comfort you. Then you can patiently endure the same things we suffer. ⁷ We are confident that as you share in our sufferings, you will also share in the comfort God gives us.

⁸ We think you ought to know, dear brothers and sisters, about the trouble we went through in the province of Asia. We were crushed and overwhelmed beyond our ability to endure, and we thought we would never live through it. ⁹ In fact, we expected to die. But as a result, we stopped relying on ourselves and learned to rely only on God, who raises the dead. ¹⁰ And he did rescue us from mortal danger, and he will rescue us again. We have placed our confidence in him, and he will continue to rescue us. ¹¹ And you are helping us by praying for us. Then many people will give thanks because God has graciously answered so many prayers for our safety.

2 Corinthians 1:3-11

Ambassador for Christ

*T*he term ambassador means that you are a representative of Jesus. You show others what His values are and what is important to Him – by the way you live. God has given you this privilege to be able to represent Him and hopefully bring others to Him by your representation.

[18] And all of this is a gift from God, who brought us back to himself through Christ. And God has given us this task of reconciling people to him. [19] For God was in Christ, reconciling the world to himself, no longer counting people's sins against them. And he gave us this wonderful message of reconciliation. [20] So we are Christ's ambassadors; God is making his appeal through us. We speak for Christ when we plead, "Come back to God!" [21] For God made Christ, who never sinned, to be the offering for our sin, so that we could be made right with God through Christ.

2 Corinthians 5:18-21

Share Your Blessings

*D*on't try to hold on to everything you have. Look around for someone who has less or someone who has a real need ... and share what God has blessed you with.

⁶ Remember this – a farmer who plants only a few seeds will get a small crop. But the one who plants generously will get a generous crop. ⁷ You must each decide in your heart how much to give. And don't give reluctantly or in response to pressure. "For God loves a person who gives cheerfully." ⁸ And God will generously provide all you need. Then you will always have everything you need and plenty left over to share with others. ⁹ As the Scriptures say,

"They share freely and give generously to the poor. Their good deeds will be remembered forever."

¹⁰ For God is the one who provides seed for the farmer and then bread to eat. In the same way, he will provide and increase your resources and then produce a great harvest of generosity in you.

¹¹ Yes, you will be enriched in every way so that you can always be generous. And when we take your gifts to those who need them, they will thank God.

2 Corinthians 9:6-11

November

New Life

*W*ill keeping a list of rules get you into heaven? Nope. Although obeying the rules your parents have is a good thing. But when it comes to obeying God, even if you keep the rules, if your heart is rebellious, you aren't really pleasing God. Let Christ, who lives in you, change your heart.

¹⁹ For when I tried to keep the law, it condemned me. So I died to the law – I stopped trying to meet all its requirements – so that I might live for God.

²⁰ My old self has been crucified with Christ. It is no longer I who live, but Christ lives in me. So I live in this earthly body by trusting in the Son of God, who loved me and gave himself for me.

²¹ I do not treat the grace of God as meaningless. For if keeping the law could make us right with God, then there was no need for Christ to die.

Galatians 2:19-21

Live By the Spirit

If you are allowing the Holy Spirit to control your life it will be apparent by how you're living. If you're not ... well, that will show, too.

¹³ For you have been called to live in freedom, my brothers and sisters. But don't use your freedom to satisfy your sinful nature. Instead, use your freedom to serve one another in love. ¹⁴ For the whole law can be summed up in this one command: "Love your neighbor as yourself." ¹⁵ But if you are always biting and devouring one another, watch out! Beware of destroying one another.

¹⁶ So I say, let the Holy Spirit guide your lives. Then you won't be doing what your sinful nature craves.

¹⁹ When you follow the desires of your sinful nature, the results are very clear: sexual immorality, impurity, lustful pleasures, ²⁰ idolatry, sorcery, hostility, quarreling, jealousy, outbursts of anger, selfish ambition, dissension, division, ²¹ envy, drunkenness, wild parties, and other sins like these. Let me tell you again, as I have before, that anyone living that sort of life will not inherit the Kingdom of God.

²² But the Holy Spirit produces this kind of fruit in our lives: love, joy, peace, patience, kindness, goodness, faithfulness, ²³ gentleness, and self-control. There is no law against these things!

²⁴ Those who belong to Christ Jesus have nailed the passions and desires of their sinful nature to his cross and crucified them there. ²⁵ Since we are living by the Spirit, let us follow the Spirit's leading in every part of our lives. ²⁶ Let us not become conceited, or provoke one another, or be jealous of one another.

Galatians 5:13-16, 19-26

Together

*R*emember Jesus said that loving one another is very important. Loving others means sharing their problems and celebrating their joys. You can't please God without loving others.

[2] Share each other's burdens, and in this way obey the law of Christ. [3] If you think you are too important to help someone, you are only fooling yourself. You are not that important.

[4] Pay careful attention to your own work, for then you will get the satisfaction of a job well done, and you won't need to compare yourself to anyone else. [5] For we are each responsible for our own conduct.

[6] Those who are taught the word of God should provide for their teachers, sharing all good things with them.

[7] Don't be misled – you cannot mock the justice of God. You will always harvest what you plant. [8] Those who live only to satisfy their own sinful nature will harvest decay and death from that sinful nature. But those who live to please the Spirit will harvest everlasting life from the Spirit. [9] So let's not get tired of doing what is good. At just the right time we will reap a harvest of blessing if we don't give up. [10] Therefore, whenever we have the opportunity, we should do good to everyone – especially to those in the family of faith.

Galatians 6:2-10

Amazing Grace

*D*o you know what grace is? Grace is when you are given something you totally do not deserve. But someone who loves you very much gives it to you anyway. Someone like God who loves you so much that His grace forgives your sins.

³ All praise to God, the Father of our Lord Jesus Christ, who has blessed us with every spiritual blessing in the heavenly realms because we are united with Christ. ⁴ Even before he made the world, God loved us and chose us in Christ to be holy and without fault in his eyes. ⁵ God decided in advance to adopt us into his own family by bringing us to himself through Jesus Christ. This is what he wanted to do, and it gave him great pleasure. ⁶ So we praise God for the glorious grace he has poured out on us who belong to his dear Son. ⁷ He is so rich in kindness and grace that he purchased our freedom with the blood of his Son and forgave our sins. ⁸ He has showered his kindness on us, along with all wisdom and understanding.

⁹ God has now revealed to us his mysterious plan regarding Christ, a plan to fulfill his own good pleasure.

Ephesians 1:3-9

Incredible Power

*P*ower – doesn't everyone want it? But, seriously, you're just a kid so how much power could you have? TONS! Because God's power is in you and His power is amazingly strong.

[18] I pray that your hearts will be flooded with light so that you can understand the confident hope he has given to those he called – his holy people who are his rich and glorious inheritance.

[19] I also pray that you will understand the incredible greatness of God's power for us who believe him. This is the same mighty power [20] that raised Christ from the dead and seated him in the place of honor at God's right hand in the heavenly realms. [21] Now he is far above any ruler or authority or power or leader or anything else – not only in this world but also in the world to come. [22] God has put all things under the authority of Christ and has made him head over all things for the benefit of the church. [23] And the church is his body; it is made full and complete by Christ, who fills all things everywhere with himself.

Ephesians 1:18-23

God's Masterpiece

A masterpiece is someone's very best work – an artist or a writer or a composer. Their masterpiece is the very best thing they have ever created. You are a masterpiece. Yep, you. God's masterpiece.

[1] Once you were dead because of your disobedience and your many sins. [2] You used to live in sin, just like the rest of the world, obeying the devil – the commander of the powers in the unseen world. He is the spirit at work in the hearts of those who refuse to obey God. [3] All of us used to live that way, following the passionate desires and inclinations of our sinful nature. By our very nature we were subject to God's anger, just like everyone else.

[4] But God is so rich in mercy, and he loved us so much, [5] that even though we were dead because of our sins, he gave us life when he raised Christ from the dead. (It is only by God's grace that you have been saved!) [6] For he raised us from the dead along with Christ and seated us with him in the heavenly realms because we are united with Christ Jesus. [7] So God can point to us in all future ages as examples of the incredible wealth of his grace and kindness toward us, as shown in all he has done for us who are united with Christ Jesus.

[8] God saved you by his grace when you believed. And you can't take credit for this; it is a gift from God. [9] Salvation is not a reward for the good things we have done, so none of us can boast about it. [10] For we are God's masterpiece. He has created us anew in Christ Jesus, so we can do the good things he planned for us long ago.

Ephesians 2:1-10

Deep Roots

You probably know that tree roots go down deep, deep in the ground and those roots pull water and nutrients into the tree. You need deep roots, too, to stay healthy and strong – roots deep in God's love.

14 When I think of all this, I fall to my knees and pray to the Father, 15 the Creator of everything in heaven and on earth. 16 I pray that from his glorious, unlimited resources he will empower you with inner strength through his Spirit. 17 Then Christ will make his home in your hearts as you trust in him. Your roots will grow down into God's love and keep you strong. 18 And may you have the power to understand, as all God's people should, how wide, how long, how high, and how deep his love is. 19 May you experience the love of Christ, though it is too great to understand fully. Then you will be made complete with all the fullness of life and power that comes from God.

20 Now all glory to God, who is able, through his mighty power at work within us, to accomplish infinitely more than we might ask or think. 21 Glory to him in the church and in Christ Jesus through all generations forever and ever! Amen.

Ephesians 3:14-21

Behaving Like a Grown-Up

*U*nfortunately not all grown-ups act like grown-ups. But you only have to answer for your own behavior. God says that a mature person is humble, gentle and patient as she lives her life with God's love at the core.

² Always be humble and gentle. Be patient with each other, making allowance for each other's faults because of your love. ³ Make every effort to keep yourselves united in the Spirit, binding yourselves together with peace. ⁴ For there is one body and one Spirit, just as you have been called to one glorious hope for the future. ⁵ There is one Lord, one faith, one baptism, ⁶ and one God and Father, who is over all and in all and living through all.

¹⁴ Then we will no longer be immature like children. We won't be tossed and blown about by every wind of new teaching. We will not be influenced when people try to trick us with lies so clever they sound like the truth. ¹⁵ Instead, we will speak the truth in love, growing in every way more and more like Christ, who is the head of his body, the church. ¹⁶ He makes the whole body fit together perfectly. As each part does its own special work, it helps the other parts grow, so that the whole body is healthy and growing and full of love.

Ephesians 4:2-6, 14-16

Reflections

*I*t's really tough to hang around with friends who don't care about God without their behavior and attitudes becoming part of your life. Be careful who you spend time with.

¹⁷ With the Lord's authority I say this: Live no longer as the Gentiles do, for they are hopelessly confused. ¹⁸ Their minds are full of darkness; they wander far from the life God gives because they have closed their minds and hardened their hearts against him. ¹⁹ They have no sense of shame. They live for lustful pleasure and eagerly practice every kind of impurity.

²⁰ But that isn't what you learned about Christ. ²¹ Since you have heard about Jesus and have learned the truth that comes from him, ²² throw off your old sinful nature and your former way of life, which is corrupted by lust and deception. ²³ Instead, let the Spirit renew your thoughts and attitudes. ²⁴ Put on your new nature, created to be like God – truly righteous and holy.

Ephesians 4:17-24

Get Rid of Anger

*E*veryone gets angry sometimes. But, what do you do with the anger? Let it grow and take root in your heart? Why? Anger, lying, stealing breaks relationships with other people and with God. Keep your emotions under control and live in love and kindness as God instructed.

[25] So stop telling lies. Let us tell our neighbors the truth, for we are all parts of the same body. [26] And "don't sin by letting anger control you." Don't let the sun go down while you are still angry, [27] for anger gives a foothold to the devil.

[28] If you are a thief, quit stealing. Instead, use your hands for good hard work, and then give generously to others in need. [29] Don't use foul or abusive language. Let everything you say be good and helpful, so that your words will be an encouragement to those who hear them.

[30] And do not bring sorrow to God's Holy Spirit by the way you live. Remember, he has identified you as his own, guaranteeing that you will be saved on the day of redemption.

[31] Get rid of all bitterness, rage, anger, harsh words, and slander, as well as all types of evil be-havior.

Ephesians 4:25-31

The Example Is Set

*W*hen you are learning something new it always helps to have an example to follow – a model. Well, God gave you a model for how to treat other people and how to live for Him. Read His Word. Study Jesus' life, then imitate what you learn.

¹ Imitate God, therefore, in everything you do, because you are his dear children. ² Live a life filled with love, following the example of Christ. He loved us and offered himself as a sacrifice for us, a pleasing aroma to God.

⁸ For once you were full of darkness, but now you have light from the Lord. So live as people of light! ⁹ For this light within you produces only what is good and right and true.

¹⁶ Make the most of every opportunity in these evil days. ¹⁷ Don't act thoughtlessly, but understand what the Lord wants you to do.

Ephesians 5:1-2, 8-9, 16-17

Dressed for Battle

*D*on't take chances by assuming you will be strong enough to fight temptation. Don't underestimate Satan's strength. Put on the armor of God that will help you stand firm.

[10] A final word: Be strong in the Lord and in his mighty power. [11] Put on all of God's armor so that you will be able to stand firm against all strategies of the devil. [12] For we are not fighting against flesh-and-blood enemies, but against evil rulers and authorities of the unseen world, against mighty powers in this dark world, and against evil spirits in the heavenly places.

[13] Therefore, put on every piece of God's armor so you will be able to resist the enemy in the time of evil. Then after the battle you will still be standing firm. [14] Stand your ground, putting on the belt of truth and the body armor of God's righteousness. [15] For shoes, put on the peace that comes from the Good News so that you will be fully prepared. [16] In addition to all of these, hold up the shield of faith to stop the fiery arrows of the devil. [17] Put on salvation as your helmet, and take the sword of the Spirit, which is the word of God.

[18] Pray in the Spirit at all times and on every occasion. Stay alert and be persistent in your prayers for all believers everywhere.

Ephesians 6:10-18

Purpose in Life

The Apostle Paul tried to put Christians in jail and literally make their lives miserable. Then he became a Christian and did a full turn-around in his life. Then his purpose in living was to live for Christ. What's your purpose?

²⁰ For I fully expect and hope that I will never be ashamed, but that I will continue to be bold for Christ, as I have been in the past. And I trust that my life will bring honor to Christ, whether I live or die.

²¹ For to me, living means living for Christ, and dying is even better.

²² But if I live, I can do more fruitful work for Christ. So I really don't know which is better.

²³ I'm torn between two desires: I long to go and be with Christ, which would be far better for me.

²⁴ But for your sakes, it is better that I continue to live.

Philippians 1:20-24

Self Image Reality

*S*elf-image is a hot topic these days. Some girls get caught up in the "I'm not skinny enough or I'm not pretty enough" struggle. Good self-image is knowing who you are in Christ and not trying to be better than anyone else. Live in a way that honors Him and treats others with respect and kindness, and have a good self-image about that.

[1] Is there any encouragement from belonging to Christ? Any comfort from his love? Any fellowship together in the Spirit? Are your hearts tender and compassionate? [2] Then make me truly happy by agreeing wholeheartedly with each other, loving one another, and working together with one mind and purpose.

[3] Don't be selfish; don't try to impress others. Be humble, thinking of others as better than yourselves. [4] Don't look out only for your own interests, but take an interest in others, too.

[5] You must have the same attitude that Christ Jesus had. [6] Though he was God, he did not think of equality with God as something to cling to. [7] Instead, he gave up his divine privileges; he took the humble position of a slave and was born as a human being. When he appeared in human form, [8] he humbled himself in obedience to God and died a criminal's death on a cross. [9] Therefore, God elevated him to the place of highest honor and gave him the name above all other names, [10] that at the name of Jesus every knee should bow, in heaven and on earth and under the earth, [11] and every tongue confess that Jesus Christ is Lord, to the glory of God the Father.

Philippians 2:1-11

No Complaining

*W*hen your parents give you a chore to do, what's your reaction? When you're out with friends, how do you speak about your parents? The question is – Are you a complainer? Complaining, even if it isn't serious, does not reflect your walk with Christ. If you have something to say – say it – then stop talking about it.

[12] Dear friends, you always followed my instructions when I was with you. And now that I am away, it is even more important. Work hard to show the results of your salvation, obeying God with deep reverence and fear. [13] For God is working in you, giving you the desire and the power to do what pleases him.

[14] Do everything without complaining and arguing, [15] so that no one can criticize you. Live clean, innocent lives as children of God, shining like bright lights in a world full of crooked and perverse people. [16] Hold firmly to the word of life; then, on the day of Christ's return, I will be proud that I did not run the race in vain and that my work was not useless. [17] But I will rejoice even if I lose my life, pouring it out like a liquid offering to God, just like your faithful service is an offering to God. And I want all of you to share that joy. [18] Yes, you should rejoice, and I will share your joy.

Philippians 2:12-18

It's a Journey

*J*ust like anything else in life, learning to live for God is a journey. You will learn things and make them part of your life, then you'll stumble and fall. Don't focus on the failures, learn from them and move forward.

¹² I don't mean to say that I have already achieved these things or that I have already reached perfection. But I press on to possess that perfection for which Christ Jesus first possessed me.

¹³ No, dear brothers and sisters, I have not achieved it, but I focus on this one thing: Forgetting the past and looking forward to what lies ahead,

¹⁴ I press on to reach the end of the race and receive the heavenly prize for which God, through Christ Jesus, is calling us.

Philippians 3:12-14

Controlling Your Thoughts

*T*here is an old saying: "Garbage in = garbage out." Put critical, mean thoughts in your mind and that is what will come out in action. Put loving, kind thoughts in and that's what will come out in action.

4 Always be full of joy in the Lord. I say it again – rejoice! 5 Let everyone see that you are considerate in all you do. Remember, the Lord is coming soon.

6 Don't worry about anything; instead, pray about everything. Tell God what you need, and thank him for all he has done.

7 Then you will experience God's peace, which exceeds anything we can understand. His peace will guard your hearts and minds as you live in Christ Jesus.

8 And now, dear brothers and sisters, one final thing. Fix your thoughts on what is true, and honorable, and right, and pure, and lovely, and admirable. Think about things that are excellent and worthy of praise.

Philippians 4:4-8

Knowing Contentment

Contentment is not very evident in society today. Everyone seems to want more stuff, more money, more success, just more of everything. Contentment means "I'm OK with what I have and where I am." Are you content?

¹⁰ How I praise the Lord that you are concerned about me again. I know you have always been concerned for me, but you didn't have the chance to help me.

¹¹ Not that I was ever in need, for I have learned how to be content with whatever I have.

¹² I know how to live on almost nothing or with everything. I have learned the secret of living in every situation, whether it is with a full stomach or empty, with plenty or little.

¹³ For I can do everything through Christ, who gives me strength. ¹⁴ Even so, you have done well to share with me in my present difficulty.

Philippians 4:10-14

Praying Friends and Family

*I*t's an amazing blessing to know that people are praying for you. Do you have family or friends who pray for you? Can you share requests with them? If you don't, why not look for someone to become prayer partners with.

⁹ So we have not stopped praying for you since we first heard about you. We ask God to give you complete knowledge of his will and to give you spiritual wisdom and understanding.

¹⁰ Then the way you live will always honor and please the Lord, and your lives will produce every kind of good fruit. All the while, you will grow as you learn to know God better and better.

¹¹ We also pray that you will be strengthened with all his glorious power so you will have all the endurance and patience you need. May you be filled with joy, ¹² always thanking the Father. He has enabled you to share in the inheritance that belongs to his people, who live in the light.

¹³ For he has rescued us from the kingdom of darkness and transferred us into the Kingdom of his dear Son, ¹⁴ who purchased our freedom and forgave our sins.

Colossians 1:9-14

The Importance of Christ

*T*here would be no world without Christ. There would be no salvation plan without Him. He is over everything. He is the reason you can have peace with God. He's important. So ... you should get to know Him.

[15] Christ is the visible image of the invisible God. He existed before anything was created and is supreme over all creation, [16] for through him God created everything in the heavenly realms and on earth. He made the things we can see and the things we can't see – such as thrones, kingdoms, rulers, and authorities in the unseen world. Everything was created through him and for him.

[17] He existed before anything else, and he holds all creation together.

[18] Christ is also the head of the church, which is his body. He is the beginning, supreme over all who rise from the dead. So he is first in everything.

[19] For God in all his fullness was pleased to live in Christ, [20] and through him God reconciled everything to himself. He made peace with everything in heaven and on earth by means of Christ's blood on the cross.

Colossians 1:15-20

Be Careful

*I*t seems like there are new beliefs and "religions" popping up all the time. Everyone thinks their own way of believing is the truth. But absolute truth is found only in Jesus and His teachings in the Bible. Be careful about listening to and following anyone else. Stay close to Jesus because that is where truth is.

[6] And now, just as you accepted Christ Jesus as your Lord, you must continue to follow him.

[7] Let your roots grow down into him, and let your lives be built on him. Then your faith will grow strong in the truth you were taught, and you will overflow with thankfulness.

[8] Don't let anyone capture you with empty philosophies and high-sounding nonsense that come from human thinking and from the spiritual powers of this world, rather than from Christ.

[9] For in Christ lives all the fullness of God in a human body. [10] So you also are complete through your union with Christ, who is the head over every ruler and authority.

Colossians 2:6-10

Knowing Christ

*Y*our real life is hidden with Christ in God. So, how are you going to discover that real life? There's only one way – by getting to know Christ. How do you do that? Read the Gospels over and over. Get to know how He related to people, how He related to God and what He taught.

[1] Since you have been raised to new life with Christ, set your sights on the realities of heaven, where Christ sits in the place of honor at God's right hand.

[2] Think about the things of heaven, not the things of earth. [3] For you died to this life, and your real life is hidden with Christ in God. [4] And when Christ, who is your life, is revealed to the whole world, you will share in all his glory.

[5] So put to death the sinful, earthly things lurking within you. Have nothing to do with sexual immorality, impurity, lust, and evil desires. Don't be greedy, for a greedy person is an idolater, worshiping the things of this world.

Colossians 3:1-5

How to Treat Others

*F*irst of all, remember that God has forgiven you so there should be no question about you forgiving others. Then, read about the other ways God says to treat people. The foundation of all relationships is love. Love others.

12 Since God chose you to be the holy people he loves, you must clothe yourselves with tenderhearted mercy, kindness, humility, gentleness, and patience. 13 Make allowance for each other's faults, and forgive anyone who offends you. Remember, the Lord forgave you, so you must forgive others.

14 Above all, clothe yourselves with love, which binds us all together in perfect harmony. 15 And let the peace that comes from Christ rule in your hearts. For as members of one body you are called to live in peace. And always be thankful.

16 Let the message about Christ, in all its richness, fill your lives. Teach and counsel each other with all the wisdom he gives. Sing psalms and hymns and spiritual songs to God with thankful hearts. 17 And whatever you do or say, do it as a representative of the Lord Jesus, giving thanks through him to God the Father.

Colossians 3:12-17

November 23

Prayer

*P*rayer is so important to your life with Christ. It's the way you communicate with Him. It gives you an opportunity to tell Him what's on your heart – what you worry about and what you care about. It's also the way you can join in the ministries of others. As you bring their needs before God, you are sharing in their work.

[2] Devote yourselves to prayer with an alert mind and a thankful heart.

[3] Pray for us, too, that God will give us many opportunities to speak about his mysterious plan concerning Christ. That is why I am here in chains.

[4] Pray that I will proclaim this message as clearly as I should.

[5] Live wisely among those who are not believers, and make the most of every opportunity.

[6] Let your conversation be gracious and attractive so that you will have the right response for everyone.

Colossians 4:2-6

Doing Your Own Thing

*I*f you live life however you want but try to convince people that you are living for God, you won't be fooling anyone – especially not God. Don't just say fancy words about obeying God. Live for Him – let your life do the talking.

[1] Finally, dear brothers and sisters, we urge you in the name of the Lord Jesus to live in a way that pleases God, as we have taught you. You live this way already, and we encourage you to do so even more. [2] For you remember what we taught you by the authority of the Lord Jesus.

[7] God has called us to live holy lives, not impure lives. [8] Therefore, anyone who refuses to live by these rules is not disobeying human teaching but is rejecting God, who gives his Holy Spirit to you.

[9] But we don't need to write to you about the importance of loving each other, for God himself has taught you to love one another. [10] Indeed, you already show your love for all the believers throughout Macedonia. Even so, dear brothers and sisters, we urge you to love them even more.

[11] Make it your goal to live a quiet life, minding your own business and working with your hands, just as we instructed you before.

1 Thessalonians 4:1-2, 7-11

Don't Get Lazy

*I*t may seem to be a strange thing to say to a young girl – but don't get lazy about the way you live. Think about how you treat others. Think about how devoted you are to serving God. This is serious business so pay attention!

[12] Dear brothers and sisters, honor those who are your leaders in the Lord's work. They work hard among you and give you spiritual guidance. [13] Show them great respect and wholehearted love because of their work. And live peacefully with each other.

[14] Brothers and sisters, we urge you to warn those who are lazy. Encourage those who are timid. Take tender care of those who are weak. Be patient with everyone.

[15] See that no one pays back evil for evil, but always try to do good to each other and to all people.

[16] Always be joyful. [17] Never stop praying. [18] Be thankful in all circumstances, for this is God's will for you who belong to Christ Jesus.

[19] Do not stifle the Holy Spirit. [20] Do not scoff at prophecies, [21] but test everything that is said. Hold on to what is good. [22] Stay away from every kind of evil.

[23] Now may the God of peace make you holy in every way, and may your whole spirit and soul and body be kept blameless until our Lord Jesus Christ comes again. [24] God will make this happen, for he who calls you is faithful.

1 Thessalonians 5:12-24

They're Watching

*E*ven when you don't realize it, people are watching how you live. Your life is a testimony of what you truly think of God. Be careful how you live.

³ Dear brothers and sisters, we can't help but thank God for you, because your faith is flourishing and your love for one another is growing. ⁴ We proudly tell God's other churches about your endurance and faithfulness in all the persecutions and hardships you are suffering. ⁵ And God will use this persecution to show his justice and to make you worthy of his Kingdom, for which you are suffering. ⁶ In his justice he will pay back those who persecute you.

⁷ And God will provide rest for you who are being persecuted and also for us when the Lord Jesus appears from heaven. He will come with his mighty angels, ⁸ in flaming fire, bringing judgment on those who don't know God and on those who refuse to obey the Good News of our Lord Jesus. ⁹ They will be punished with eternal destruction, forever separated from the Lord and from his glorious power. ¹⁰ When he comes on that day, he will receive glory from his holy people – praise from all who believe. And this includes you, for you believed what we told you about him.

¹¹ So we keep on praying for you, asking our God to enable you to live a life worthy of his call. May he give you the power to accomplish all the good things your faith prompts you to do. ¹² Then the name of our Lord Jesus will be honored because of the way you live, and you will be honored along with him. This is all made possible because of the grace of our God and Lord, Jesus Christ.

2 Thessalonians 1:3-12

Stand Firm

Salvation is a gift from God. You did nothing to earn it – it is offered only by His grace. So thank Him, learn from Him. Stand firm in your salvation. Don't let anything pull you away from Him.

[13] As for us, we can't help but thank God for you, dear brothers and sisters loved by the Lord. We are always thankful that God chose you to be among the first to experience salvation – a salvation that came through the Spirit who makes you holy and through your belief in the truth. [14] He called you to salvation when we told you the Good News; now you can share in the glory of our Lord Jesus Christ.

[15] With all these things in mind, dear brothers and sisters, stand firm and keep a strong grip on the teaching we passed on to you both in person and by letter.

[16] Now may our Lord Jesus Christ himself and God our Father, who loved us and by his grace gave us eternal comfort and a wonderful hope, [17] comfort you and strengthen you in every good thing you do and say.

2 Thessalonians 2:13-17

Training Time

*J*ust as an athlete trains to stay in good physical condition, a believer trains to be a stronger follower of Christ. This training comes from reading God's Word, learning about Him, having a mentor to help you learn how to live. Don't put this off just because you're young ... start training now!

⁷ Do not waste time arguing over godless ideas and old wives' tales. Instead, train yourself to be godly. ⁸ "Physical training is good, but training for godliness is much better, promising benefits in this life and in the life to come." ⁹ This is a trustworthy saying, and everyone should accept it. ¹⁰ This is why we work hard and continue to struggle, for our hope is in the living God, who is the Savior of all people and particularly of all believers.

¹¹ Teach these things and insist that everyone learn them. ¹² Don't let anyone think less of you because you are young. Be an example to all believers in what you say, in the way you live, in your love, your faith, and your purity. ¹³ Until I get there, focus on reading the Scriptures to the church, encouraging the believers, and teaching them.

¹⁴ Do not neglect the spiritual gift you received through the prophecy spoken over you when the elders of the church laid their hands on you. ¹⁵ Give your complete attention to these matters. Throw yourself into your tasks so that everyone will see your progress. ¹⁶ Keep a close watch on how you live and on your teaching. Stay true to what is right for the sake of your own salvation and the salvation of those who hear you.

1 Timothy 4:7-16

Thank Your Parents

If your parents shared God's love with you, thank them. Appreciate their continued prayers and support of you and be courageous in sharing your faith, as your parents shared with you.

³ Timothy, I thank God for you – the God I serve with a clear conscience, just as my ancestors did. Night and day I constantly remember you in my prayers. ⁴ I long to see you again, for I remember your tears as we parted. And I will be filled with joy when we are together again.

⁵ I remember your genuine faith, for you share the faith that first filled your grandmother Lois and your mother, Eunice. And I know that same faith continues strong in you. ⁶ This is why I remind you to fan into flames the spiritual gift God gave you when I laid my hands on you. ⁷ For God has not given us a spirit of fear and timidity, but of power, love, and self-discipline.

⁸ So never be ashamed to tell others about our Lord. And don't be ashamed of me, either, even though I'm in prison for him. With the strength God gives you, be ready to suffer with me for the sake of the Good News. ⁹ For God saved us and called us to live a holy life. He did this, not because we deserved it, but because that was his plan from before the beginning of time – to show us his grace through Christ Jesus. ¹⁰ And now he has made all of this plain to us by the appearing of Christ Jesus, our Savior. He broke the power of death and illuminated the way to life and immortality through the Good News.

2 Timothy 1:3-10

November 30

December

Foolish Talk

*D*o you enjoy making your friends laugh? That's OK. But does the laughter sometimes come at the expense of another person? Making fun of someone else is foolish talk. It's not worth a cheap laugh.

¹⁵ Work hard so you can present yourself to God and receive his approval. Be a good worker, one who does not need to be ashamed and who correctly explains the word of truth.

¹⁶ Avoid worthless, foolish talk that only leads to more godless behavior.

¹⁹ But God's truth stands firm like a foundation stone with this inscription: "The Lord knows those who are his," and "All who belong to the Lord must turn away from evil."

²⁰ In a wealthy home some utensils are made of gold and silver, and some are made of wood and clay. The expensive utensils are used for special occasions, and the cheap ones are for everyday use. ²¹ If you keep yourself pure, you will be a special utensil for honorable use. Your life will be clean, and you will be ready for the Master to use you for every good work.

²³ Again I say, don't get involved in foolish, ignorant arguments that only start fights. ²⁴ A servant of the Lord must not quarrel but must be kind to everyone, be able to teach, and be patient with difficult people.

2 Timothy 2:15-16, 19-21, 23-24

God's Holy Word

*G*od's Word – the Bible – is not just another book. Its writers were inspired by God to write down things that help people know God and live for Him. Don't take God's Word lightly. Read it. Study it. Know it.

¹⁴ But you must remain faithful to the things you have been taught. You know they are true, for you know you can trust those who taught you.

¹⁵ You have been taught the holy Scriptures from childhood, and they have given you the wisdom to receive the salvation that comes by trusting in Christ Jesus.

¹⁶ All Scripture is inspired by God and is useful to teach us what is true and to make us realize what is wrong in our lives. It corrects us when we are wrong and teaches us to do what is right.

¹⁷ God uses it to prepare and equip his people to do every good work.

2 Timothy 3:14-17

The Prize Ahead

*T*he Apostle Paul could look back over his life and his work for Christ and know that he did everything he could for Jesus. He finished the race well and the prize for his good race was waiting for him. Wouldn't that be a good way to face the end of one's earthly life and look toward heaven?

[1] I solemnly urge you in the presence of God and Christ Jesus, who will someday judge the living and the dead when he appears to set up his Kingdom: [2] Preach the word of God. Be prepared, whether the time is favorable or not. Patiently correct, rebuke, and encourage your people with good teaching.

[3] For a time is coming when people will no longer listen to sound and wholesome teaching. They will follow their own desires and will look for teachers who will tell them whatever their itching ears want to hear. [4] They will reject the truth and chase after myths.

[5] But you should keep a clear mind in every situation. Don't be afraid of suffering for the Lord. Work at telling others the Good News, and fully carry out the ministry God has given you.

[6] As for me, my life has already been poured out as an offering to God. The time of my death is near. [7] I have fought the good fight, I have finished the race, and I have remained faithful. [8] And now the prize awaits me – the crown of righteousness, which the Lord, the righteous Judge, will give me on the day of his return. And the prize is not just for me but for all who eagerly look forward to his appearing.

2 Timothy 4:1-8

New Life

*T*hank God for His generous gift of the Holy Spirit to live in your heart and teach you about God. The whole opportunity to even know God at all is a gift. Is your heart truly thankful?

[1] Remind the believers to submit to the government and its officers. They should be obedient, always ready to do what is good. [2] They must not slander anyone and must avoid quarreling. Instead, they should be gentle and show true humility to everyone.

[3] Once we, too, were foolish and disobedient. We were misled and became slaves to many lusts and pleasures. Our lives were full of evil and envy, and we hated each other.

[4] But – "When God our Savior revealed his kindness and love, [5] he saved us, not because of the righteous things we had done, but because of his mercy. He washed away our sins, giving us a new birth and new life through the Holy Spirit. [6] He generously poured out the Spirit upon us through Jesus Christ our Savior. [7] Because of his grace he declared us righteous and gave us confidence that we will inherit eternal life." [8] This is a trustworthy saying, and I want you to insist on these teachings so that all who trust in God will devote themselves to doing good. These teachings are good and beneficial for everyone.

Titus 3:1-8

God's Beloved Son

*I*t's hard to understand how very much God loves you. He has one Son. One holy Son. He gave that Son to humanity to go through all kinds of terrible things. He didn't have to do that. He did it because He loves you. Jesus is God and He was willing to go through all that stuff ... because He loves you.

[1] Long ago God spoke many times and in many ways to our ancestors through the prophets. [2] And now in these final days, he has spoken to us through his Son. God promised everything to the Son as an inheritance, and through the Son he created the universe. [3] The Son radiates God's own glory and expresses the very character of God, and he sustains everything by the mighty power of his command. When he had cleansed us from our sins, he sat down in the place of honor at the right hand of the majestic God in heaven. [4] This shows that the Son is far greater than the angels, just as the name God gave him is greater than their names.

[5] For God never said to any angel what he said to Jesus:
"You are my Son. Today I have become your Father."
God also said,
"I will be his Father, and he will be my Son."
[6] And when he brought his supreme Son into the world, God said,
"Let all of God's angels worship him."

Hebrews 1:1-6

One of Us

*J*esus did what He had to do to make salvation possible for us. He became one of us. So, He knows what life is like as a human. He understands the temptations and struggles.

[11] So now Jesus and the ones he makes holy have the same Father. That is why Jesus is not ashamed to call them his brothers and sisters. [12] For he said to God, "I will proclaim your name to my brothers and sisters. I will praise you among your assembled people."

[13] He also said, "I will put my trust in him," that is, "I and the children God has given me."

[14] Because God's children are human beings – made of flesh and blood – the Son also became flesh and blood. For only as a human being could he die, and only by dying could he break the power of the devil, who had the power of death. [15] Only in this way could he set free all who have lived their lives as slaves to the fear of dying.

[16] We also know that the Son did not come to help angels; he came to help the descendants of Abraham. [17] Therefore, it was necessary for him to be made in every respect like us, his brothers and sisters, so that he could be our merciful and faithful High Priest before God. Then he could offer a sacrifice that would take away the sins of the people. [18] Since he himself has gone through suffering and testing, he is able to help us when we are being tested.

Hebrews 2:11-18

Helping Each Other

*I*t is an incredible gift to have a friend or family member you trust who can point out when you are turning away from God. This person can help you stay on track in the journey of living for God.

¹² Be careful then, dear brothers and sisters. Make sure that your own hearts are not evil and unbelieving, turning you away from the living God.

¹³ You must warn each other every day, while it is still "today," so that none of you will be deceived by sin and hardened against God.

¹⁴ For if we are faithful to the end, trusting God just as firmly as when we first believed, we will share in all that belongs to Christ.

¹⁵ Remember what it says:

"Today when you hear his voice, don't harden your hearts as Israel did when they rebelled."

Hebrews 3:12-15

The Living Word

The Bible is like God's letter to you. It's a personal message that is inspired by His Spirit. So, yes, it is alive and powerful. When you take the words of Scripture to heart, it will change your life.

[12] For the word of God is alive and powerful. It is sharper than the sharpest two-edged sword, cutting between soul and spirit, between joint and marrow. It exposes our innermost thoughts and desires.

[13] Nothing in all creation is hidden from God. Everything is naked and exposed before his eyes, and he is the one to whom we are accountable.

Hebrews 4:12-13

Jesus Understands

*N*o other religion makes the claim that its leader is divine and also human. But, Jesus experienced what it's like to be human. So He understands temptations, sorrow and all the emotions you have. That means He can help you through them!

¹² For the word of God is alive and powerful. It is sharper than the sharpest two-edged sword, cutting between soul and spirit, between joint and marrow. It exposes our innermost thoughts and desires. ¹³ Nothing in all creation is hidden from God. Everything is naked and exposed before his eyes, and he is the one to whom we are accountable.

¹⁴ So then, since we have a great High Priest who has entered heaven, Jesus the Son of God, let us hold firmly to what we believe. ¹⁵ This High Priest of ours understands our weaknesses, for he faced all of the same testings we do, yet he did not sin. ¹⁶ So let us come boldly to the throne of our gracious God. There we will receive his mercy, and we will find grace to help us when we need it most.

Hebrews 4:12-16

Maturity

*G*rowing up is a process. As you mature you become wiser. You become able to make better choices and decisions. You are able to handle bigger responsibilities. You have to do your part to mature physically by eating healthy food and taking care of yourself. The same is true with spiritual maturity. You should read God's Word, pray and do all you can to grow up in Him.

[11] There is much more we would like to say about this, but it is difficult to explain, especially since you are spiritually dull and don't seem to listen.

[12] You have been believers so long now that you ought to be teaching others. Instead, you need someone to teach you again the basic things about God's word. You are like babies who need milk and cannot eat solid food.

[13] For someone who lives on milk is still an infant and doesn't know how to do what is right. [14] Solid food is for those who are mature, who through training have the skill to recognize the difference between right and wrong.

Hebrews 5:11-14

Examples of Faith

*T*here are wonderful examples in Scripture of people who had great faith. That faith helped them accomplish great things for God. Reading about their faith can help you grow your own strong faith.

¹ Faith is the confidence that what we hope for will actually happen; it gives us assurance about things we cannot see. ² Through their faith, the people in days of old earned a good reputation.

³ By faith we understand that the entire universe was formed at God's command, that what we now see did not come from anything that can be seen.

⁴ It was by faith that Abel brought a more acceptable offering to God than Cain did. Abel's offering gave evidence that he was a righteous man, and God showed his approval of his gifts. Although Abel is long dead, he still speaks to us by his example of faith.

⁵ It was by faith that Enoch was taken up to heaven without dying – "he disappeared, because God took him." For before he was taken up, he was known as a person who pleased God. ⁶ And it is impossible to please God without faith. Anyone who wants to come to him must believe that God exists and that he rewards those who sincerely seek him.

Hebrews 11:1-6

Don't Give Up!

Sometimes you get tired. Like when you're working out to improve your athletic skills or when you're working to learn new things in math or a foreign language or when you are learning difficult musical pieces. Any skill you work to improve takes effort and sometimes you get tired and discouraged. Don't give up, though. Take a firm grip and keep on going!

¹² So take a new grip with your tired hands and strengthen your weak knees.

¹³ Mark out a straight path for your feet so that those who are weak and lame will not fall but become strong.

¹⁴ Work at living in peace with everyone, and work at living a holy life, for those who are not holy will not see the Lord.

¹⁵ Look after each other so that none of you fails to receive the grace of God. Watch out that no poisonous root of bitterness grows up to trouble you, corrupting many.

²⁸ Since we are receiving a Kingdom that is un-shakable, let us be thankful and please God by worshiping him with holy fear and awe. ²⁹ For our God is a devouring fire.

Hebrews 12:12-15, 28-29

Celebrate Troubles?

*P*roblems can teach you a lot of things. You can grow stronger through what you learn from them. If you need help, ask God. He will gladly help you!

² Dear brothers and sisters, when troubles come your way, consider it an opportunity for great joy. ³ For you know that when your faith is tested, your endurance has a chance to grow. ⁴ So let it grow, for when your endurance is fully developed, you will be perfect and complete, needing nothing.

⁵ If you need wisdom, ask our generous God, and he will give it to you. He will not rebuke you for asking. ⁶ But when you ask him, be sure that your faith is in God alone. Do not waver, for a person with divided loyalty is as unsettled as a wave of the sea that is blown and tossed by the wind. ⁷ Such people should not expect to receive anything from the Lord. ⁸ Their loyalty is divided between God and the world, and they are unstable in everything they do.

¹² God blesses those who patiently endure testing and temptation. Afterward they will receive the crown of life that God has promised to those who love him.

James 1:2-8, 12

Looking in a Mirror

*Y*ou check the mirror before you leave the house, right? You make sure your hair looks nice and that your clothes look good. What if you could look in a mirror to see what your life looks like? What would you see? It might make you more honest about admitting whether or not you are obeying God!

[19] Understand this, my dear brothers and sisters: You must all be quick to listen, slow to speak, and slow to get angry. [20] Human anger does not produce the righteousness God desires. [21] So get rid of all the filth and evil in your lives, and humbly accept the word God has planted in your hearts, for it has the power to save your souls.

[22] But don't just listen to God's word. You must do what it says. Otherwise, you are only fooling yourselves. [23] For if you listen to the word and don't obey, it is like glancing at your face in a mirror. [24] You see yourself, walk away, and forget what you look like. [25] But if you look carefully into the perfect law that sets you free, and if you do what it says and don't forget what you heard, then God will bless you for doing it.

[26] If you claim to be religious but don't control your tongue, you are fooling yourself, and your religion is worthless. [27] Pure and genuine religion in the sight of God the Father means caring for orphans and widows in their distress and refusing to let the world corrupt you.

James 1:19-27

December 14

Going for the In Crowd

*E*very school has an "in crowd." That's the popular crowd that everyone wants to be a part of. They are the standards of what's "cool." If you have the chance to hang with an "in crowd" girl or stick with an "ordinary" girl, what would you do?

¹ My dear brothers and sisters, how can you claim to have faith in our glorious Lord Jesus Christ if you favor some people over others?

² For example, suppose someone comes into your meeting dressed in fancy clothes and expensive jewelry, and another comes in who is poor and dressed in dirty clothes. ³ If you give special attention and a good seat to the rich person, but you say to the poor one, "You can stand over there, or else sit on the floor" – well, ⁴ doesn't this discrimination show that your judgments are guided by evil motives?

⁵ Listen to me, dear brothers and sisters. Hasn't God chosen the poor in this world to be rich in faith? Aren't they the ones who will inherit the Kingdom he promised to those who love him? ⁶ But you dishonor the poor! Isn't it the rich who oppress you and drag you into court? ⁷ Aren't they the ones who slander Jesus Christ, whose noble name you bear?

⁸ Yes indeed, it is good when you obey the royal law as found in the Scriptures: "Love your neighbor as yourself." ⁹ But if you favor some people over others, you are committing a sin. You are guilty of breaking the law.

¹² So whatever you say or whatever you do, remember that you will be judged by the law that sets you free.

James 2:1-9, 12

December 15

Sticks and Stones

*W*ords are powerful. Words of criticism and sarcasm lay on a person's heart and damage self-esteem. Watch how you speak to others. Your words have a lot of power.

² Indeed, we all make many mistakes. For if we could control our tongues, we would be perfect and could also control ourselves in every other way.

³ We can make a large horse go wherever we want by means of a small bit in its mouth. ⁴ And a small rudder makes a huge ship turn wherever the pilot chooses to go, even though the winds are strong. ⁵ In the same way, the tongue is a small thing that makes grand speeches.

But a tiny spark can set a great forest on fire. ⁶ And the tongue is a flame of fire. It is a whole world of wickedness, corrupting your entire body. It can set your whole life on fire, for it is set on fire by hell itself.

⁷ People can tame all kinds of animals, birds, reptiles, and fish, ⁸ but no one can tame the tongue. It is restless and evil, full of deadly poison. ⁹ Sometimes it praises our Lord and Father, and sometimes it curses those who have been made in the image of God. ¹⁰ And so blessing and cursing come pouring out of the same mouth. Surely, my brothers and sisters, this is not right! ¹¹ Does a spring of water bubble out with both fresh water and bitter water? ¹² Does a fig tree produce olives, or a grapevine produce figs? No, and you can't draw fresh water from a salty spring.

James 3:2-12

What Are You Fighting About?

*F*ighting with others is really a waste of time. Fighting because of jealousy is a bigger waste of time. If you're fighting or arguing with someone now, stop. Let God take care of your problems. You just take care of you.

[1] What is causing the quarrels and fights among you? Don't they come from the evil desires at war within you? [2] You want what you don't have, so you scheme and kill to get it. You are jealous of what others have, but you can't get it, so you fight and wage war to take it away from them. Yet you don't have what you want because you don't ask God for it. [3] And even when you ask, you don't get it because your motives are all wrong – you want only what will give you pleasure.

[7] So humble yourselves before God. Resist the devil, and he will flee from you. [8] Come close to God, and God will come close to you. Wash your hands, you sinners; purify your hearts, for your loyalty is divided between God and the world. [9] Let there be tears for what you have done. Let there be sorrow and deep grief. Let there be sadness instead of laughter, and gloom instead of joy. [10] Humble yourselves before the Lord, and he will lift you up in honor.

[11] Don't speak evil against each other, dear brothers and sisters. If you criticize and judge each other, then you are criticizing and judging God's law. But your job is to obey the law, not to judge whether it applies to you. [12] God alone, who gave the law, is the Judge. He alone has the power to save or to destroy. So what right do you have to judge your neighbor?

James 4:1-3, 7-12

Respect Authority

*O*ne of the toughest things in our world today is respecting authority. This standard seems to be losing respect. What does God say about authority and your place as a servant?

13 For the Lord's sake, respect all human authority – whether the king as head of state, 14 or the officials he has appointed. For the king has sent them to punish those who do wrong and to honor those who do right.

15 It is God's will that your honorable lives should silence those ignorant people who make foolish accusations against you. 16 For you are free, yet you are God's slaves, so don't use your freedom as an excuse to do evil. 17 Respect everyone, and love your Christian brothers and sisters. Fear God, and respect the king.

18 You who are slaves must accept the authority of your masters with all respect. Do what they tell you – not only if they are kind and reasonable, but even if they are cruel. 19 For God is pleased with you when you do what you know is right and patiently endure unfair treatment. 20 Of course, you get no credit for being patient if you are beaten for doing wrong. But if you suffer for doing good and endure it patiently, God is pleased with you.

21 For God called you to do good, even if it means suffering, just as Christ suffered for you. He is your example, and you must follow in his steps.

1 Peter 2:13-21

The Process

Growing in the Christian life is like stacking building blocks. As you learn each thing, you grow to be stronger and stronger.

[3] By his divine power, God has given us everything we need for living a godly life. We have received all of this by coming to know him, the one who called us to himself by means of his marvelous glory and excellence. [4] And because of his glory and excellence, he has given us great and precious promises. These are the promises that enable you to share his divine nature and escape the world's corruption caused by human desires.

[5] In view of all this, make every effort to respond to God's promises. Supplement your faith with a generous provision of moral excellence, and moral excellence with knowledge, [6] and knowledge with self-control, and self-control with patient endurance, and patient endurance with godliness, [7] and godliness with brotherly affection, and brotherly affection with love for everyone.

[8] The more you grow like this, the more productive and useful you will be in your knowledge of our Lord Jesus Christ. [9] But those who fail to develop in this way are shortsighted or blind, forgetting that they have been cleansed from their old sins.

2 Peter 1:3-9

Be Honest with Yourself

*Y*ou sin. That's it. That's the bottom line. Be honest with yourself about admitting that. You can try fooling yourself, but you will just be lying to yourself and to God.

⁵ This is the message we heard from Jesus and now declare to you: God is light, and there is no darkness in him at all. ⁶ So we are lying if we say we have fellowship with God but go on living in spiritual darkness; we are not practicing the truth. ⁷ But if we are living in the light, as God is in the light, then we have fellowship with each other, and the blood of Jesus, his Son, cleanses us from all sin.

⁸ If we claim we have no sin, we are only fooling ourselves and not living in the truth. ⁹ But if we confess our sins to him, he is faithful and just to forgive us our sins and to cleanse us from all wickedness. ¹⁰ If we claim we have not sinned, we are calling God a liar and showing that his word has no place in our hearts.

1 John 1:5-10

Obedience Is Evidence

*I*f a girl brags that she speaks French fluently but when asked she can't utter one correct sentence ... the evidence shows she was lying. Follow the evidence to get the facts. Obedience to God's laws is evidence of your relationship with Him.

¹ My dear children, I am writing this to you so that you will not sin. But if anyone does sin, we have an advocate who pleads our case before the Father. He is Jesus Christ, the one who is truly righteous. ² He himself is the sacrifice that atones for our sins – and not only our sins but the sins of all the world.

³ And we can be sure that we know him if we obey his commandments. ⁴ If someone claims, "I know God," but doesn't obey God's commandments, that person is a liar and is not living in the truth. ⁵ But those who obey God's word truly show how completely they love him. That is how we know we are living in him. ⁶ Those who say they live in God should live their lives as Jesus did.

1 John 2:1-6

A New Old Commandment

*F*rom the very beginning Jesus taught that loving others is very important. He never wavered from that. Petty differences with your friends and being difficult with your family needs to stop. Love one another. That love is the evidence that you love God.

[7] Dear friends, I am not writing a new commandment for you; rather it is an old one you have had from the very beginning. This old commandment – to love one another – is the same message you heard before. [8] Yet it is also new. Jesus lived the truth of this commandment, and you also are living it. For the darkness is disappearing, and the true light is already shining.

[9] If anyone claims, "I am living in the light," but hates a Christian brother or sister, that person is still living in darkness. [10] Anyone who loves another brother or sister is living in the light and does not cause others to stumble. [11] But anyone who hates another brother or sister is still living and walking in darkness. Such a person does not know the way to go, having been blinded by the darkness.

1 John 2:7-11

Stop Sinning

Sin is when you disobey God's laws. Practical examples are dishonesty, unkindness, selfishness ... you get the idea. God says to stop sinning. Not easy to do, but you can ask His help.

⁴ Everyone who sins is breaking God's law, for all sin is contrary to the law of God. ⁵ And you know that Jesus came to take away our sins, and there is no sin in him. ⁶ Anyone who continues to live in him will not sin. But anyone who keeps on sinning does not know him or understand who he is.

⁷ Dear children, don't let anyone deceive you about this: When people do what is right, it shows that they are righteous, even as Christ is righteous. ⁸ But when people keep on sinning, it shows that they belong to the devil, who has been sinning since the beginning. But the Son of God came to destroy the works of the devil. ⁹ Those who have been born into God's family do not make a practice of sinning, because God's life is in them. So they can't keep on sinning, because they are children of God.

¹⁰ So now we can tell who are children of God and who are children of the devil. Anyone who does not live righteously and does not love other believers does not belong to God.

1 John 3:4-10

Love in Action

*H*elping others by giving a few dollars or an hour of time is OK. But sacrificial giving of money you could use or time that takes away from something you would rather be doing – that is a special kind of love. Let your actions show your love.

[16] We know what real love is because Jesus gave up his life for us. So we also ought to give up our lives for our brothers and sisters. [17] If someone has enough money to live well and sees a brother or sister in need but shows no compassion – how can God's love be in that person?

[18] Dear children, let's not merely say that we love each other; let us show the truth by our actions. [19] Our actions will show that we belong to the truth, so we will be confident when we stand before God. [20] Even if we feel guilty, God is greater than our feelings, and he knows everything.

[21] Dear friends, if we don't feel guilty, we can come to God with bold confidence. [22] And we will receive from him whatever we ask because we obey him and do the things that please him.

[23] And this is his commandment: We must believe in the name of his Son, Jesus Christ, and love one another, just as he commanded us. [24] Those who obey God's commandments remain in fellowship with him, and he with them. And we know he lives in us because the Spirit he gave us lives in us.

1 John 3:16-24

Love as God Loves

*W*ords of love must be matched with action. Don't just speak love, put love to work to help others. Love grows more love. Start where you can and ask God to help you love more and more.

⁹ God showed how much he loved us by sending his one and only Son into the world so that we might have eternal life through him. ¹⁰ This is real love – not that we loved God, but that he loved us and sent his Son as a sacrifice to take away our sins.

¹¹ Dear friends, since God loved us that much, we surely ought to love each other. ¹² No one has ever seen God. But if we love each other, God lives in us, and his love is brought to full expression in us.

¹⁶ We know how much God loves us, and we have put our trust in his love. God is love, and all who live in love live in God, and God lives in them. ¹⁷ And as we live in God, our love grows more perfect. So we will not be afraid on the day of judgment, but we can face him with confidence because we live like Jesus here in this world.

¹⁸ Such love has no fear, because perfect love expels all fear. If we are afraid, it is for fear of punishment, and this shows that we have not fully experienced his perfect love. ¹⁹ We love each other because he loved us first.

²⁰ If someone says, "I love God," but hates a Christian brother or sister, that person is a liar; for if we don't love people we can see, how can we love God, whom we cannot see? ²¹ And he has given us this command: Those who love God must also love their Christian brothers and sisters.

1 John 4:9-12, 16-21

Back Up

*Y*our friends are important to you, aren't they? The Bible says they aren't just important because of the fun you have, but also because good Christian friends will help you stay on track in living for God, and you can do the same for them.

17 But you, my dear friends, must remember what the apostles of our Lord Jesus Christ said. 18 They told you that in the last times there would be scoffers whose purpose in life is to satisfy their ungodly desires. 19 These people are the ones who are creating divisions among you. They follow their natural instincts because they do not have God's Spirit in them.

20 But you, dear friends, must build each other up in your most holy faith, pray in the power of the Holy Spirit, 21 and await the mercy of our Lord Jesus Christ, who will bring you eternal life. In this way, you will keep yourselves safe in God's love.

22 And you must show mercy to those whose faith is wavering. 23 Rescue others by snatching them from the flames of judgment. Show mercy to still others, but do so with great caution, hating the sins that contaminate their lives.

24 Now all glory to God, who is able to keep you from falling away and will bring you with great joy into his glorious presence without a single fault. 25 All glory to him who alone is God, our Savior through Jesus Christ our Lord. All glory, majesty, power, and authority are his before all time, and in the present, and beyond all time! Amen.

Jude 17-25

The Revelation

*J*esus will come back one day to take His children to be with Him. He gave information about what that day would be like and encouraged people to keep living for Him as that day grows closer.

¹ This is a revelation from Jesus Christ, which God gave him to show his servants the events that must soon take place. He sent an angel to present this revelation to his servant John, ² who faithfully reported everything he saw. This is his report of the word of God and the testimony of Jesus Christ.

³ God blesses the one who reads the words of this prophecy to the church, and he blesses all who listen to its message and obey what it says, for the time is near.

⁴ This letter is from John to the seven churches in the province of Asia.

Grace and peace to you from the one who is, who always was, and who is still to come; from the sevenfold Spirit before his throne; ⁵ and from Jesus Christ. He is the faithful witness to these things, the first to rise from the dead, and the ruler of all the kings of the world.

All glory to him who loves us and has freed us from our sins by shedding his blood for us.

¹⁷ When I saw him, I fell at his feet as if I were dead. But he laid his right hand on me and said, "Don't be afraid! I am the First and the Last. ¹⁸ I am the living one. I died, but look – I am alive forever and ever! And I hold the keys of death and the grave.

¹⁹ "Write down what you have seen – both the things that are now happening and the things that will happen."

Revelation 1:1-5, 17-19

The Message of Love ... Again

*O*nce again the message of loving others is first and foremost. Jesus knew that it's easy to get caught up in the stuff of life and stop working on love.

¹ "Write this letter to the angel of the church in Ephesus. This is the message from the one who holds the seven stars in his right hand, the one who walks among the seven gold lampstands:

² "I know all the things you do. I have seen your hard work and your patient endurance. I know you don't tolerate evil people. You have examined the claims of those who say they are apostles but are not. You have discovered they are liars. ³ You have patiently suffered for me without quitting.

⁴ "But I have this complaint against you. You don't love me or each other as you did at first! ⁵ Look how far you have fallen! Turn back to me and do the works you did at first. If you don't repent, I will come and remove your lampstand from its place among the churches. ⁶ But this is in your favor: You hate the evil deeds of the Nicolaitans, just as I do.

⁷ "Anyone with ears to hear must listen to the Spirit and understand what he is saying to the churches. To everyone who is victorious I will give fruit from the tree of life in the paradise of God."

Revelation 2:1-7

Correct Teaching

*D*on't get sucked into watering down what you know is the truth. Stay true to what God's Word teaches.

[12] "Write this letter to the angel of the church in Pergamum. This is the message from the one with the sharp two-edged sword:

[13] "I know that you live in the city where Satan has his throne, yet you have remained loyal to me. You refused to deny me even when Antipas, my faithful witness, was martyred among you there in Satan's city.

[14] "But I have a few complaints against you. You tolerate some among you whose teaching is like that of Balaam, who showed Balak how to trip up the people of Israel. He taught them to sin by eating food offered to idols and by committing sexual sin. [15] In a similar way, you have some Nicolaitans among you who follow the same teaching. [16] Repent of your sin, or I will come to you suddenly and fight against them with the sword of my mouth.

[17] "Anyone with ears to hear must listen to the Spirit and understand what he is saying to the churches. To everyone who is victorious I will give some of the manna that has been hidden away in heaven. And I will give to each one a white stone, and on the stone will be engraved a new name that no one understands except the one who receives it."

Revelation 2:12-17

Lukewarm Believers

*D*on't try to ride the fence by behaving Christian when you're with Christians but doing whatever you want when you're with others. Make a choice – live for God or stop pretending!

[14] "Write this letter to the angel of the church in Laodicea. This is the message from the one who is the Amen – the faithful and true witness, the beginning of God's new creation:

[15] "I know all the things you do, that you are neither hot nor cold. I wish that you were one or the other! [16] But since you are like lukewarm water, neither hot nor cold, I will spit you out of my mouth! [17] You say, 'I am rich. I have everything I want. I don't need a thing!' And you don't realize that you are wretched and miserable and poor and blind and naked. [18] So I advise you to buy gold from me – gold that has been purified by fire. Then you will be rich. Also buy white garments from me so you will not be shamed by your nakedness, and ointment for your eyes so you will be able to see. [19] I correct and discipline everyone I love. So be diligent and turn from your indifference.

[20] "Look! I stand at the door and knock. If you hear my voice and open the door, I will come in, and we will share a meal together as friends. [21] Those who are victorious will sit with me on my throne, just as I was victorious and sat with my Father on his throne.

[22] "Anyone with ears to hear must listen to the Spirit and understand what he is saying to the churches."

Revelation 3:14-22

Forever and Ever

*T*he promise of Scripture is that God's children will one day be with Him in heaven – forever and ever. The day is coming ... Jesus will return!

[1] Then I saw a new heaven and a new earth, for the old heaven and the old earth had disappeared. And the sea was also gone. [2] And I saw the holy city, the new Jerusalem, coming down from God out of heaven like a bride beautifully dressed for her husband.

[3] I heard a loud shout from the throne, saying, "Look, God's home is now among his people! He will live with them, and they will be his people. God himself will be with them. [4] He will wipe every tear from their eyes, and there will be no more death or sorrow or crying or pain. All these things are gone forever."

[5] And the one sitting on the throne said, "Look, I am making everything new!" And then he said to me, "Write this down, for what I tell you is trustworthy and true." [6] And he also said, "It is finished! I am the Alpha and the Omega – the Beginning and the End. To all who are thirsty I will give freely from the springs of the water of life. [7] All who are victorious will inherit all these blessings, and I will be their God, and they will be my children.

22[20] He who is the faithful witness to all these things says, "Yes, I am coming soon!"

Amen! Come, Lord Jesus!

[21] May the grace of the Lord Jesus be with God's holy people.

Revelation 21:1-7; 22:20-21

About the Author

Carolyn Larsen is an author, actress, and an experienced speaker with a God-given passion for ministering to women and children. She has spoken at conferences and retreats around the United States, Canada, and India. Carolyn has written over 40 books for children and adults. Her writing has won various awards, including the C. S. Lewis Silver Award. Carolyn lives in Glen Ellyn, Illinois, with her husband, Eric.

Words of Jesus for Girls

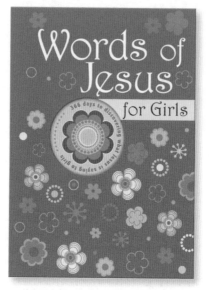

Also available as an eBook!

ISBN 978-1-4321-0131-2
eISBN 978-1-4321-0502-0

Words of Jesus for Girls is ideal for girls who are serious about following Jesus. Each devotion features a Bible verse, a lesson for the day, and a practical "Living It" section in a funky colorful layout. This 366-day devotional will help girls to make sense of the tough decisions they are faced with every day by listening to Jesus' words.

365 Days to
Knowing God for Girls

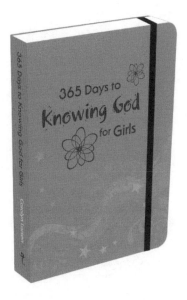

Also available as an eBook!

ISBN 978-1-77036-148-5
eISBN 978-1-4321-0377-4

Written especially for girls who want to get to know God better, this 365-day devotional will help them to focus their thoughts on God as they learn more about His greatness.